DOGS 'n STUFF

by J. Francis Bradley

EDITORIAL

Andrew De Prisco — Editor-in-Chief
Amy Deputato — Senior Editor
Jonathan Nigro — Associate Editor

PRODUCTION

Sherise Buhagiar — Graphic Layout
Bill Jonas — Digital Design
Joanne Muzyka — Concept and Digital Design
Matthew Strubel — Production Coordinator
Dana Stravelli — Properties Manager

Kennel Club Books®
A DIVISION OF BOWTIE, INC.

40 Broad Street, Freehold, NJ 07728 • USA

Library of Congress Cataloging-in-Publication Data

Bradley, J. Francis.
  Dogs 'n stuff / by J. Francis Bradley.
    p. cm.
  ISBN-13: 978-1-59378-659-5
  ISBN-10: 1-59378-659-X
  1. Dogs—Pictorial works. 2. Photography of dogs. I. Title.
  SF430.B73 2008
  636.7022'2—dc22

                                    2008001899

Printed in Singapore

10 9 8 7 6 5 4 3 2 1

The Stuff of Dog Dreams

Everyone's seen his or her dog dream! Legs stretching as Fido swims to shore, growls and teeth bared as Poochie assails a giant teddy bear, paws twitching as Rover digs for lost treasures. We'll never truly know what dogs are dreaming about!

Dogs 'n Stuff, however, is the stuff that dog dreams are made of! Our photo team, along with many warped and willing owners, managed to create dream settings for dozens of hungry, fun-loving dogs. Bulldog Rosie will never know why she was being buried in her favorite treat, Milk-Bones. Most dogs rarely get to even sniff a Swedish Fish, no less eat one, and Bichon Frisé Bina was offered thousands of them all at once! Would it be fun to be buried in confetti? You betcha, as a dozen of our models reveled in the experiences of the noisy, scratchy stuff! *Dogs 'n Stuff* was bound to happen, and every dog in this book is sure glad he or she was a part of this inevitable messy endeavor.

While the photographs in this book seemingly have no redeemable value, they are indisputable evidence of the twisted mind of this photographer, a lasting testament to the good humor of the dogs' owners and a colorful tribute to the patience and silliness of our canine models.

If you have a fraction of the fun we all had creating this important addition to canine literature, then surely *Dogs 'n Stuff* is a dream come true!

— J. Francis Bradley

No dogs were harmed in the
creation of this book.

Chocolate Tootsie Rolls
Tootsie Roll
America's Favorite Candy

Mangia bene!

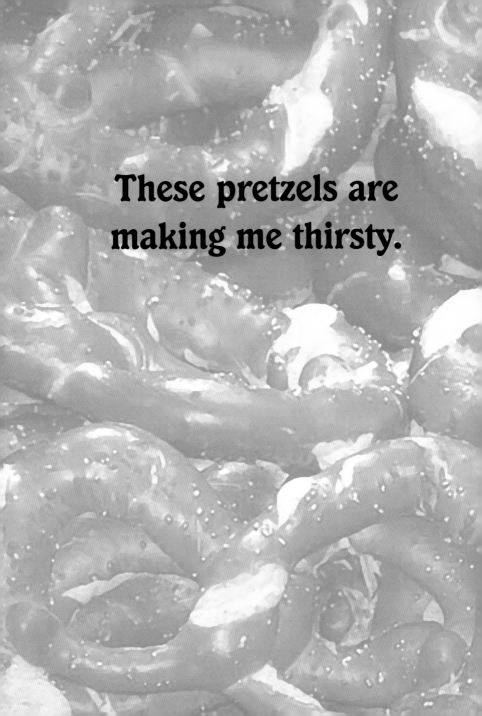

These pretzels are
making me thirsty.

No bones about it!

Sometimes
you feel like a ...

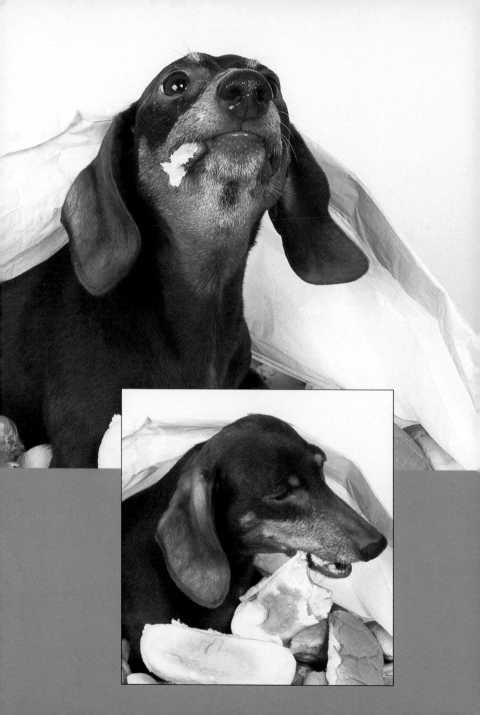

Bubble bath, anyone?

The devil made me do it!

Cheesy does it!

SAY CHEESE!

GONE FISHING

Lions and tigers...

oh my!

Avalanche!

Coffee and...

Munchkins to go

¡Quiero mis Lucky Charms!

What!

No lox?

Oy.

CALIFORNIA ROLL...

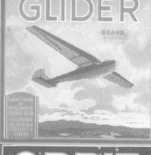

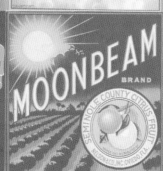

Dog Bless America

Confetti is...

exciting

colorful

SURPRISE!

Dog
Beach
USA

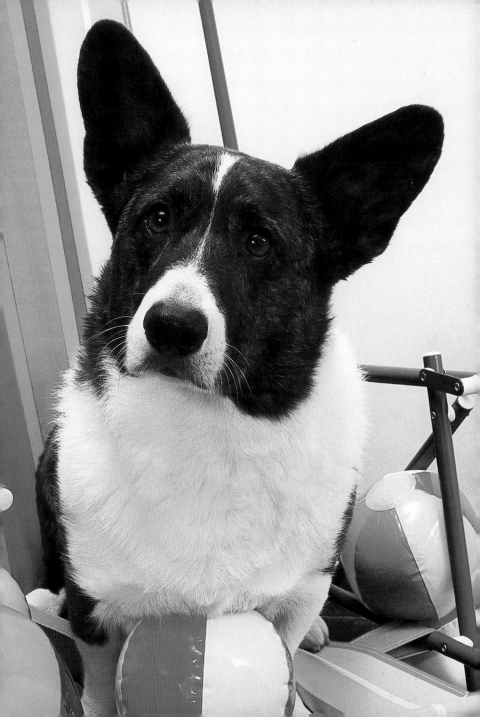

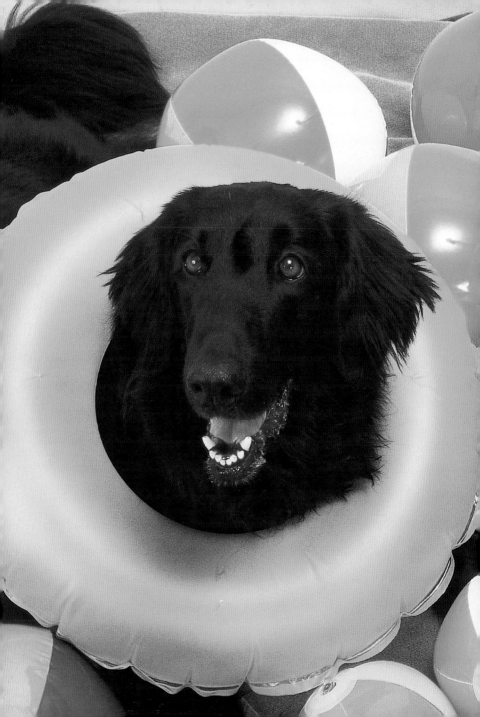

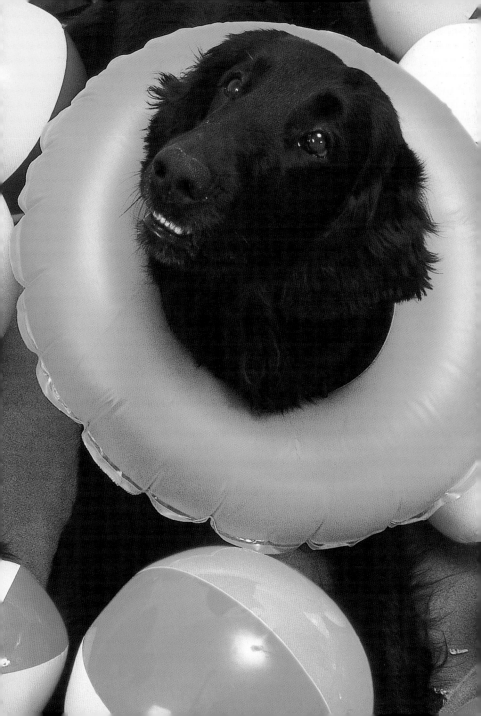

MUCH "COOLER" IN HERE.

Bring on the waves...

A-low-howl!

Purebred
Hula Hound

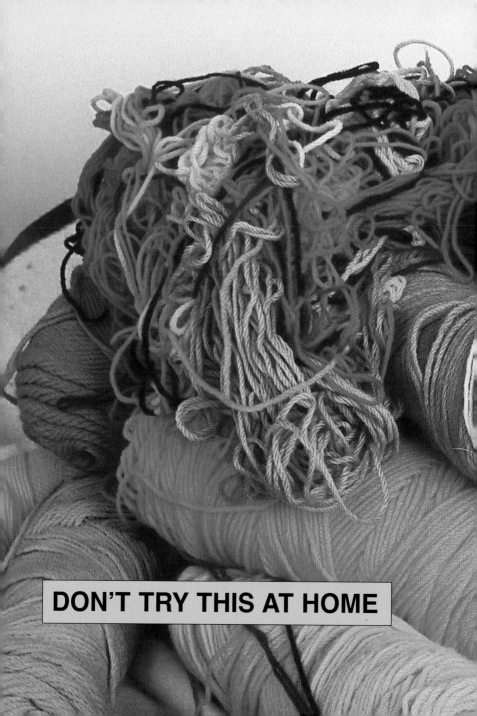

DON'T TRY THIS AT HOME

Foiled.

UNWINDING A HARD DAY'S NIGHT...

Having a ball!

Yes, we're house-trained...

can't you tell?

Swab...

and debon·ear!

T

F I D O

D

Y

The broom looked like a "rug."

What price glamour?

From sea to shining sea...

Hide 'n seek

Stop looking at me like I have two heads!

No, we're not *toy* fox terriers.

Welcome to the office

Memo

Re: Unexplained
    shortage of
    rubber bands

THIS END UP

Here comes the...

runaway bride

Does this nose
make my hat look big?

Does anyone know how to tie one of these things?

Ooh, la, la!

Feathers make the mastiff.

Topless on Bourbon Street

NOW PLAYING

EXTRA BUTTER,
PLEASE.

Get hooked!

A Big Thank You!

The *Dogs 'n Stuff* production team wishes to thank all of the owners and their patient, wonderful, fun-loving (and hungry!) dogs who participated in the photo shoots for this book, including:

David Alba (Sonny), Ron Assoian (Cody), Peter & Cindy Bauer (Penny), Ellen Beris (Andrew), Jim & Suzy Brown (Molly), Maritza Bush (Bina), Jill Bergmann (Sydney & Keaton), Brian & Cindy Buck (Max), Patricia Byrne (Monty), TJ & Nicole Ceballos (Wiley & Dallas), Danielle Chudy (Willie & Benjamin), Liz Clancy (Maizy), Carollyn Carson (Annie), Dana Deraney (Casey), Joseph DiSanto (Gia), Cindy Dodeles (Chester), Norman & Nina Forrest (Rosie), Holly Freimark (Thadeus), Lynn Farruggio (Gizmo), Greg & Sherree Gerzanics (Annie), Carol Glotzbier (Gracie), Susan Hart-White (Dwight), John & Carole Hessels (Reingold & Tilburg), Kay Hornung (Zoey), Eileen Jones (Sparkle), Susan Klie (Duncan), Ari Lash (Archie & Sydney), Brianna Leary (Rafi), Susan Lynch (Callie), Christine & Ron Macchione (Red), Charlie & Mary McGee (Bruno), Lynn Mendelon (Tigger), Laurel Mengarelli (Rafi), John Merriman (Astrid, Buzzi, Carmen & Steffi), Frances Shirley Miller (Flair, Teko & Piper), Pamela L. Miller (Jace), Michael Monks (Keller & RJ), Amy Murray (Luella May), Matthew S. Musicant (Scooter), the Panaccione family (Miya), Lauri Pine (Spencer), Shirley Pittman (CoCo, Gizmo & Lola), Susan Poff (Wheatleigh), Jaylynn Prince (Ryan), Reyna Prosnitz (Hailey), Alan Rubenfeld (BJ, Captain Jack, Dolores, Delago & Sir James), Derek & Shanelle Sager (Parker), Martin Schreiber (Oscar), Stuart Schreiber (Madison), Richard & Amy Scotti (Rocky), Liz Shakalis (Annie), Stacey Shevlin (Oliver), Kevin Smith (Bosco), Charlotte Tiarnaigh (Luna & Pixie), Charles & Toniann Tortoriello (Haley), Charlotte Trainor (Robin), Frank & Denise Vacchiano (Buca), Denise Visco (Hunter, Lexie & Gidget), Karen Wheatley (Angus), Robert White (Azuki), Jodi Woolley (Trixie), Joyce Yaccarino (Emmy Lou & Tug), Kim Yow (Maggie).

Special thanks to Isabelle Francais, Kathy Hall, Michael Monks and the team at Camp Bow Wow of Midland Park, NJ, Jayne and Toni of the Dunkin' Donuts of Neptune, NJ and Dana Stravelli for their contributions to the creation of this book.

DOGS 'n STUFF

THE END

REMNANTS:
SEASON OF FIRE

REMNANTS: SEASON OF FIRE

BOOK 2 IN THE REMNANTS SERIES

BY LISA T. BERGREN

BLINK

BLINK

Remnants: Season of Fire
Copyright © 2015 by Lisa T. Bergren

This title is also available as a Blink ebook. Visit www.zondervan.com/ebooks.

Requests for information should be addressed to:
Blink, 3900 *Sparks Drive SE, Grand Rapids, Michigan* 49546

ISBN 978-0-310-73565-6

Any internet addresses (websites, blogs, etc.) and telephone numbers in this book are offered as a resource. They are not intended in any way to be or imply an endorsement by the publisher, nor does the publisher vouch for the content of these sites and numbers for the life of this book.

Cover design: *Brand Navigation*
Cover photography: *©sakura-Fotolia.com*
               LuminaStock-istock
Interior design: *David Conn*

Printed in the United States of America

15 16 17 18 19 20 /DCI/ 20 19 18 17 16 15 14 13 12 11 10 9 8 7 6 5 4 3 2 1

"If you will not fight for right when you can easily win without bloodshed; if you will not fight when your victory is sure and not too costly; you may come to the moment when you will have to fight with all the odds against you and only a precarious chance of survival. There may even be a worse case. You may have to fight when there is no hope of victory, because it is better to perish than to live as slaves."

—Sir Winston Churchill (1874–1965)

CHAPTER
1

ANDRIANA

I found the ship we want. A merchant vessel with supplies for Catal, the *Far North*." Chaza'el cast a worried glance back through the maze of crates — three times taller than we were — and then to us again. "One little problem — she's loaded with soldiers."

"Perfect," Vidar said, crossing his arms. "It's been a little dull around here."

I smiled at him, my eyes tracing the lingering bruises on his olive skin, then sighed heavily, wishing again Niero was with us. He'd know how to go about this — seeking to free Kapriel from the island prison, as well as how to board a ship loaded with sailors who wouldn't exactly welcome us.

"You're sure that's the one, Chaz?" Vidar asked, gesturing toward the ship. "The one you saw in your vision?"

The shorter man nodded once, and his dark, silken hair

washed forward and back. "And as far as I can tell, it's the only one heading out any time soon."

"We're too obvious, all together," Killian groused, pushing his blond dreadlocks over a shoulder. He looked at Ronan, my knight, who had assumed leadership in Niero's absence. "Send me. And Bellona. We'll slip in, spring Kapriel, and bring him back to you. The rest of you can find shelter in the meantime."

Ronan's green-brown eyes hovered over Killian a minute, then at the rest of us. "Look, I know this seems like the most idiotic thing we've done. But Kapriel is the key to us winning this war. Niero said so. He's the only one who can really go head to head with Keallach. And if he's ill …" He looked at each of us in turn again and we seemed to collectively hold our breath. "We all need to go," Ronan said, "because we all might not return." His lips clamped together and avoided my gaze. "We're never going to be closer to Kapriel than this, right? Anyone disagree that this is where the Maker has led us?"

We all shook our heads, even Killian, clearly miserable at the idea of putting his Remnant in such danger. But ever since we'd seen the broad band of the blue ocean, we'd felt the undeniable pull toward Catal and Kapriel, as impossible as it seemed.

"Get down," Bellona suddenly growled. Her long, brown braid hit my shoulder as she whirled to crouch beside me.

We ducked, and a second later heard two men walk by, just one crate away from us. They were laughing under their breath and murmuring to each other. We'd seen the whistles every worker wore around their necks. The dockyard's air filled with the sound of them, long and short blasts, a wordless language that sounded eerie and foreign to our ears. I had no doubt that there was a unique blast for alarm — a call that would send some of the gray-clad soldiers stationed on each corner, armed with automatic weapons, after us.

The men paused on the far side of the crate that separated Chaza'el, Killian, and Tressa from them. My fellow Ailith were breathing shallowly, eyes wide, backs to the crate. We all had our hands on the hilts of our weapons, but my ears strained for the bits of conversation from the dockworkers. They were speaking in low tones about the *Far North*, the merchant ship Chaza'el said we had to board if we were to get to Catal today. Only the transports and supply vessels were allowed around the island; any others were immediately destroyed.

I could feel Ronan's stare. Ever since we'd kissed, he seemed somehow more *present*. Vivid. Like he was an extension of me, in a way. I met his gaze and his brows knit together. He vacillated between concern and understanding what I was after — to learn more from the two dockworkers nearest us. If either felt alarm, I'd be the first to know it.

An empath, Niero had called me once. It was my gift to feel what others felt. Just as it was Tressa's gift to heal, Chaza'el's gift to see the future, and Vidar's gift to know light or darkness in another. We knew that somewhere ahead of us was Kapriel, with a miraculous power of his own; and others too. If they yet lived. I knew it as surely as Ronan did that this — this mad need to get to Kapriel, our brother, our prince, and free him — was what we had to get done.

Somehow.

"Shoving off soon ..." said one of the dockworkers as I dared to edge closer, crawling down low in order to hear better.

"Yeah. All the freight's loaded already," said the other.

Their conversation over, they turned to go and I slowly pulled back, freezing as they came into view — with me in plain sight — but they passed on. My heart hammered in my chest, but I grinned. I rolled to my side, and around the corner of the crate. Ronan gripped my upper arms, half in consternation at the risk I took, half in hope I'd gained good information.

"We have to get aboard tonight. They're to leave soon," I whispered.

"Bellona and Vidar," he said, "make your way over to the *Far North* and see if you can spot a way for us to steal our way aboard."

The two nodded and immediately moved out, each carrying a dagger in their hands. If they came up against a dockworker, they'd be best dispatched in silence. Ronan and Killian watched their progress, ready to spring to their aid if necessary. The rest of us stayed down.

"What if we got into some crates?" Tressa asked, pushing her red ponytail over her shoulder. "Like we did in Castle Vega?"

"It sounds like they're all loaded already," I said.

She sighed. I knew what she was after — avoiding a fight. And I couldn't blame her. She found it nearly impossible to hurt another — with her gift of healing, it felt completely wrong, regardless of how much danger she faced. I had encountered something similar. As my empathy gifting grew, I knew what it was to feel what my enemies felt, and their fear or fury tangled with my own heart in alarming fashion. The mere thought of it sent bands of panic around my chest, and I fought to breathe. But I couldn't help it. Were Tressa and I as much an impediment as a boon to the Ailith? Might we not endanger the others, in their efforts to protect us as well as themselves?

Chaza'el caught my eye. He studied me, searching me, seeing me in a way that I hadn't often been seen. It reminded me of Niero, and my heart panged anew with worry for our lost leader. Was he all right? Hurt? Even alive?

"We are on the Maker's path," Chaza'el said, a hint of compassion in the lines of his moon-shaped eyes, as well as within him. "And this is his next step for you, Andriana. I've seen it."

I nodded, once, not really feeling like I wanted to get into it. But his choice of words — *you*, not *us* — and then the cold wave of hesitation from him, gave me pause. What else had he seen in his vision? We'd already lost Niero. Were we about to lose others on this mission too?

Chaza'el moved away, edging past Ronan as if he didn't want to stay close to me, giving me further opportunity to question him. Ronan absently ran his fingers along his ribs, where I'd seen the massive bruise days ago, even as he watched our companions make their way through the labyrinth of the dock's crates.

"Hey," I said, touching his hand lightly. "How're you healing?"

"It's getting better," he said distractedly. But he dropped his hand.

"Can you still see Bellona and Vid?"

"No. They disappeared a couple rows away from the ship."

I listened to the whistles that continued to fill the air, and prayed we wouldn't hear an alarm.

■ ■ ■

Two hours later, we all moved over toward the ship, with Bellona and Vidar leading the way. After sunset, the docks grew mostly quiet, with only the wash of waves against the docks; by nightfall, the workers' whistles and wheeling gulls all grew silent. Every so often, we heard a short whistle, and I came to understand that it was a sort of clock — the means for guards on duty to know how much time had passed . . . and how much was left before their watch was over.

Vidar gestured for most of us to hide along a line of triple-stacked crates, and Ronan and I took up opposite guard flanks, watching for patrolling guards. I grabbed Vidar's arm as he passed me. "Anything?" I whispered, wondering if he sensed any of the Sheolite nearby.

He shook his head, and I released him. For this being enemy territory, we'd run into very few that alarmed Vidar, and our armbands remained oddly neutral. Mostly, Vidar said he sensed a vague void, which seemed to unsettle him more than the looming cold threat that the scouts and trackers brought with them.

He and Bellona went on alone, slipping to the edge of the docks row by row. Under the light of a half-moon, I could see their shadowy figures pause a moment, then one leaped out over the water. Vidar. He grabbed hold of the heavy rope, wound his legs around it, and shimmied up the arc toward the ship. When he was a third of the way, I saw Bellona leap for the rope beneath him and do as he was doing — climbing her way up to the ship, but at a greater speed.

I smiled. It galled Vidar that his knight, Bellona, was better at such things than he, and I could almost hear the stifled wisecrack forming in his mind now.

He was nearing the top, and I held my breath as his dark form disappeared against the broad side of the ship. "C'mon, Vidar," I whispered.

I could hear Tressa and Chaza'el praying, probably a much better use of energy. But I couldn't bring my mind to anything but staring as hard as I could, trying to discern one shadow from the other.

There, I thought, watching a lump slide over the edge of the rail. Shortly afterward I saw Bellona lift herself up and over in a far more graceful manner. But they were both aboard.

I smiled and dared to take a breath. "They're on," I whispered, and felt the others' relief meld with my own.

Then there were sounds of a fight — gasps and groans that carried across the water — and we all waited through long, slow seconds for an alarm whistle or sailors to come running to the aid of those who were attacked. But none came.

"They'll call us in a moment," Chaza'el whispered, a second before Vidar whistled lowly.

A shiver ran down my back. "Are you going to be doing that a lot?" I whispered back to him.

He smiled without showing his teeth. "If the Maker is generous with what he allows me to see." He turned to follow Tressa and Killian, and I trailed them through the maze of crates, staying low as they were. Before leaving the relative safety of each row of crates, we paused, made sure we were clear, then scurried to the next bank of them. Ronan brought up the rear.

Killian, Tressa, and Chaza'el took to the rope without hesitation, and I was getting ready to leap from the tar-covered wood to the rope next, when Ronan grabbed my arm and yanked me to the side and down.

The hair on my neck stood on end as I realized my armband had grown cold.

I'd been so focused on the Ailith that led us … I'd missed that there were Sheolites nearby.

"How?" I whispered. Ronan hovered over me, his face an inch from mine. We both stared in the same direction, to an opening between the crates. "How'd they know we were here?"

"Maybe they didn't until now," he whispered back. "If the Maker smiles, they won't. C'mon." He grabbed my hand and led me, hunched over, away from the ship, and I saw what he was doing. If we couldn't join our fellow Ailith, we'd either distract our enemies with a chase or hide again.

The moon disappeared behind a bank of clouds and the dockyard became twice as eerie. I could barely see anything ahead of us and couldn't imagine how Ronan knew where to go. Maybe he was feeling his way forward.

I nervously glanced down each aisle we passed, my eyes wide and straining in the pitch-dark. I glimpsed the ship, with new lanterns glowing beside her, illuminating her prow. But there had been no soldiers or Sheolites near her. "Ronan," I panted, feeling my arm cuff turn from the chill of warning to the painful icy cold that demanded I flee, or prepare to fight.

"I know," he said, turning to face me. His words came out strangled. He pulled me to the next corner. "You keep looking left. Draw your dagger." Then he stood in front of me and slowly withdrew his sword, trying to remove it silently from its scabbard. I knew he'd be watching the aisle in front of us and to the right.

The flesh around my armband ached with the numbing cold. Only one person had made it this frigid before.

"Sethos," I whispered, the name distant to my own ears.

The moon emerged from the drifting clouds and Ronan and I both heard the low laugh of the man. I peered over

Ronan's shoulder as my knight moved into a defensive position. All we could see was the dark robe and hood, Sethos's face hidden in shadow.

"To the left," I grunted, seeing the two scouts, one carrying a lantern.

"And to the right," returned Ronan. I knew there were others, behind us, without looking.

Sethos laughed again and tugged on a glove, as if straightening it. "Come, Ailith. You are surrounded. Surrender your blades and accompany us. The emperor seeks to speak with you. He intends you no harm. At least not yet."

He dared to walk right up to the point of Ronan's blade, his hands outstretched, as if approaching in peace. I saw teeth flash in a smile, though I still could not see his eyes hidden beneath the hood.

"I should end you now," Ronan growled.

"You realize it would only result in your own death," Sethos said in bored tone.

"At least I'd die satisfied, knowing that I took you with me."

I glanced nervously from one side to the other, seeing the others were steadily closing in. Those with the lanterns set them down, and edged nearer, swords drawn. Was Ronan really intent on fighting our way out of here? Would it even be possible?

"You'd risk your own life, yes," Sethos said, his hooded head shifting as if he was looking me over. "But you won't risk hers. Bring them," he sniffed, turning in an assuming whirl of red fabric and striding away from us.

Ronan glanced over his shoulder at me, a knot of agitation and grudging defeat. "It's all right," I said, putting a hand on his shoulder. "We will fight another day. For now, we must try other methods."

Slowly, he crouched and laid his sword on the ground. The Sheolites had their hands on us in seconds, one grabbing my wrist and slamming it against the crate to force me to drop my dagger. He then roughly turned me around, put my hands against the crate, and methodically searched my body for other weapons. There was no lust in him, only single-minded duty. He set one dagger after another on the crate by my left hand, then yanked me to the right, handing me to two others. They each grabbed hold of an arm and rushed me forward. Sethos had already reached the end of the crates ahead of us, his form a dark silhouette backlit by another lamp.

Madly, I thought through one move after another that could take both my guards down. But I knew it would be a short-lived victory. Others would catch us again in a few paces. The only way to get through this was to face Keallach. I could see him standing beside Sethos in a clearing at the edge of the yard. There were twenty or more guards around them, and my last vestiges of hopeful escape disappeared.

"Andriana," Keallach said softly, as we appeared before him. Four men stood with oil-burning lamps on rods in intervals around us. "And Ronan."

We remained silent.

"I am glad to see you alive," Keallach tried again with a tentative smile.

I reached out to search him, and knew truth in him. He was genuinely glad. It took me aback.

"We didn't know if you'd died in the desert or in the mountains. There are still men out there, trying to find you. We lost your trail. But I feared the worst."

The worst? What was worse than Keallach's minions capturing us?

"Where are your companions?" he asked.

"For all we know, they are dead," Ronan said.

"I doubt that," Sethos said, pulling back his hood. His long, dark hair was in a braid, as all Sheolites wore it. He turned to four scouts in red behind him. "Search all quadrants of the docks. Quickly."

"It surprised us, when I sensed you here, tonight," Keallach said quietly. "What brought you here?"

"We sought an escape from Pacifica," I pretended to admit, stalling for time, hoping our companions were safely hidden aboard the *Far North*, and the Sheolites would not think to search the vessel.

"To where?" Keallach asked wryly, lifting one brow. "The far off countries are in no better shape than our own, though we are working on assisting them. If you'd like to book passage, I'd be more than happy to help you." He stepped closer to me, his keen green eyes searching mine.

"You didn't seem anxious to help us last time we met," I said.

He frowned, as if troubled. "My men . . . are very protective of me. Especially in the sanctuary. They thought the Ailith presented a mortal danger to my life."

"So they very nearly took ours. They may have even killed some of our brothers and sisters."

"No," Keallach said. "None of the Ailith have been captured or killed. You have my word."

"I find it difficult to believe," Sethos said, bringing a hand to his chin, "that if your mind was on escape, you wouldn't flee back to your precious Valley. If you thought the emperor your enemy, why make your way deeper into his territory?"

"Have you ever crossed the Great Expanse on foot?" Ronan grunted. "We're not anxious to do that again."

I dared to look Keallach's way. I detected no malice in him. Only curiosity. Longing. Hope. It was so obvious in contrast with Sethos's seething hatred. Even Keallach's small niceties toward us were agitating the dark master.

"I suspect," Keallach said, glancing down to his boot and kicking at a clump of grass growing among rotting, tar-laced boards, "that you didn't intend to board a ship bound across the sea." His eyes moved again to meet mine, and I fought the urge to shift nervously. "I suspect you were instead trying to board this ship to Catal," he said, nodding behind me.

"Catal?" I asked, feigning ignorance.

The hint of a smile teased the corners of his full lips. "Catal, the island prison. Where my brother Kapriel is held."

I tried to swallow, but my mouth was dry. I stared back at him for a long moment, deciding.

"Yes," Ronan broke in. "We wanted to see Kapriel."

"And free him?" he asked, cocking his head. I felt the arrow of pain, of betrayal, when he thought of his brother. Why could I read him so well tonight when I could not in Wadi Qelt? It was as if he'd decided to let me in. He looked away from us, to the side, to the sea, glittering in the moonlight.

"Possibly," I said, knowing that saying anything else would be a known lie. The men all around us erupted in jeering laughter but Keallach's face remained sober.

"I can allow you to see Kapriel," he said softly to me, his tone edged in pain. "But you will spend the journey, to and from, in my cabin so that you can hear what I have to say too. And when we leave Catal, Kapriel will remain behind us."

"I don't think — " Ronan began.

"I don't think you are in any position to negotiate, Knight," Keallach interrupted, with a flick of his fingers. All along, he kept his eyes on me. "Do we have a deal, Andriana?"

I sighed, contemplating our options. Really, we had none. And perhaps if Ronan and I distracted these men, they wouldn't search the *Far North* for our companions. Perhaps this was all in the Maker's design ... the perfect distraction for our enemy.

The word stuck in my mind. Despite what had happened at the winter palace, Keallach didn't feel like an enemy. Not really. He was surrounded by the fallen, chiefly the loathsome Sethos, but maybe I could reach him, influence him. Each of the brothers, Kapriel and Keallach, was a force — I'd gathered that much. But together?

With both of them on our side, the Ailith would be unstoppable.

CHAPTER 2

ANDRIANA

We walked up a steep plank to board the *Far North*, and I fought to keep my eyes from looking at the rope that tethered the ship to the dock, then nervously around the deck, for the other Ailith. Where had they hidden themselves? Were they safe? Or had they been captured? Did Keallach and Sethos sense them, as they had us? And how were we going to get out of this mess?

One step at a time, Dri, I told myself, trying to calm my fluttering heart. *One step at a time.*

Just as Keallach led me into the captain's cabin, I thought I saw a female sailor in the gray Pacifican soldier's uniform, sporting a long braid that looked suspiciously like Bellona's, but I didn't dare look again, for fear of exposing her. When the Sheolite scouts had returned with nothing to report, Sethos had peered over the dockyard one more time, scowling suspiciously, and then seemed to decide that Ronan and I had indeed set off on this mission alone. But where had our friends stashed the bodies of those they'd overtaken? Were they soon to be discovered?

The two guards who still held my arms jostled me left, then right, heading toward the captain's cabin. They let me go as we were forced to climb single file up a narrow, steep set of steps, and I looked back to make sure Ronan was behind us. I took a deep breath as I saw him crest the stairs too, then saw that the door to the captain's cabin was open. Warm light poured out toward us in welcome, and I could hear the crack of firewood burning in a small stove. There was a couch that looked brand new against the far wall and to the right —

The door abruptly closed behind me, and I glanced back to see a burly Sheolite guard, arms folded, in front of it. Outside, I heard Ronan cry out, the sounds of a scuffle, then silence. I took a step toward the door, but Keallach's hand grabbed my shoulder. "Andriana — "

I whirled again to face him, fists up in preparation to fight.

"Take your ease," he said lifting his hands, palms up. "Your knight has been detained, solely so you and I can speak in private, for once." He nodded at me slowly. "I gave *you* permission to visit Kapriel, *not* a Knight of the Last Order. And something tells me that if I have Ronan within my grasp, you won't wander far. Am I right?"

He gave me that teasing, knowing grin again, head half-cocked. I was furious with him and yet grudgingly understood. If I were in his shoes, would I not do the same thing? My cheeks grew warm, flushing in embarrassment that he'd been able to tell there was something more than Knight-Remnant connection between Ronan and me. I ignored it, lifting my chin and folding my arms. "You will not harm him?"

He shook his head. "Nothing more than it takes to keep him apart from you for a while. If he's as smart as he is strong, he'll see the likelihood of that soon enough."

"Where will you hold him?"

"Belowdecks."

"In chains?"

"Not unless it's absolutely necessary." He moved over to a table and poured two goblets full of wine, then brought one back to me. I wasn't partial to the red liquid, but my mouth was terribly dry, so I drank just a bit to ease my discomfort, then set it aside.

His green eyes lingered on the goblet for a moment, and I felt a wash of dismay. What had he intended? To get me to imbibe until I relaxed? I remembered the Drifters by the river, drunk to the point of passing out in the cave. Had he hoped that I'd soon be the same? I narrowed my eyes at him.

But again, I detected no malice within him.

"Please, Andriana, sit," he said, gesturing to a chair beside the couch, covered in a deep, rich red fabric that reminded me of the Sheolites' capes. Swallowing my distaste, I forced myself to do as he asked. He went to the table and picked up a platter, covered in a hammered bronze dome. "You must be hungry after your long journey."

He sat on the corner of the couch nearest me and placed the platter on the table between us. Delicious smells of garlic and butter wafted upward as he lifted the dome and set it aside. Underneath was a steaming tureen of soup beside a ladle and two bowls. A round of brown bread was beside it, along with a small ramekin full of fresh-churned butter, which was glistening on the surface. In spite of myself, I licked my lips. It had been a full day since we'd last eaten, our supplies from the mountain camp all consumed.

Keallach tore off a chunk of bread, picked up a knife, and slathered the bread with butter, then passed it to me. I watched him carefully as he ladled some of the thick stew — heavy with meat and carrots and potatoes — into my bowl, then served himself. I liked that he didn't have a servant for this. I also liked that I could watch his every move, so that I might have confidence that what I was eating, he too ate. He was about to take his first bite when he saw my hesitation. His spoon lowered. "What's this? Does it not look appetizing? Or ..." His eyebrows lifted. "You wait to pray? Please. Allow me."

He bowed his head and I tentatively did the same, still keeping my eyes on him, even as he closed his own. "Thank you that you have brought us together, Maker. Thank you for this day and for this food. Amen."

"Amen," I whispered, my mind racing in confusion. This one prayed? And I'd felt genuine gratitude from him. I was certain of it. Hope surged in me and I found myself smiling just as Keallach took a bite of soup and looked up at me. My armband had grown neutral, its incessant cold ache fading to blood temperature again.

"What is it?" he said, after he swallowed. A smile warmed his handsome face, and I thought of him again on the night we'd first met in the Wadi sanctuary.

"Nothing," I dodged, giving my head a little shake. I eagerly took my own first bite, scalding my mouth but not caring. The meat was tender, the vegetables and broth delicious. I took a bite of the bread and found it was freshly made and soft. I shoved away guilty thoughts of Ronan and the rest without food, and decided to look for a way to hide part of the bread to share with them later. I'd ask for seconds on my stew and fill up on that instead ... and slide my own remaining bread into my sleeve.

"Andriana?" Keallach asked softly.

I looked up at him, feeling caught in my own plans.

"Are you all right?"

"I am," I said slowly, wondering what he was getting at.

"You aren't just hungry. You're ravenous. Your friends ... in the mountains. They did not feed you?"

I took another bite and considered the lack of alarm within him. There was still no sense of menace. Did he already know about Chaza'el's village among the treehouses and mountain caves? Or did he consider them harmless? Chaza'el said they'd never been visited by Sheolites, but that didn't mean they hadn't known they were there.

"We found no friends in the mountains. Ronan and I managed to forage for enough food to sustain us," I lied, fearful I'd betray Chaza'el. "But this is far more delicious than anything I've had in days." I took another bite and met his gaze. "I'm here to hear about you, not tell you about me, right? Wasn't that our deal in order to secure passage and see Kapriel? To hear your side of things?"

He set aside his empty bowl and leaned back against his chair, crossing one leg over his other knee. "Truthfully, I'd hoped to learn as much about you as I shared about myself. My story is terribly ... public. Yours is far more secretive ... and therefore, intriguing."

I swallowed my last bite and leaned toward the tureen. "May I?"

"Please," he said, waving a generous hand toward the stew.

24

I could feel his curious eyes cover me, from the tips of my nails up my arms, to my neck and face, then down. I ignored the sensation even as a shiver ran down my neck.

"You might think of your story as public. For Pacificans," I said. "But for those of us living in the Trading Union, we know far less."

"Even among the Ailith?" he asked, cocking one brow again. A shadow of his defensiveness laced his tone.

"I have heard some about you," I allowed. "But I think I'd like to hear it straight from the source."

The muscles in his cheeks worked as if he tensed at the thought. "I'll ask you to keep an open mind, Andriana. Undoubtedly, they've told you half-truths. That's always what gets shared. Half-truths and lies."

I felt the bitterness in him. The hurt. The wounding.

"Half-truths?" I said. In spite of my empathy for him, I couldn't deny my own rising anger. "Tell me what is untruthful. That you denied all you'd been taught by your trainer, imprisoned your twin, and seized the Pacifican throne for yourself? Tell me how you could ignore the Call. How you could possibly turn away from it on that night of nights?"

His eyes shot to mine again and hardened. Then he lifted his chin, took a deep breath, and leaned forward. "I haven't denied what I have been taught. I simply disagreed with our parents. There have never, in the entire history of our world, been brother kings. It would never work. One always has to take the lead, or divide their realms. And I am the eldest … the first out of the womb. By rights, the throne is mine. By rights."

I nodded slowly. I could see why he'd consider it that way. "But Keallach, we are not like any others that have come before us. We Ailith were born entirely for this purpose … to save the world. What if you got in the Maker's way by turning from the path laid before you?"

Keallach tapped his fingertips together, still leaning forward. "I pray that I did not." He bowed his head and scratched the back of his neck, then lifted his face. "You must believe me, Andriana. My intention is for good. For the good of all."

I searched him, then. His words were true. Or at least he believed what he was saying. "But Keallach, you are … the Sheolites. Sethos …" I gestured to the guard at the door, feeling suddenly heavy, weary, utterly exhausted.

"Leave us," Keallach said.

"Highness?" the guard responded.

"Stand outside if you must. But my friend shall speak more freely without you here. Leave us."

"Yes, Highness."

I watched as the burly man disappeared into the night, closing the door with more grace and care than expected. Then I looked to Keallach. "Those men are lost. They are of the dark. And you are surrounded by them."

"You judge them harshly," he said evenly, quietly.

I scoffed. "If you had seen what I have seen —"

He held up a hand. "Perhaps there is a way that is between us. A place where the forked path unites again."

I frowned. What he said made as much sense as water turning to dust. Not after what I'd felt on that battlefield when we fought the Sheolites. The depths of darkness, despair. Death itself, fighting to take me down, hold me down until I suffocated, choking on my own loss of hope.

"Don't you see, Andriana?" he asked, rising and pacing the short room, one hand on his head, one gesturing to me. "All people respond to power. It is what drives them. And what am

I on the cusp of? Ultimate power. Within months, the entire Trading Union will bow to me as emperor. We will claim the rebels and outliers in time. Together, we shall rebuild this country, and begin to claim others. Together, we will establish unification of the entire world. Peace. This is the moment to seize it. Upon its rebirth. I wager you've learned enough of humanity's history to know that once each power is developed, they will resist bowing to another. But right now ..." His eyes danced with possibility. "It's like the opportunity to train up a child rather than try and remake a man. I really think it could work."

I stared at him. So his quest for ultimate power was true. But the way he put it, the goal was not for glory and riches, but rather for something we all might cheer for — peace. My mind whirled, grasping for truth, trying to make sense of what I'd learned. "But what of Pacifica? What of your methods of stealing children in Georgii Post? Wrenching them away from their parents and spiriting them off to be adopted in your own land or put to work in the factories and mines?"

He stilled and stared at me, mouth agape. "What? What are you talking about?"

"The children. The reaping. I saw it for myself. Armed guards, stealing away children to be adopted by the childless across the Wall."

He shook his head, and I felt the confusion in him. "We adopt children who have no hope, no future. But the children are brought to us, given to our soldiers. It is sad, the conditions that leave them in such a desperate place —"

"No," I said, shaking my head. "That's not how it happens there. We saw children ripped from an orphanage ourselves."

"There are no sanctioned orphanages in Georgii Post.

Perhaps a few good-hearted people showing kindnesses, but I assure you, we take far better care of them in Pacifica. Most are put into our very own homes; some are given a place to eat, sleep, work."

I shook my head again. "Why is that? Why not sanction an orphanage? And what right does Pacifica have, dictating what goes on at Georgii Post?"

Keallach lifted a brow. "I just told you. In time, it shall be part of the greater empire, for their own good."

"For their own good? Keallach, I saw soldiers rip a child from his parents' arms! If that is what it means to be part of your 'empire,' I'll be certain to lead the rebels against you."

Keallach frowned and seemed to take a moment to gather himself. "If what you say is true, I want to get to the bottom of it. It's not how I want it," he said, slicing his hand in the air, a red blush arriving at his jawline. "But it is exactly those sorts of things that I seek to remedy. Don't you see?" he asked, stepping closer to me. "You've likely glimpsed enough of Pacifica's prosperity en route to the wharf. I will gladly show you more of our success here, myself. Eventually, places like Georgii Post will be more like Pacifica. The entire Trading Union will institute laws and have governance that will bring about needed change. Castle Vega. Even Zanzibar, in time."

I stared at him. He honestly believed it. He thought he was on a righteous, true path. I reached for my goblet and took a swallow. "What of your brother? Why did he not agree with this plan?"

"I have not spoken to my brother in many seasons," he said. His eyes were on the dark porthole as if he could peer through the night.

"Why?"

He shook his head and sat down again heavily.

"But you happened to choose this night, this ship, to go to him?"

"I'd heard … There are some that say …" His eyes moved back to the porthole again, and he took a deep breath and let it out slowly. "Word reached me that Kapriel was unwell. Frail. He's refused food for some time." He looked at me, miserable. "Andriana, I wanted Kapriel out of my way. Far out of my way. But I never wanted to see him die."

Again, I felt the longing, the pain within him. Love for his brother. I was lost in a tornado of thought. Could it be? Had the elders misunderstood about Keallach? Might I be able to broker peace? Bring Keallach into the Ailith fold, even now when he was considered lost to us?

I felt his eyes on me, the desperation, the hope, the desire for connection, and rose quickly, hoping a little pacing of my own might straighten out my thoughts. But then a question stilled me.

"Keallach, where is your knight?" Every Remnant had been paired with a Knight upon their twelfth year. Where was his? I half turned to face him and felt a pang of fear run through him. My eyes narrowed. Fear?

His face darkened, and he looked away again. I could feel pain in his memory. "My knight was killed at the same time Kapriel was sent to the Isle of Catal." He looked me full in the face. "He killed Kapriel's knight in the same battle."

I swallowed hard. "They killed each other." My words came out in a whisper. Such a waste, such a loss. My Ailith brothers or sisters …

"It was a terrible day," he said, grief lacing his voice. "And it got worse. My parents would not abide by my decision."

I stared at him, wondering if he'd be willing to be fully honest. "What happened to them?"

"They ... died."

"You killed them."

His blue-green eyes shot up to meet mine. "No," he said with a shake of his head. "No. I did not."

I frowned. "Then who did?"

He took a breath, then a second. "Another."

Another. I had a good idea who that might be. "Keallach ... When did Sethos enter your court?"

"Sethos was the captain of my father's guard. I asked him to take ... my knight's place."

I stared at him, thinking that I might've misheard him. My arm cuff seemed to grow colder at the mere mention of the man's name. "You asked him to?"

He nodded once, his eyes on mine, measuring my reaction, even as pain and grief continued to lance through him.

"And ... before you asked him to do so ... Were you ... friends?"

His lips clamped together as he stared at me. "You're asking if he influenced my decisions."

"Yes."

"No more than I allowed. And now ... Andriana, if you could see Pacifica, see my court, see my people, you would see a *good* kingdom. My kingdom," he said, touching his chest. "A kingdom worthy of leading an empire. And it's my doing. Not Sethos's."

I turned away and stared at the crackling fire dancing behind a soot-covered screen. Was this the fissure I sought? Had Sethos been the one to influence my brother? Turn him away from the right path? Was this why Sethos had wanted to destroy us before we got anywhere near him?

I turned again to him. "Sethos is of the dark," I said carefully. "He is our enemy."

Keallach sat down heavily and sighed. "I know it must appear that way, to you. You've judged him harshly, because of that. But I sent him to seek you out. To bring the Ailith to me. I knew you wouldn't come willingly so — "

"No," I said, stepping toward him, frowning. "You still don't understand. Your man," I said, gesturing past the guard at the door to where I assumed Sethos was, "is of Sheol." I leaned in, searching him as hard as I could. Again, the confusion in him was clear.

"Sheol?" he said blankly. "Now you've given in to superstition."

"Trust me," I said, crossing my arms. "He is. I don't know how he has remained cloaked to you, a Remnant. But he is, Keallach. And it was the Sheolites who ..." My voice cracked with sudden tears, and I swallowed hard. Keallach reached out, as if to comfort me, but I stepped away, alarmed. "It was the Sheolites who murdered my parents," I spat out.

He visably paled. "Wh-what?"

I nodded. "The night of our Call, they came after me and discovered my parents. They tortured them, Keallach. Tortured ..." My voice broke again and tears ran down my cheeks. I angrily brushed them away as I stared at him, furious, wanting to blame him. To find anything in him that verified that he was as much my enemy as Sethos was. But there was nothing. Still, I pressed forward. "What was it?" I asked bitterly. "After you killed your own parents was it so easy to order the deaths of ours?"

He scowled and reached out to grab hold of my upper arms, just beneath the cuff. "Again, such lies! Have they fed you nothing but lies your whole life? Is this evidence of what the Community elders preach?"

I scanned his eyes, so close that I could see brown flecks in one. My head was beginning to pound. *Too much empath work all at once*, I assessed.

I shook off his hands and sank back to my chair again, trying to make sense of what I was learning. "So you deny it? Killing your parents?"

"Yes, I deny it," he said bitterly, pacing with one hand on his hip, one on his head. "It wasn't me. I mean, I was there. And you have to believe me, Andriana ... there isn't a day that goes by that I don't wish I'd found a way to stop it. It ..." He shook his head. "It's a long, complicated story." He looked into my eyes, and in them I saw his grief, his regret.

I stared at him, grudgingly feeling my walls crumbling a little. "And you did not send the Sheolites to kill us?"

"My guard. Not ... *Sheolites*, as you call them. To find you. Not to kill you."

"Keallach, they are Sheolites. How can you be so blind? Does your Ailith blood not tell you that they are enemies? Do you not feel it in your bones?"

He stared back at me in confusion.

"If you had been there ... If you had seen them. Keallach, they were intent on murder, not capture. I'm sure of it. I-I think." My thoughts came slowly, as if muddled. I felt the weight of my responsibility in this moment merely as increased exhaustion — another burden to bear. "Keallach, you need to separate from Sethos. Send him as far from you as possible. I fear ... I fear he's influenced you. And done things you weren't aware of. Perhaps it was his idea to send Kapriel to the Isle of Catal?"

Keallach frowned at me. "Sethos? No, as much as I'd like to pass off the responsibility, it was my own order."

I thought back to Castle Vega and the Council of Six I'd encountered. Men easy in Sethos's company. Men who moved among the Trading Union with an air of ownership. "Keallach, how did you choose your council?" I picked up my goblet again and sipped, pretending to still be relaxed, even though my stomach roiled.

"The Six?" he asked in surprise.

I nodded.

"They are my most trusted friends, as well as from highly influential families in Pacifica. They have helped me unify Pacifica and make her stronger. Strong enough to lead the entire empire. They shall be my generals when we bring the Union under our wing. Together, we will wipe out starvation and illness. Together, we will all prosper."

I stared at him. He truly believed in the philanthropy of his mission. That it was for the good of all. But I'd had firsthand experience with his most trusted friends. They were intent on eradicating any competition; hadn't they destroyed the Hoodite farm?

He took a sip of his wine and gave me a small smile. "I hear you met them, at Castle Vega. That all the Ailith managed to sneak in and disguise themselves as servants."

"We did," I said, waiting for the rest of it, my muscles tensing. We'd tried to kill Maximillian on our way out. And failed.

Keallach's eyes casually drifted over my neck and shoulder and arm for a moment, and then back to my face, and his smile grew, forming deep dimples in his cheeks. "Max thought

I should find you again and we should be betrothed. A daughter of the Union, married to the emperor. Both of us Ailith. It would help ease our cause, among the commoners."

I frowned and he laughed, lifting his hands, choking on a new sip of wine. He managed to swallow and then said, "Forgive me. I only meant to tease. Clearly, I am not to your taste."

His eyes were merry, and I shook my head. "It's not that. It's just ..."

His smile faded, and he looked almost sad for a moment. "Just ... *Ronan*, right?"

I shivered. There was some emotion just beyond where I could reach in him ... something that made me pause. And I had the clear thought that it wasn't good that he knew how deeply I felt for my knight. That I didn't just love Ronan as a brother, but that I *loved* him.

"When we get back to Pacifica," he said, rising to pour more wine from a carafe, "I will bring you to the palace, and you can give the Six another chance. I think you'll find them quite likable, when you aren't fearing discovery or harm. I think your fear gave you the wrong idea about them."

I thought back to the men, cavorting about in the courtyard with half-dressed women. Drinking wine as if it were water. Leering at me. All so hungry for power. "Perhaps," I lied.

He pursed his full lips and tapped them. "You are an empath, are you not? That is your gift? That is what Sethos judged you to be."

"I am. What is your gift?"

He ignored my question. "And so you sensed something in them that made you dislike them?"

"Yes. And trust me when I say that I had ample *outward* reasons too."

He shifted his head back and forth and tapped his lips, as if still trying to sort it out. "Castle Vega is where people let loose. Trust me, they are far more refined when at home in Pacifica. Gentlemen."

"Gentlemen?" I said with a laugh, the archaic word sounding odd on my own tongue, and especially so when applied to the men I'd met.

"Yes," he insisted, irritated.

I took another sip of my wine and, with some surprise, found my goblet empty. "It is my opinion that a gentleman is a gentleman, even when no one else expects it of him."

Keallach stared at me so intently that I wished I had more wine so I'd have something to do with my hands.

"What do you think I am like, Andriana?" he asked softly, setting down his goblet. "When no one has expectations of me?"

I felt his burden, then. Understood that expectations followed him everywhere. I blinked at him, trying to steady my vision. There seemed to be two of him for a bit, then one. "I … I don't know."

He leaned forward, took my hand in both of his, and stared at our fingers intertwined. His palms were warm and dry, comforting. Dimly, I thought I should pull away. But I couldn't summon the power to truly care or figure out why.

He smiled softly. "You are as lovely as the Six say, Andriana. And it is my hope that I will someday prove to you that I am a gentleman, wherever I am."

I looked back at him, and three of his tentative, tender smiles danced before me, rotating in a circle. "I … I … Perhaps I had too much wine."

"One glass? I doubt it. You are simply weary after so great a journey. Come. I will show you where you can sleep for a while."

He pulled me to my feet and then rested warm, strong hands on my hips when I swayed, unsteady. My head was spinning. "Keallach, I ... I ..."

He swept me up into his arms, which just made it worse. I was floating, flying, colors imploding in my brain like fireworks. We moved, and the lights turned into a swirl of light. I heard him murmuring in my ear, comforting me, and then felt him lay me down, felt the whisper of cool night air before a soft blanket covered me, warding it off, then heard the click of a door behind him.

And by the time I recognized that I lay atop soft, silky sheets and had sunk into the recesses of a feather pillow, I thought of protesting, of forcing my head clear and making my way to Ronan.

But it was no use. My head spun faster and faster.

It was over before it began.

RONAN

"Once again, divided from your precious Remnant," Sethos whispered, smiling at me as I struggled to break free. We were in a small room belowdecks. Two men held me, one on either arm, with another behind me, as they worked to chain my wrists. "You are not so good at staying by her side, are you?"

"Better than you are with Keallach," I returned. "You leave him vulnerable and often alone, I see."

One wrist was chained and the other was nearly clasped

when he struck, ramming his fists to my side in two swift punches that made me double up, and gasp for breath. Tears streamed from my eyes. He'd aimed directly for the wound I'd sustained in the Wadi.

He wrenched back my head, holding my ponytail in his hand. "You shall never threaten the emperor again," he grit out.

"I'll make you a deal," I said, panting, trying to get on top of the pain. "You never threaten Andriana again, and I'll try to leave your boy alone."

He let go of my hair with a sneer. "What are you really doing here in Pacifica, Knight? Tell me."

"We did," I said, lifting my chin.

"You came all this way merely to *see* Kapriel. To *talk* to him," he mocked, pacing a bit before me, chin in hand.

"Exactly."

"And where are the others?"

"What others?"

"The Remnants," he said, turning to face me, his dark eyes narrowing. "The other knights."

"I don't know," I said.

He punched me again, connecting with the lower left of my jaw so hard that I wondered if he'd cracked all of my teeth. My head swung to the right and he was pulling back to give me a second blow from the other side. But I'd anticipated it, and turned just in time so that when his fist connected, it was with skull rather than cheek, as our trainer had taught us.

We all clearly heard the sounds of cracking bones. My vision tunneled and I fought to keep conscious.

Sethos roared in complaint, cradling his broken hand in the other and staggering far enough for me to reach up on the chains, lift my body, and kick.

My boots caught him, one in the throat and one in the chest. My left arm had given out at the last second, the agony in my side weakening me. I looked up in time to see Sethos reel back and hit the far wall, bouncing off it and nearly going to his knees before he regained his equilibrium. He shook off the men who rushed to his aid and slowly straightened.

My armband was colder than ever, practically ringing with frigidity. But I could clearly see the evil in my midst. "You are poison, Sethos."

"And it's a pity that I can't lead you to poison's end, Knight. All I can do is extract the information I seek. But someday soon, I shall have your life." He stepped toward me, but not close enough for me to reach him with a kick again. "Bind his legs," he told his men. "We will have the truth from him, one way or another."

The malice in the room was palpable as he carefully bound his wounded hand, and casually waved his other to indicate he wanted his men to beat me again.

I continued to fight unconsciousness. Blood dripped into my eye. Another cut seeped blood into my mouth. Sethos came closer and pulled my head upright, holding my hair again. "What will it take, Knight? Shall I bring your pretty little Remnant down here?"

His eyes glinted when I glared at him. "Ah, yes. She's the key to opening your mouth, isn't she?"

"You'll find that she's stronger than I," I said. "Within."

"In some ways, yes," he said, releasing me and then pacing slowly before me again, chin in hand. He lifted one brow. "And in other ways, not." He turned to face me. "I tire of our games, Ronan. I'll ask one more time. Where are the others?"

"I do not know," I said. It was the truth. I only hoped

to the Maker that they were somewhere aboard this ship. Protecting Dri. And poising to free me. But I'd seen enough to know. We were outnumbered. We'd have to surprise them. The longer they tortured me, the farther out to sea we went, the more relaxed they became, the better our chances.

The thought made me smile.

I didn't see his fist. Only heard his growl. And then his good hand connected with my jaw again and I was spinning, spinning, knowing it was impossible, feeling the distant tug of chains, still holding me, but spinning anyway.

Until I felt and saw nothing at all.

CHAPTER

3

ANDRIANA

I awakened and felt the lift and drop of the ship. *Oh no*, was my first thought. Too much time had passed since I last remembered anything. Far too much time.

I gasped and sat up, eyes wide, looking all around me, my heart thundering in my chest. The captain's bedroom was as finely appointed as his sitting room, full of lush fabric, an ornate oval mirror in the corner — that swayed on its hinges with the rise and fall of the ship emitting an irritating creak — an overstuffed chair, and a highly polished side table. I scanned it all for signs of Keallach, thinking he had to be here somewhere. But I found no evidence of him.

It was with some relief that I looked over at the other side of the wide bed and saw that it hadn't been slept in. *I will prove to you that I am a gentleman*, he'd said. Had he been speaking the truth?

But then I looked down and gasped. Not only had my hair been loosed from its knot and set into waves around my shoulders, but it had been washed. How had I slept through that? And I'd been changed into one of the white, ethereal gowns of Pacifica. I could see the gleaming cuff on my arm through the gossamer material, but at least the thin sheath that covered my body provided a measure of modesty. A slim measure. I jumped out of bed and pulled at the material in anger, as if it had betrayed me more than Keallach.

After a brief knock, the door opened and I whirled.

Keallach leaned against the doorjamb with a grin, appraising me from head to toe. Had he said he thought me beautiful last night? Or had I dreamed it? I was taken back to that morning in the Wadi Qelt sanctuary, when I'd realized he'd left the purple flower I'd set in my hair, not Ronan. Keallach had looked so pleased, seeing it behind my ear ...

He looked twice as drawn to me now, and I knew his desire then, in full. There were no walls today, only full access.

"Keallach!" I said, seizing on anger, trying to fish my thoughts out of the swirl of his emotion. "Did you ... Did you do this to me?" I said, gesturing down at my gown.

"Well, there's no need to say it like I molested you," he said with a scoff. "I didn't tend to you. Not that I would've minded," he said, cocking one brow, his grin returning.

"I—I—"

He held up a hand. "Andriana. I had a maidservant wash you and change you. You were sleeping in my bed, after all. Who knew what vermin you'd brought in after your weeks on the road?"

My mouth dropped open, half in surprise, half in embarrassment. His revulsion at the thought of my uncleanliness nearly usurped his physical draw toward me. He narrowed his eyes. "Are you reading me, Andriana? What I'm feeling? Thinking?"

I abruptly shut my mouth and grimaced as I felt the heat of a blush on my cheeks. "I cannot read your thoughts, only your emotions."

"But you can take an educated guess on thoughts, based on feelings."

I didn't acknowledge his question. I'd already said too much.

He lifted a hand. "You apparently have never had Pacifican evening wine."

"I've had very little wine at all," I said.

"Evening wine has a mild sedative in it to help us sleep," he said, and I felt the contrition within him. "Forgive me. I should've known to warn you."

"Yes," I said, lifting my chin, agitated, furious, somehow doubting it had been an accident. My stomach clenched and twisted. "You should have." I strode to the door to pass him, but he blocked it with one strong arm.

I hesitated, but stared at the worn planks of the deck, rather at him. "I'd like to go outside. I think I'm going to be sick."

The arm immediately dropped and I rushed through the sitting room, out the cabin door, and to the railing of the ship. Immediately, all the contents of my stomach joined the swirling, frothy waters beneath us. I coughed, spit, and straightened, then vomited again. My stomach heaving but empty, I gasped and closed my eyes, slowly straightening. Still, I gripped the rail, feeling empty, a tad faint, but far better than moments before.

Keallach stood beside me, silent for a time. He was so close that I could feel the hair of his arm tickling my skin. "That's more likely due to the sea rather than the evening wine. Keep your eye on the horizon. It'll help."

"How can you stomach the stuff?" I said, squinting outward, blinking against the sheen of the sun on the water's surface.

"The evening wine? We've been given sips of it since we were learning to walk. You'll become accustomed to it too."

I frowned and yet said nothing. Why did he assume that I would be in Pacifica long enough to become accustomed to anything?

He looked over at me, and I felt his grin, even though I didn't meet his gaze. "The maidservant found this in the sleeve of your sweater," he said, lifting the half-eaten piece of bread and offering it to me. "Are you in the habit of stashing away food?"

"I'm in the habit of avoiding starvation," I sniffed. I wiped at my nose with the back of my hand, and a handkerchief appeared in my line of vision. Did he have to be so … attentive? But I took the cloth and angrily swiped at my nose.

"Did you fear we wouldn't feed Ronan?" he asked softly.

"Yes," I lied. The last thing I needed was him getting the truth out of me — that I hoped to give a little to every Ailith aboard this ship. Five more than just Ronan.

At least I hoped they were aboard. It felt like they were here. My arm cuff was curiously warm — was that their presence? Or Keallach's? "Where is Ronan?" I asked.

"He's belowdecks, as I said he'd be," he said, his tone overly light. I tried to read him again, but the walls were back. I couldn't get anything. How did he do that? And did I dare touch him to see if that would penetrate the wall?

I turned to run my eyes down the length of the *Far North*, over one sailor and then another in gray. Soldiers. Sheolite. But all carefully kept their gazes out of Keallach's business here with me, and none were familiar. The Ailith were near. They had to be. I sensed them; I just couldn't see them.

"It's beautiful, isn't it?" Keallach asked, gesturing outward to the waves again. "As a daughter of the Valley, I assume you've never been at sea. We left port only a few hours ago, and now this — it's as if we're alone on a watery planet. It's as mesmerizing as the stars in the desert, is it not?"

Though I didn't say it aloud, I had to admit that it was an exhilarating, otherworldly experience. To see nothing but green-blue waves, rolling and cresting with tiny whitecaps, for as far as my eyes could see. The ocean did appear as its own world. The air was cold and crisp, even with the sun warm on our skin, and I shivered and rubbed my arms.

"Are you cold?"

"A bit," I said. "If I had my own clothes — "

"They'll be given back to you. The maids are laundering them. Not that I'm anxious to see you change out of that lovely gown. Here," he said, fiddling with the button of his light, taupe-colored cape.

"No, no, that's not necessary," I said, lifting a hand. But he was already wrapping it around my shoulders, and I had to admit the warmth was welcome.

He had on a billowing white shirt beneath, tied at the base of his throat, and tucked into brown leather breeches. He looked every part the dashing prince — like someone out of a storybook.

"Look, there!" he said, leaning close, so close I could feel the heat of his skin. He pointed below us, down near where the edge of the ship was slicing through the waves.

"What? What are those?" I asked. I could see the flip of a tail, the curve of a body. Then another, and another.

"A pod of dolphins," he said, pleasure lacing his tone.

One of the creatures crested then, racing with the ship, and jumped out of the water in an arc, then dived back in. Right behind him, two others did the same. Surprised, I laughed, and then laughed again when they repeated the exercise.

I felt Keallach's surge of admiration toward me and edged away, facing him. I shook my head a little in warning.

He laughed under his breath, peered out to the ocean's horizon for a moment, then back to me. "This reading my emotions is a bit … disruptive," he mused. "It'll take me a while to get used to that. But women always complain that men won't express their feelings, right? I take it that's not an issue for you. You know everything I feel."

I clamped my lips shut, absorbing his words. We wouldn't be keeping company for long. The agreement had only been for time together to and from the island. And with any luck, we'd be on separate ships when we left Catal.

"What is your gifting?" I asked. "And how is it that you can block me from reading your feelings at times?"

He studied me, weighing whether he trusted me or not. He took a deep breath, as if fearing I might laugh at him when I heard. "I occasionally have curious powers. To do things — move objects and the like, with my mind."

I thought about this, my mouth dry, no trace of humor teasing my lips. "And your brother?" I managed to ask.

"The power to command nature. Summon rain and such." His eyes perused me and drifted down to my arm. The cape had blown back over one shoulder, leaving my cuff exposed. "But we have not received the full gifting our trainer spoke of." He glanced over at me and turned. "Max told me that several of you wore these armbands in Castle Vega," he said, reaching up to lightly touch mine with two fingers. I stood stock-still and his eyes shifted back and forth, as if he could read me. "I assume it has something to do with that?"

"It is a trinket," I said idly, staring out to sea as my stomach grew unsettled again. "Something the Ailith wear as a sign of our solidarity." I tried to casually put some space between us and pulled the cape back over my shoulder. Would he have felt the heat with it that told me my friends were here nearby? Or did he know that anyway—recognizing fellow Ailith as we always could? Maybe he'd lost the ability in his separation.

He laughed under his breath and leaned his arms against the rail. "Where are the other cuffs, then? For the Remnants you've yet to meet?"

"I don't know."

He frowned. "You don't know?"

"No," I said, shaking my head, thinking of Raniero, and the small bag at his waist that had held them. He had given them to Ronan, but where they were now, I didn't know.

"Was there—" he paused, taking a moment to choose his words, "some sort of ceremony that unlocked your gift, Andriana? That fused the cuff to your skin?" He leaned a few inches back, to examine my entire face. "You are far more mature in your gifting than I. And there is word from Zanzibar that your healer conquered even the Cancer. Is that true? Sethos ... he says that the boy named Vidar knew he was present before he was visible. Something has ... changed for you all. Tell me what that was."

I knew I had to tread carefully. To tell him too much was to give him a weapon against us. And yet if I told him too little, he'd guess I was lying or holding back. And there was such longing within him … that hunger that would only be assuaged by a reunion with the Maker. An answer to his own Call.

To join us. Was there a chance? Had the Maker made this conversation possible so that I might draw him back in? I felt the pull of him, the magnetic draw I felt with every one of my Ailith kin. Did he feel it too?

"It is the Maker who unlocks our gifting, Keallach," I said, rejoining him at the rail. I closed my eyes, and dared to slide my hand next to his, letting our hands touch. "That and being in community. You are so far from us. You've set yourself apart from your kin … both of the blood and of spirit." I let my hand cover his briefly, lightly, and in that small touch, I felt the grief within him, the separation.

A lump formed in my throat as I took on his burden as my own. I glanced up to find him staring at me. It was a pure moment of knowing and being known, as only I could do with other Ailith. I swallowed hard, feeling our bond. I held onto it and then cast it toward him, wanting him to feel the full force of it too.

He abruptly pulled his hand from mine and stepped away, holding it as if I'd burned him. "How … How did you do that?"

"What?" I asked, pretending ignorance.

"You know," he said. "You just won't tell me." The soft lines of the ache, the longing I could see on his face turned into the hard lines of resentment. The wall slid neatly upward, dividing us again. And our separation made me feel nauseated, as I might with any other of my Ailith brothers or sisters. It was so clearly wrong — wrong that he wasn't with us. That we'd been divided.

He continued to stare at me, and my sorrow seemed to anger him most.

"Do not pity me, Andriana," he bit out, leaning toward me. Any trace of grief and loneliness quickly morphed into agitation. "I made my choices with a clear mind and heart," he whispered harshly again in my ear, his breath hot. "Do you understand me?"

I nodded once. Other than that, I stayed utterly still.

Then he turned and left the small deck, charging down the ladder to the bigger deck below.

My mind swirled as I thought about Keallach and all he'd said. How close he was, and yet how distant.

I watched the white bubbles beneath me eddy in wide, dissipating circles as the boat continued to slice through the water toward the island prison.

And then I vomited again.

CHAPTER
4

ANDRIANA

We reached the Isle of Catal a little while later. I exited Keallach's cabin, leaving his cape behind, when I heard the shouts and felt the steam engine slow. Clouds were gathering on the horizon, a great wall of billowing gray. More troubling was the view of the prison itself: aging white stone in straight walls extending from island cliffs, washed by waves, allowing little purchase for climbers, few ledges for ladders. *At least from this side ...*

Sailors came together at the rail to watch the approach of the island, and behind them great puffs of steam emerged from a smokestack—the apparent power for our speed. All along the way, the ivory sails had remained furled and tied to their beams, seemingly only a backup in case the steam failed. I felt a chill on my cuff and saw Keallach speaking to Sethos on the broad deck below with his arms crossed. At one point, both looked up at me. I willed myself not to look away until they did, and then searched the others. There was still no sign of my companions.

I moved to climb down from the upper deck via the small ladder-like stairwell, but a sailor stepped in my way and lifted one hand. "You are to remain here, miss," he said.

My heart thudding, I noticed the other man on the far side of the deck, plainly another guard. "So I am a prisoner?"

The first man gave me a small shrug. "Hardly a cell," he said, waving back toward the cabin with a grin. "Could be worse. Just sit tight. We'll dock shortly."

I lifted my chin. "I'd like to see Ronan, my companion."

He glanced at the other guard and smiled, crossing his arms. "As I'm certain he'd like to see you." He let his dark eyes drift down to my toes and back, slowly, and I blushed, recognizing that the wind made the thin fabric cling to every line and curve of my body. Anger quickly rushed through me and I was moving before I thought about it, punching him in the gut, kneeing him in the nose when he bent over, then driving him back against the wall of the captain's cabin, pinning him against it, leaning as hard as I could with both hands encircling his neck. His nose dripped blood.

"I would like to see Ronan," I grit out, my fingers clenching around his throat. "And I demand you treat me with more respect."

A low laugh behind me pulled me out of my fog of fury. *Keallach.*

I dropped my hands, knowing I couldn't handle much more of the guard's growing panic, and not wanting Keallach to note my weakness. I glanced over my shoulder at him. Sethos was right behind him, scowling, but Keallach was shaking his head, bemused, all traces of his previous irritation evaporated. "That's hardly ladylike, Andriana," he said, almost teasing in his tone.

"Yes, well, ladylike manners are hardly my first priority."

"You've gone and gotten this man's blood all over your pristine white skirts," he noted.

"Cleanliness is not quite my priority either," I said, brushing past him, pacing, hoping he wouldn't see my trembling. I'd been too furious to notice that my armband had grown painfully cold with Sethos so near. I tried to get as far from him as the small deck space allowed, but I could feel his dark eyes on me, taking in far more information than I liked.

"All I wanted was to see Ronan," I said, speaking only to Keallach. "Will you allow him to accompany me on the island?"

"No," Keallach said, as friendly as if he'd said yes. "I promised that *you* would see Kapriel. Ronan will stay belowdecks to insure you return with us and don't try anything foolish." He gestured to the guard, scowling as he held a handkerchief to his dripping nose. "You are apparently more lethal than your beauty would lead one to believe. Your trainer did well." He nodded in appreciation, his dimple deepening.

I had to make a conscious effort not to bite my lip as I tried to think my way through this. I couldn't do it all alone — freeing Kapriel, that is. Not with so many of Keallach's men about. And Sethos. The man would stick as close as a leech. Here on a ship, or on the island … we'd be too easily entrapped. We'd need to return later for Kapriel. For now, all I could do was meet him and hopefully gather information to help us later.

"Do not trust her, Highness," Sethos said slowly, arms folded, squinting at me.

"Her?" Keallach said, frowning. "What could an empath do? Here on the island? Alone?" But I saw the shadow of doubt cross his face, as if he'd remembered how I'd cast emotion into him.

Sethos strode over to me and when I tried to evade him, he grabbed hold of me, forcing me to look him in the face. "What are you planning, girl?"

"Sethos, stop," Keallach said, but the larger man ignored him.

Sethos's features were angular, sharp, his nose long and thin, and there was devastating strength within him. With him so near, a chasm seemed to open within me — a gaping hole that made me gasp — and I remembered the feeling of darkness encapsulating me on the battlefield.

"Sethos! Stop at once!" Keallach commanded, enraged. He gripped Sethos's arm.

Finally, the man gave me a brief look of understanding and let go of me. Involuntarily, I reached up and touched my cuff; it almost hurt, it was so cold. Like it felt in the Valley when I was a child, holding my hand beneath the frozen crust of the river, hoping to catch a fish. His eyes followed my movement with interest, and something kindled in his dark eyes. I let out a breath of exasperation and turned, striding to the railing.

Neither of them said another word to me as shouts and commands and whistles filled the air. We were entering the tiny harbor of the island, and two guard boats came out to circle us, each with a machine gun mounted on the top. When they spotted Keallach and Sethos, they saluted and sped off.

A loud noise came from belowdecks, and I could feel the big ship begin to slow. Churning sounds emerged from the back, and we came to a neat stop in the slip of a huge dock. Sailors tossed down heavy ropes, and soldiers below tied them to enormous cleats on the pier. The gangplank emerged and Keallach stopped beside me. "Ready?" he said, looking excited, as if he was truly eager to reunite with his brother, not face a man he'd sent away to prison.

I stared at him for several seconds. He was utterly confounding. One moment standing as leader of his menacing forces, the next as close to my heart as any other of my Ailith kin.

"Come," he said, turning to shimmy down the ladder.

I followed him down to the main deck, well aware that Sethos had disappeared. As much as I detested his presence, having him away from my line of vision made me all the more nervous. Taking a chance on the moment's camaraderie, when I reached the end of the ladder, I touched Keallach's arm. He glanced down at my hand in surprise.

"May I have a quick word?" I said.

He frowned and then nodded, pulling me a bit away from the nearest soldiers. He folded his arms and faced me, cocking his head as if waiting, clearly wary of my touch.

I licked my lips. "Keallach, you need to dismiss Sethos. Send him away. He is vile — the very definition of evil."

His frown deepened. "More of this, now? What can you know of Sethos?"

"I know that he fights against everything — and everyone — who fights for the Maker. And he has powers …" I shook my head. "Fearsome powers."

"And you know this by …"

"Because every time I've been in his presence, I've felt it."

"He was after you," Keallach said with a dismissive shrug, pulling away. "On my orders, he was out to capture any Ailith he could and bring you to me. Perhaps you confuse his intense drive with something more grave."

"I don't think so."

"This is a conversation for another time." He turned to leave and I grabbed his arm. Pointedly, he looked from my hand to me.

I dropped my hand but edged closer. "It's a conversation for now," I pressed. "Don't you see? It's he who has drawn you away from the Ailith cause and calling. He who divides us."

"Nonsense. Has he not allowed you and Ronan to be aboard my very ship?"

"Only to see if he might find a way to stop us. Or destroy us."

Keallach let out a dismissive noise. "You feel *too* much, Empath. It has confused you."

"There is no confusion in this," I insisted, following him when he strode away from me.

He folded his arms and turned toward me again. "You've gotten the wrong idea of Sethos, Andriana. He is … *challenging* at times. But there is good in him. If not for him, I don't know if I'd be here today."

My mouth dropped open, ten different retorts tying my tongue.

Taking in my expression, he scanned the docks to make sure we were still out of earshot of any of the men and then turned back to me. "It is Sethos who masterminded the public health operation that keeps Pacifica Cancer-free. It was he who began imports and exports with the Trading Union, which have saved countless families from starvation. From *both* sides of the Wall." His hand pierced the air in angry emphasis. And then he dropped his voice. "It was he who came to me and told me that Kapriel was ill, and convinced me I ought to reach out to him again. Does that sound like the voice of evil to you?"

My mind whirled and I shook my head in confusion.

"Come," he said, gesturing toward the gangplank.

I passed him, agitated and angry. It made no sense. Sethos was wholly evil. Wasn't he? Again, I looked for him, and a shiver ran down my back when I couldn't find him. My armband was cool, but not frigid. He and the Sheolites were present … just not where I could see them.

"Where is he?" I asked him, panting as we left the sun-bleached slats of the pier and took to the steep, cobblestone road that presumably led up to the prison. "Sethos and his men?"

"Sethos and his men tend to upset my brother," Keallach said. "I thought it best if they wait for our return down at the docks."

I turned away before he could see my small smile. It was good to put some distance between me and the Sheolites, and it gave me hope about finding some way — some crazy way — to free Kapriel. Mentally, I sized up Keallach, wondering if I could take him, if we could somehow ditch the guards. He was taller than I by several inches, and certainly broader at the shoulders. And yet maybe my training had been better than his own. Hadn't he just admired how I took down that guard with a few swift moves?

But the thought of Sethos back aboard the ship, with Ronan tied up and unable to defend himself … any small sense of hope I'd felt was immediately snuffed out. I slowed alongside Keallach, sensing his trepidation, his fear over what I assumed was the coming meeting with his brother. Anger and frustration were present within him too. Was he preparing his defensive argument to present to his twin?

Around the next bend, there was a heavy gate. We stopped and the others — six guards in gray — gathered around me.

Keallach glanced at me and then gestured to two men. "Chain her and see that you never let go of her arms." His eyes met mine again. "Forgive me. But I can take no chances."

"What? Wait —" I began, but my protests were buried beneath the soldiers' quick agreement.

"Yes, my liege."

"Right away, Highness."

It rankled, their titles for him. His claim on any measure of royalty had sent his brother here, to this cold prison isle, for season upon season. I hoped guilt would rot within Keallach, tear at him, poke at him. Perhaps it would open him up to his brother — and to his fellow Ailith — anew.

Heavy, rusting iron rings clamped down on my wrists, tiny anomalies in the steel poking at me. A chain spread between them and then down to meet another, which they clamped around my ankles. I looked to Keallach in disbelief, playing upon my femininity. "Is this truly necessary?"

"From what I know of you and yours, yes," he said abruptly, then moved on ahead of me and up a winding staircase. He looked over his shoulder. "You will wait out here," he said, gesturing to the platform beside him. "When I am done speaking with my brother, you will have your turn to meet him."

He disappeared then, and I shuffled over to the staircase and made my way up it with some effort, given the extra thirty pounds of chain and long gown that encumbered me. I could hear the soldier behind me, snickering, and ignored him. At the top at last, I moved over to the far wall and looked down.

We were on the very edge of the prison wall, and far below the sea crashed against dark gray rocks. I quickly edged away, my stomach flipping.

A soldier pretended to push me, with a shout meant to startle me, but I managed to not cry out. I looked at him with as much loathing as I could muster, and he gave a small, nervous laugh and looked to his friend, who chuckled with him. But he took a step away from me, even as he continued to toss out derisive comments I chose to ignore. My eyes moved to the horizon and the gathering storm building there. Would we be trapped on the island? Already the swells of the sea were growing, much bigger than when we'd crossed, with whitecaps on their long crests.

I put my chained hands on the wall and closed my eyes, reaching for my Ailith brothers, feeling the damp wind whip across my face and send my dark hair flying behind me. There was the scent of rain on the wind, and I welcomed it like a message from home. It had been days, even weeks, since I had felt the comforting droplets from the sky, so much a part of most of our days at home in the wet Valley.

That was when I felt the emotion from within the very walls, it seemed. I actually pulled my hands away, so fierce was the hurt, the anger. After a second, I put my hands down on the stone and concrete again, and there it was ... explosive and excruciating. It was Keallach, I knew, and his twin. I could feel my Ailith brothers' emotions, almost as clearly as if I was in the same room with them. Agitation. Frustration. And yet beneath it all, still, love. It was such a cacophony of emotion I couldn't bear it and pulled away. The storm over the sea seemed to echo what was happening inside the prison, the clouds climbing in a billowing, angry mass. I inhaled deeply.

The air carried the spicy tang of lightning even before I could see it. I shivered, the chill sending goosebumps over my arms. Or was the chill internal?

I forced myself to touch the wall again, knowing I had to learn what I could. But what I felt then was only a deep, harrowing sorrow. I wanted to weep it was so strong, like diving into a dark pool of grief itself. The door opened behind me and I turned. Keallach, ragged, his eyes red-rimmed, emerged. He paused when he saw me, and even in that moment, he seemed to really *see* me, enough to notice me rubbing away the cold along my arms. He again pulled his tawny cape from his shoulders and wrapped it around me. "My brother will see you now," he muttered to me as he passed.

I stared at the dark doorway, partially afraid.

Because it wasn't only his grief, fear, and agitation I felt. But his twin's too.

CHAPTER 5

ANDRIANA

I paused at the threshold of the door, feeling Keallach's trepidation and sorrow — sorting it out from his twin's. Ahead, Kapriel promised nothing of that to me. All along, he'd been nothing but hope to me — the lost prince — the end goal in every Ailith's mind. Somehow we knew that in freeing Kapriel, our destiny would be that much closer, a key piece in place. But now, in trying to extricate my own feelings from what Keallach had experienced, I battled anxiety on several levels and fought to separate myself. *It is his pain, not mine*, I reminded myself. *His frustration, not mine.*

Half of me wished I'd been present to hear their conversation.

Half of me was glad I hadn't.

I pressed through the doorway and felt the relief of being out from the howling wind, even with the protection of

Keallach's cape. I glanced backward, but no guard accompanied me, apparently on the emperor's order. I supposed they figured that in chains, within the very prison, I wasn't able to go far. I shivered and moved forward, the metal between my ankles scraping over the stone. I sniffed and regretted it, my nostrils filling with the scent of human waste as well as the foul scent of rotting flesh.

I turned a corner and heard the weeping, then, over the wind, so gut-wrenching that tears immediately sprang to my own eyes. It was an honest cry, the sort of wail that didn't care who heard, who knew. Total brokenness.

It made my decision to move forward an act of will. Half of me was drawn to my brother, crumbling, and half of me was repelled, overcome by the desire to run away. Far away. It was as if the memory of Keallach's feelings had left an imprint, a place to live within me, even now that I was disconnected. And all I hungered for was my prince. A strong, stalwart prince.

Regardless of what you feel, Niero had once fiercely told me, *remember what you know*. I began to repeat silently what I knew for certain.

I am a Remnant.

I was born to serve with my brothers and sisters.

To save the world, one at a time.

And we are called to save Kapriel now.

The Ailith were on the ship, somewhere, along with Ronan. And if they couldn't make it to me, I had to find some way to free myself and Kapriel and make it back to them. Maybe we could fight off the soldiers and force the sailors to take us to safety? But with the chains ...

Kapriel's weeping waned, and yet his grief was still visceral. I went back to repeating the things I knew to be true in my mind so that I would not be lost amidst the tsunami of his sorrow. I rounded the corner and saw him then, face turned toward the tiny window. "Why?" he muttered, his voice ragged. "Why, Maker? Will you not do something? Even now? How is *this* your way?"

I was rendered mute by his similarity to Keallach. But he was so much thinner, so bedraggled and weary, it was like seeing a skewed reflection of his brother. It struck me then that Keallach carried his own ragged weariness too, but it was carefully hidden away deep inside him, rather than on his flesh.

I clenched the rusting bars in both hands, and the chain between my wrists clanged against them. I froze, as did Kapriel, and his blue-green eyes turned to me. Relief washed through him as he recognized me as a fellow Remnant, and he turned toward me on weak, shaking legs. He reached out a hand toward me, and there was such anguish, such joy, such immediate *love* in the gesture, that tears welled in my own eyes, then crested and ran down my cheeks. My arm cuff warmed, as if in pleasure.

"You have come, my sister," he said, and took another step.

"Such as I am," I returned, lifting my chains. "Hardly the rescuer you imagined, I'd wager."

He covered the few remaining steps between us and covered my hands with his own, as if we were old friends — kin, rather than strangers. And it was exactly right. It was as if I'd known this man my whole life, just as I'd known the other.

"It matters not," he said. "The Maker specializes in unlikely heroes."

"And impossible odds?"

"Especially those," he said, smiling. He was close enough for me to see the tracks of his tears through the dirt on his thin face. The smudges where he'd wiped them away. How long since he'd had a bath?

"I am Andriana," I said.

"And I am Kapriel."

I glanced back to the empty stone hallway, amazed that Keallach was giving us this time alone. Perhaps he was still too grief-stricken to move. But undoubtedly he was making plans. Pulling himself together again. When I turned back, Kapriel had moved to a stone in the floor and was removing it. Beneath it, he pulled out a shard of iron and quickly returned to the bars between us.

"Give me your hands, quickly." He set upon the lock at my wrist, his fingernails caked with dirt. "This was too small to jimmy the lock of my cell, but it might be just right for — "

A *click* stopped him and he grinned. The manacle popped open, and I carefully eased it from my arm, trying not to jostle the chain too much and alert those outside with the noise.

"Keep talking as if nothing is going on," he whispered, kneeling to reach through the bars to my ankles.

"He cannot keep you here forever," I said, more loudly than before. "Surely there is some way for you two to come to an agreement."

"He'll hear none of it," Kapriel muttered, and it sounded like he spoke as much from the heart as for the stage. "It's either his way or nothing. It's always been so."

"He needs you, though," I said urgently, almost forgetting that others might be listening. "You two were born together for a reason. Together, you would bring balance to the throne. You could rule Pacifica, and even beyond, in a manner that would please the Maker."

"I'm rather certain"—a second *click* freed my ankle—"that is the farthest thing from my brother's mind."

He rose and I stepped out of my chains, relief flooding through me.

"Maybe. Maybe not," I said.

Sounds of a scuffle outside brought my head up. A man cried out, another swore. I reached for my cuff and felt the alternating waves of both cold and heat.

The Ailith had come.

But our enemies had too.

I looked around madly for another loose rock, anything to arm myself with, but there was nothing. Grimly, I leaned down to gather the skirt of my long Pacifican gown and sheath and tore them to the knee, freeing my legs.

Three soldiers backed into the prison hallway, as if to defend their precious prisoner. The closest one caught sight of me and his eyes widened. I whirled and caught him in the throat with a roundhouse kick, just as he brought his sword up. He fell back against the one behind him, choking, and I turned to the third man, ignoring the warm trickle of blood running down my leg where the man had nicked me. It was only because he hadn't time to fully raise his sword that I hadn't suffered a mortal wound.

But this one before me now was fully ready.

We circled each other, and it ate at me, the precious seconds that were evaporating, allowing the other two to rise and gather themselves. I caught a glimpse of another soldier falling into the far end of the passageway, but he was immediately on his feet and back out again. My fellow Ailith clearly were bringing the fight to them outside. Could I hold these three off in the meantime?

The soldier before me flicked his sword back and forth in a teasing pattern. "Come now, girl. You can't hope to make it out alive. Give yourself up. The emperor will be dismayed if he finds we had to kill you."

"And what will he do when he finds you three dead?" I snapped back. "Will he give you a second thought?"

"Not likely," he said, waving his sword, "but what choice do I have? Die here in the fight, or die later for losing. My only hope is to fight and win, if I want to live."

I frowned. Keallach would kill his men for losing? I'd never heard of such a vicious thing. And it didn't square with what I'd learned of him.

The man swung his sword at me and I leaned back. It just barely missed my belly. "You said you're intent on taking me alive, right?"

He smiled and continued to circle me. "Alive, but with a memory of why you shouldn't fight a Pacifican soldier."

Kapriel caught my eye and gestured toward him. He wanted me to maneuver the man closer to the bars.

I scurried to the left as the second soldier grabbed at me from the right, then bent low as the first swung his sword again. The tip swished through my hair. I needed a sword of my own or I'd be sliced and diced before this was over. I eyed the man still on the ground, gasping for breath. It was possible I'd crushed his windpipe. I had to physically push away the feelings of his panic, and kicked at my attacker. I connected with his stomach, then punched him. But as I reached for his sword, now held in a slack hand, the second man was up on his feet again and wrapped huge arms around me, lifting me from my feet.

"There you go, woman. It's over now," he said. "Come along

quietly and I'll see that no more harm comes to you." His words were sweet but his tone was smarmy, sticky in my ear. I had no doubt what would happen to me if he had me alone in a room, or worse, a cell. I pretended to relax, as if I was giving up, but as his tension eased, I rammed my head back into his nose.

He immediately released me, groaning and backing up to the bars, his hand on his bleeding, broken nose, his mouth open in horror and anger.

Kapriel reached through the bars, grabbed hold of his head, and took a curious hold where neck met shoulder. After a few seconds, the big man went down heavily, clearly unconscious.

The second man drove toward the bars, enraged, sword extended. At the last possible second, Kapriel edged aside, took hold of the man's arm, and swiftly pressed forward with all of his weight. The man screamed, and the sickening sound of bone breaking echoed against the stone walls. His sword skittered to the ground. The soldier went to his knees, his arm at such a terrible angle that he couldn't extract it, essentially trapping him. He shrieked.

Kapriel took the sword, tossed it to me, then reached through to take hold of the second man at the curve of his shoulder, sending him into merciful unconscious. His pitiful gasps and cries came to a stop and I dared to take a breath.

"You're going to have to teach me how you do that," I panted.

"Gladly," he said with a grin. "I've been trying to reach them for some time. Turns out ..." Kapriel's words trailed off as he reached through to fumble along the belt of the man with the broken arm, and I smiled, seeing what he was after. He had been Kapriel's jailor. And now Kapriel held up his keys. "I just needed you to distract them long enough to accomplish it."

The first man I'd hit in the throat was crawling toward the doorway.

As I stared in his direction, I recognized his terror. I hurried over to him, gripped his feet and dragged him back across the stone floor and into an empty cell. He was too weak from lack of breath to put up any fight, but he was heavy. Once the door clanged shut and I latched the lock, I looked in on him, panting. "May the Maker preserve you, if you have a heart worth salvaging."

"Every soul is worth salvaging," Kapriel said quietly beside me.

I turned and smiled at him. "You're free!"

"With your help," he said. He frowned and looked down at the growing red stain on my ivory gown. "How bad is your wound?"

"Not too bad," I said, ignoring the stinging pain. "Come on. Let's see if the others are still outside." The sounds of ongoing battle met us as we peered around the corner of the doorway from either side. We both had swords now, but Kapriel looked even worse in the light of day, and gray and sweaty from his efforts inside. He was a great deal lighter than his brother, all sinew and light muscle where his brother was brawn.

I saw Keallach then and took a step farther out.

He was battling Ronan. My knight. Our brothers and sisters had obviously freed him. One of Ronan's eyes was swollen shut, and a deep purpling bruise colored his cheek, but he appeared anything but weak. I frowned as he drove Keallach backward with one fierce strike after another, all pent-up fury funneling toward its target.

My eyes narrowed at his single-minded focus. His rage was fierce enough to make him want to kill Keallach.

"Ronan!" I cried. "Don't!" Keallach had done something … reprehensible. But he was one of us. Reachable. Redeemable. He wouldn't hurt any of the Ailith, not lethally anyway. He couldn't. He was one of us. "Ronan, stop!"

Ronan cast a mad glance at me, eyebrows furrowed — did a double take, seeing me in the bloody Pacifican gown — and in that second, Keallach turned and pierced him, his strike as fluid and natural as if he'd practiced it a hundred times before.

I screamed, my voice sounding distant and hollow to my own ears.

Ronan sank to his knees and Kapriel shoved past me, moving toward his brother as Keallach pulled the sword free from Ronan's shoulder, using his foot to pry it loose in time to meet his brother's charge. He brought it up and around just in time, and the two battled back and forth. But I knew Kapriel wouldn't last long, in his weakened state. Even now he faltered.

Ronan was still on his knees, trying to rise again and falling. I hurried to him and came under his opposite arm. "Hold on, Ronan. Come. Just over here, against the short wall, behind you," I directed. Clumsily, we got up and over to where I wanted. At least here no one could get behind us. I could defend Ronan.

All the Ailith were in the courtyard and stairwell around us, fighting two gray-clad soldiers for every one of them, steadily driving them away from us. Tressa knelt on the other side of Ronan, praying, but largely distracted. One by one the others killed or wounded their adversaries, leaving only the twins, Kapriel and Keallach.

Wordlessly, Tressa helped me get Ronan's leather breastplate unstrapped and cut away the shoulder of his shirt to look at the wound. "Press here," she said, placing a thick cloth in my hand and pushing it across the nasty gash.

I did as she asked, but had to swallow back a wave of nausea when I felt Ronan's pain. My own nick was long forgotten in the face of his terrible wound. He was pale, and the cords in his neck stuck out as Tressa examined his back, where the sword had exited. She pressed another cloth on the other side and leaned toward his face. "Ronan, how is your breathing? Did he get your lung?"

Ronan breathed in and out slowly, once, twice, then shook his head.

"Good, good," she said soothingly. "You'll heal up nicely, then."

Logically, I knew she was right, that with some stitches and rest, he'd likely be fine, in time. But seeing him there, bleeding, hurting — and clearly having suffered terrible abuse belowdecks — made me want to hurt someone else. I grabbed hold of the sword again and turned toward Keallach, striding toward him, even as he continued to battle his brother.

He had to have known they were hurting Ronan. Sethos couldn't have acted without the emperor's approval, could he?

The storm was on us, blowing my hair this way and that, and I felt a few droplets of rain. But I could see little other than the man who had so convinced me that he was one of us that I endangered my knight by coming to his defense. Had it all been an act? It was one thing to fool me with words; how could he have fooled me with his feelings?

Red-hot fury seemed to fill me, then began to cool, like freshly forged iron thrust into a river. Keallach nicked Kapriel with his sword and I broke into a charge, determined that Kapriel not be further injured.

It was then that Sethos jumped from the rooftop above us, landing in a crouch, directly in my path.

Two other Sheolites landed beside their master, and it was only because I knew the rest of the Ailith were turning toward me that in that moment I didn't turn tail and run. *But together, we are strong.* I repeated it over and over in my mind.

Sethos rose, his crimson robes plastering against his side in the fierce wind. My heart pounded in fear as his wrath seeped toward me, surrounding me, tangling with my own fury. Choking me ... once again, opening something dark and insidious within ...

Behind him, Keallach whirled and struck his brother. Kapriel fell, clutching his upper arm and I saw his sword clatter to the cobblestones.

"No! Kapriel!" I cried.

Together, we attacked the Sheolites, and nearly overcame them, when I saw Keallach raise a hand toward us, palm out. He clutched his chest and dropped his head. A second later, it was if we all had hit a brick wall. As one, we crumpled or fell backward. My head slammed to the stones and my vision tunneled toward black for a moment, then cleared. Only Killian and Bellona managed to hold on to their swords and leap back to their feet, blocking the oncoming Sheolite scouts.

Sethos advanced on me, but Ronan labored to his feet and stepped in his path. "You shall not have her," he bit out as I still struggled to rise.

"We shall see," Sethos returned fiercely, whirling and striking in one fearsomely powerful move.

Ronan narrowly blocked his blow, the metal clanging and scraping as the swords separated. Again and again, Ronan parried, but just barely. I wearily lifted my sword, intent on going to his aid and driving Sethos back, when I saw Kapriel drop, eyes wide and to the sky, lips moving in silent prayer. He lifted his arms, palms up, and Keallach turned on him, his face an angry sneer.

"Kapriel!" I screamed, my voice distant and slow to my own ears. Rain pelted us, so hard it felt as if each droplet was piercing, more like hail than rain. It came so hard and so fast that the stones at our feet became slippery, awash in water, blood trailing from bodies on the ground, red rivulets making their way toward the stairs in tiny, ghoulish waterfalls.

Keallach staggered against the sheets of rain, blinking repeatedly to try and see his adversary, but a great wind blew us all to the side, and he stumbled, lost his footing, then came down heavily on one hip.

I fell, rolled, and rolled again, shoved by the wind like a tumbleweed until I was lodged against the far wall. I watched the water in the courtyard before me clearly seeing the swirling motion. I looked up, blinking against the heavy rain. It was as if a small cyclone arose from it, and at its center were Sethos and the two scouts, with Keallach at their feet. They were glaring at his brother, then us.

They're in the eye of the storm, I thought, trying to make sense of it. But the small storm moved, herding them, in effect, closer and closer to the prison doorway. The rest of us regained our feet and followed behind, finding it difficult to believe what we were seeing. But when the small funnel turned into a massive blast that sent our enemies somersaulting inside, we charged after them.

Inside, the men seem dazed and out of breath. We quickly took hold of them and slammed them inside Kapriel's old cell.

"See how *you* like being left in here," I said to Keallach.

He rushed toward the bars, all trace of the deadly fury I'd

seen moments before now gone. "Andriana, you don't understand. There's still so much I need to explain."

I backed away, trying to ignore the pain and loss within him that muddled the sheer loathing I'd felt toward him a moment ago. "We leave you to the Maker's mercy," I muttered. With that, I strode out.

"Andriana!" he cried. "Wait! Andriana!"

But I managed to ignore him. If he was to be redeemed, it would have to be later. Our immediate call was to get Kapriel to safety. Every one of us knew it.

Outside, we found the prince curled up on the wet stones, eyes closed. Ronan was beside him, on his knees. Above us, the sky was clearing, the clouds lifting before our eyes. Here and there, shafts of sunlight met the sea.

"Kapriel," I said, kneeling beside them. I took his hand but it was cold and lifeless.

His eyes rolled as Tressa turned him to his back, his head in her lap. She leaned forward to put her ear to his mouth, and her mass of auburn curls hid them for a moment. "He breathes," she said briskly, straightening, feeling for a pulse at his neck, and I think we all took a collective breath with him.

"Was it too much?" Vidar asked. "Him using his gifting to such a level, before he received the blessing?"

Shouts from inside the prison echoed out to us, but we ignored them.

Kapriel coughed, closed his eyes, then coughed again — so hard it turned to retching — then rolled back, gasping. When he opened his eyes, he looked about at each of our faces encircling him, then slowly grinned. "It's all right. Help me rise," he said, his voice raspy.

Vidar reached forward, took his hand, and helped him to

his feet. The two stared at each other for a long moment, then briefly embraced. "I'm Vidar," he said, thumping Kapriel on the back.

I came up under Ronan's arm, preparing to help him down the stairs, when Kapriel reached us. "She is special, this one," he said to Ronan, wanly gripping his arm.

"I know," Ronan said, a tiny smile edging his lips. His good eye shifted to me, then back to our new brother. "I am Ronan." The others quickly introduced themselves.

"Come, my friends," Kapriel said. "We must make haste. If we make our escape on Keallach's ship before word reaches the mainland that there has been trouble here, we may be able to disappear."

"I'm afraid the *Far North* isn't in working order," Bellona said with an impish smile that betrayed a dimple on her normally sober face. She and Vidar shared a sly look that told me they'd laid waste to the ship's engines. "We'll need alternate transportation."

"And I think we have it," Chaza'el said, looking over the wall. Ronan and I stepped up beside him and looked down to the churning ocean, a brilliant turquoise under the bright, sudden sun. I squinted down at the long, sleek motorboat, wondering if I could trust my eyes.

"Am I seeing things?" I whispered. "Is that ..." I couldn't bear to say his name, raise their hopes, in case I was wrong.

"You're not," Ronan said with a grin. "It's him!"

CHAPTER 6

ANDRIANA

Raniero. I let out a breathy, shocked laugh as Vidar hooted and Bellona and Tressa shouted his name.

Killian tied a quick knot in a thick rope and sent the heavy coils over the side. My stomach sank. I wanted to get down to the beach as fast as anyone. But did we really have to do it this way? Ronan's hand covered my arm. Looking up at his handsome face, marred by the obvious beatings he'd taken, I felt more cowardly than ever.

"It's stupid, Ronan," I began.

"Hey," he said, interrupting. "It's just part of you, for now. Not that you won't ever get past it ..."

His good eye met mine and we shared a rueful smile. "All right," he amended. "Maybe you won't ever get past it. But we can deal with it." His warm, full lips curved into a smile and he winced, just as I saw the crack at the corner, shedding fresh blood.

I eyed the curving stone road we'd taken up here from the harbor. "Can't Niero meet us at the docks?"

Ronan shook his head quickly. "Ah, we took out a fair number of the soldiers down there, and the rest are trying to save the *Far North* from sinking. But we want them to stay focused on that, rather than head up here to see what's taking the others so long, right? Buy us time to get away."

I nodded, silently cursing my odd fear of heights. If the Maker was going to gift us, why saddle us with something else that might endanger the group? Bellona passed by us, guessing what was going on, and gave me a dubious look.

And why was it that *I* had to have the handicap?

"Ignore her," Ronan said, squeezing my arm. "Look at me."

"I can't," I said, facing him in misery. "All I see is the beating you obviously took. While I was free."

I tried to ignore my stomach twisting as Bellona casually dropped over the wall with Vidar right behind her. Then Killian and Tressa were next.

"Look at me," Ronan growled.

I looked up into his good eye, so tender with love, and it made me both want to laugh and cry at the same time.

He smiled and then winced again. "There. That. Hold on to that, Andriana. Hopefully that will keep you distracted for the time it takes for me to get you down."

"But Ronan, your wound. You can barely get yourself down with one good arm. You can't —"

"Andriana," he interrupted. "I have you. Think no more of it."

I nodded and looked down as he turned, unwilling for him to see my face and guess my doubt. But I tried really hard as he crouched down to let me climb on his back. I wrapped my arms over his massive shoulders, trying to avoid his right side, clasping my hands tightly under his chin and clenching his hips with my legs.

"Yes, good," he said, patting my leg. "If you can keep most of your weight centered there, around my hips, it'll help."

Then he was up on the wall, turning and dropping, rappelling down the side of the prison that had looked so fearfully high from down below when we sailed in. *No*, I told myself. *Stop thinking about your fear. Think about good things. Concentrate on Ronan, as he said. His love, his crazy-fierce devotion. His love! He loves me!*

And then we were down on the ragged, black rocks, crashing waves sending a fine mist over us. Killian gently lifting me off of Ronan's back and supported me when my trembling legs threatened to give out. Ronan turned and gave me a tremulous smile as he loosed the ropes. I could see what it had cost him, this last effort, when he hurt so. We dived shallowly into the water, and swam out to the boat, Killian helping Ronan along. "Him first," I insisted, scared that Ronan was so weak he might drown right there beside us. Killian scrambled in, and together with Raniero, leaned down, grabbed hold of Ronan, and heaved him up and in. It was only then that Ronan cried out. It was a gasping, guttural cry.

Vidar and Bellona grasped my arms and effortlessly lifted me in, and then Raniero was before me. It was really him. *Alive. Well.* "Niero!" I fell into his burly arms, inhaling the dry, strong scent of him, feeling my limp legs gain instant strength.

After a moment, I made myself step away and look at him. Fading bruises were still visible, even on his mahogany skin. Killian wrapped a blanket around me, and I realized I was shivering and that the ripped, wet Pacifican gown left little to hide. But I was too wrapped up in Niero's miraculous appearance to worry. "How, Niero? How did you get away?"

"It's not important," he said, taking my hand in his, then looking to the rest. "What's important is that we need to put some miles between us and this cursed prison." He leaned down and clasped Kapriel's hand, something unspoken moving between them. Tressa, wrapped in a blanket, moved between Kapriel and Ronan as she tended to their wounds.

"The farther we can get from here the better," Kapriel said weakly, even as Niero moved to the steering wheel and pressed down on a lever at his side. Some sort of ancient engine roared to life, making the entire boat rattle and yet surge forward at a frightening speed. We soon skimmed across the water, bouncing across the waves.

Chilled, I settled into a seat beside Ronan, nestled into the crook of his armpit, half against his chest and well away from his wound, as we watched the Isle of Catal disappear behind us, the wake of the boat like a dissipating road of white, soon absorbed by the teal-colored sea.

We'd done it.

We'd freed the man that Keallach had held prisoner for season upon season.

I turned and looked at him again, to make certain it was real, that I wasn't dreaming. How odd it was, to begin the day on one ship with Keallach, then end the day on another with his twin. A shiver ran down my back.

We'd won the battle.

But we'd also just openly declared war.

■　■　■

For hours we drove through the waves, at times so big that it felt as if we were aloft for seconds at a time. Tressa stitched and bound Ronan's wound at the shoulder, and mine on the leg. While there was a great deal of blood over the white gown I still wore, my wound was superficial. Ronan's piercing wound would take a great deal longer to heal. I watched Tressa as she worked on him, so intent that she could ignore the way he winced and shut his eyes tightly against the pain. And yet here and there, she would lay a delicate hand on his other shoulder or whisper "almost done," encouraging him through. She was thorough and quick, and my admiration for her grew alongside a deep gratitude that the Maker had brought her to us.

To the west, the sun was beginning to set, and a deep, gray mist had moved in from the ocean as if it was bent on blanketing the entire coast. Just when I was craning my neck, trying to get a glimpse of the fuel gauge on Niero's console, he banked right and headed toward the beach, where we could see a limp tendril of smoke rising from a fire.

He turned in a tight circle, and then again, then brought the engine to an idle. We all stared at him as the mist began to turn into a light rain. "Uh, Niero," Vidar began. "Are we going to—"

Niero lifted a hand, shushing him. And in a moment, a boat emerged from the coastline—a river mouth, I realized—and came toward us. At the back was a dark-haired woman, perched behind a massive machine gun. We hadn't seen anything like it since the Drifters, on land.

"Uh, Niero …" Vidar said again.

"It's all right," Kapriel said, sharing a look with Niero. "They are friends. I'll explain everything once we're clear."

I stared at Vidar as he rubbed his cuff, as I did too. And

neither of us knew foreboding or worry in those moments. Only warmth. Gladness. Promise.

Niero and Kapriel's new friends circled us, and when they'd exchanged a hand signal with him, they pulled alongside. "Everyone in that boat," Niero said, and we made our way into the larger vessel. The small, sandy-haired captain with light amber eyes helped each of us aboard, and when Kapriel crossed onto her deck, she knelt.

"My prince," she said. "I am Aleris. It is an honor to serve you."

"I shall find a way to repay you, friend," he replied, and I started at the royal edge that now laced his tone. "I understand that you and your tribe have taken great risk to assist us." I studied Kapriel, and reached out, wondering if I would detect pride, arrogance. But there was nothing but joy and gratitude within him.

Niero was last aboard, and after he clasped arms with the new captain, he turned and stared at the boat we'd just left as it drifted away on a swift current.

Were we just going to let it drift out to sea? Such a valuable commodity? Surely we could sell it to somebody, even for a fraction of its worth —

He turned and nodded at the woman behind the machine gun, and she lifted something from her belt, pressed a red button, and we heard the pop of a light explosion. Immediately afterward, the boat's nose began rising, faster and faster, even as the bottom sank. In ten breaths, she was entirely under.

"Oh, I *need* one of those," Vidar said, sidling up to the machine gunner and gesturing toward the remote triggering device. "And tell me about this beauty," he added, running his fingers along the massive shaft of the gun. But his eyes were solely on the dark-haired girl.

She tossed Vidar a saucy smile as a wave hit our boat and almost sent him to his knees. "I'd sit down if I were you."

He straightened. "Nah. I'll get my sea legs soon enough," he began.

But Aleris pushed her boat into action, and we all lurched with the motion. Vidar wasn't ready, and careened forward, making Bellona laugh. He landed half on a cushioned seat beside the gunner. He flipped and shifted as if he'd planned to do just that, all along, and then winked up at her. "Me falling at your feet. How can you resist?"

"Right," she said, rolling her eyes. But I could see the hint of a smile behind them.

■ ■ ■

The captain took us back into the river mouth and expertly maneuvered up the winding waterway, dodging rocks and sandbars, which became progressively more challenging the farther we went. The banks narrowed inward, and in places we moved against a current so strong that we slowed. But then the river widened again and we surged forward. The gunner moved to the front and turned on a powerful light that illuminated the obstacles before us, which were hard to spot with only the last vestiges of twilight.

We traveled so long, I wondered if this river might eventually reach the eastern border of Pacifica. Where had they obtained such boats, and the petrol to run them? They were relics of the age before the Great War, and I had a hard time believing that Pacifica would knowingly let such machines go to anyone but loyalists. I shivered in the cold; even Ronan's hands were like ice. I found myself praying we'd soon run out of fuel so that the wind would cease, at least. But then, around the next bend, the river spread even wider and almost stilled, reflecting the stars above. The captain brought her boat to a swift stop. She cut the engine, cupped her hands around her mouth, and made the bright chattering sound of what I guessed was a local bird.

We paused, all searching the riverbank, and the collective tension I felt made me want to close my eyes and scream. But at last an identical call sounded from the riverbank. There was rustling among the reeds, and I blinked, trying to see if I was really seeing what I thought I was seeing. It was as if a gate had opened, and what once appeared as just part of the river became another dark waterway.

Aleris smiled and started the engine again, moving slowly toward the channel and into it.

I felt Ronan tense beside me, then edge between me and the channel bank, just a leap away. Bellona moved in front of Vidar. Killian in front of Tressa, on the other side. Raniero, I noted, stood between Chaza'el and Kapriel, but he seemed relaxed, confident. We could see the movement in the shadows, heard the stretch of a bowstring pulled taut, again and again. But as soon as they saw the captain and the gunner, the bows were lowered and we could hear the murmuring of excited chatter as we passed.

"They're Aravanders," Chaza'el whispered, so quietly I almost missed it.

"What?" I said, not knowing if I should look at him or the many people who now followed our progress up the channel. But his excitement and sense of glory was tangible.

"Rebels, people of the river," he said, "on Pacifica's north-ern border. We're now farther north than even my mountain is. I ... I'd thought Aravand a myth, legend," he said, staring into the dark, towering trees that now surrounded us.

Aleris laughed, the sound of it rich and full of joy. "Our tribe is worthy of the stories people tell," she said, grinning over her shoulder at him. "As you shall soon see."

The engine was cut and two boys leaped aboard with ropes, gradually pulling the boat to a smooth stop by wrapping them around trees along the edge, as if they'd done it a hundred times before. Perhaps they had.

We gazed up at the gathering crowd, covered in what appeared to be pelts of some river animal. Otter? Beaver? Did they survive in this part of the country? I didn't know. The Aravanders' faces were mostly a uniform brown with dark eyes, and they stared at us hungrily, as if we were characters rising from the pages of a book. Half of them were armed with bows, arrows nocked.

A chiding voice cut through the din of their chatter, and the crowd split. A tall, elegant woman about my mother's age moved toward us. She smiled in welcome even as she spread her arms wide, then clasped her hands quickly, in wonder. With the movement of her robe, I saw that she was heavy with child, though she moved as lightly as a girl. It shocked me; I'd never seen a woman so old — well past her third decade — pregnant. There was a wide gap between her top front teeth, and yet she seemed exquisitely beautiful. Behind her were three men, one who edged closer to her as if intent on protec-tion. Her husband?

She seemed unaware of him, her eyes only on Kapriel as he exited the boat. Just as the captain had done earlier, she sank to her knee, every bit of her movement full of grace and dignity. Her people immediately imitated her action, each taking a knee and bowing their heads. "My prince," their leader said, eyes to the pine needles before her. "You have no idea how long we have prayed for this day."

"The Maker has heard those prayers, Latonia," he said, resting a hand on her shoulder. "And others'. Our day has come," he said. "The night has been cold and long, but now morning is upon us."

CHAPTER 7

ANDRIANA

Once we were out of the boat, the others covered it with many dirt-colored tarps and then laid branches across them, effectively disguising it. I looked upward, wondering what they feared from the air, or how anyone could see anything beyond the river. There was good reason that Aravand had remained hidden, "a myth," as Chaza'el had called it, for decades. While seemingly settled, it appeared that the tribe could pull up stakes and leave within minutes.

I inhaled deeply and smiled. It felt so good to be in the forest again, the scents different in this place so far from the Valley but similar enough to feel like home. I sensed Ronan's pleasure too, as well as Bellona and Vidar's, and yet the reminders made me feel a pang of melancholy too.

I shoved away thoughts of my home. Of the blood, so much blood. Mom's handprint near mine...

We padded along the path, winding our way through the woods in utter darkness now. I wondered how Ronan could see enough through his one good eye to so confidently lead me forward, but then his night vision had always been sharper than mine. For a moment, I remembered that terrifying first night when we'd felt the Call and known the Sheolites were near, hunting us. In some ways it felt like years before. So much had happened over these last months as Harvest faded, edging nearer and nearer to Hoarfrost, that it felt almost as if both seasons had come and gone rather than just a few cycles of the moon. Even now, our breath clouded before our faces.

I smelled the fires before we saw them, and I shivered in anticipation of getting out of the thin white gown that marked me as a prior prisoner of Pacifica and into the warm robes of the Aravanders. I wished we had had the opportunity to wash the salt of the ocean away in the river before we'd left the fresh water. Perhaps we'd have the chance come morning. Though, truth be told, I felt too weary to truly care about anything more than food and sleep and a warm change of clothes, and my companions were much the same.

Ahead of us, Kapriel stumbled — plainly spent — and Raniero wrapped his arm around the smaller man's waist. There was something about the way Niero moved that told me he hurt, but my eyes remained on Kapriel. "It is too much," I said, wrapping my hand around Ronan's arm. "He's not been out of his cell for so long. And now ..."

Ronan put his other hand on mine, reassuring me. Ahead, we could see the dark shapes of the tree trunks against the approaching fires. "It'll be all right. It's a lot," he said, "but our prince draws from a deeper well than most. After a night's sleep we'll all feel better."

"I hope so," I said, forcing myself to form the words. Even the thought of it made me want to plead for a place to rest and eat and talk come morning. But I knew propriety wouldn't allow it.

Boys with torches joined us, and we entered a village of small huts, one on each side of the small path we walked. The huts were uniform in appearance, each with a low doorway only waist-high, their roofs made of what looked like pine branches tightly wound together. People poured from them as we passed, and shouts of celebration kept erupting from one or the other as word spread that Kapriel was here, and with him his Ailith kin. The villagers stared at us in barely concealed awe, and over and over again, they clapped, eyes bright in the firelight. A song began from somewhere behind us and overtook those around and in front, until we were surrounded by such a sweet, haunting song that we all came to a halt.

I listened, their combined voices sending shivers down my back. They sang of the Maker, of hope, of promise. And every note brought the words into vivid color.

Kapriel collapsed to his knees and I gasped, thinking he'd fallen again, but then saw his face turning to the skies above. Niero immediately took a knee beside him. The rest of us did the same, feeling the song swell to a crescendo, and I stared up at the stars the Maker had put into place, then around at friends — unmet brothers and sisters — he'd placed here too. For their sakes, and ours. And there was such an overwhelming surge of joy, within and without, that I found tears streaming down my face.

We continued to lift our hands to the skies as the villagers reached the end of their song. With the last note fading, we were silent, and the silence was almost more a moment of sheer, perfect praise than the song that preceded it. I scarcely dared to breathe, wishing it could go on.

It was Kapriel who tried to rise first, and faltered. Niero gained his feet and helped him up. As before, he wrapped his arm around Kapriel's waist and I was again struck by how oddly my friend moved. I'd spent enough long days on a trail following the man and the rest of the Ailith that I'd be able to know their movements by shadow alone. Was Niero suffering from an injury? What had they done to him, back at Wadi Qelt, when he was captured? What had he endured in order to escape?

My mind went back to seeing his bare back and chest in the soft, flickering firelight of the Hoodites. The hundreds of scars ... and the swiftly healing wound he'd just sustained. He'd been bathing alone, when he thought us all long asleep. Would he wait for a similar opportunity here? I doubt he'd allow me to surprise him again, even though I longed for another glimpse of his back, a mystery I longed to unravel. He was only a little over two decades old. And yet his skin looked as if he had been in constant battle for centuries.

Huts, covered with bound, green tree limbs, were nestled here and there, usually against taller underbrush. There was no uniform circle, but there were greater numbers of the huts as we neared what had to be the center of the Aravander camp. In a small clearing was the huge fire that we'd glimpsed through the forest. Women and men were tending to spits that surrounded the bigger fire, some turning meat that splattered hissing grease to the coals beneath while others fed the flames with more dried wood. Cries of welcome moved through them along with the murmuring of news shared, so that soon all knew what had transpired on this day.

The village chief, Latonia, gestured to blankets folded into squares in a large circle among the trees, and Niero helped lower Kapriel to the first one, then settled wearily on the one beside it. We quickly followed suit, and when we were all seated, Latonia's man helped her sit, then settled beside her. It was clear then, just how late in her pregnancy she was. I looked around the circle as other villagers took seats that we left vacant. Tressa was gazing in an oddly intent manner toward Latonia, as was Chaza'el. But then shallow wooden bowls, still sticky with pitch underneath, were passed, and in each was a thick slice of meat, a spoon, and a chunky stew beneath. It smelled rich and savory, and my mouth watered.

But we all had to wait as some ceremonial liquid was poured into wooden cups. Latonia lifted hers when all were served. "We welcome you, sisters and brothers. Long have we awaited this day." She lifted her cup with both hands to her lips and we did the same.

I nearly choked as the thin, bitter berry wine seemed to pucker my tongue and burn all the way down my throat. I had obviously taken too big of a sip. But Latonia and the Aravanders weren't done. Together, we took two more sips, and I was careful to make them the tiniest possible. Would it be considered rude to leave the rest in my cup? I was dying for water, but no one was pouring from the earthen jugs. My eyes returned to my stew and meat.

"Please," the chieftess said, setting aside her cup and lifting a hand. "Eat. And then when your bellies are full, we shall have your story from beginning to end, yes?"

"Gladly," Niero said. He nudged Kapriel, who looked glassy-eyed and slack-jawed with weariness, and bent to whisper something in his ear. I saw Kapriel rouse and bring the meat to his mouth with a leaden hand. He bit off some and chewed slowly, but it was obvious it took a supreme effort. I knew he was far more tired than I felt, which seemed impossible. But again and again, Niero whispered encouragement in his ear, and I could almost sense what he said to Kapriel, or moreover, the feel of what he would say, as if he were saying it to me. An arrow of jealousy and bitterness shot through me. A week ago, he had looked after me. Us. But now it was all about Kapriel?

Niero looked sharply in my direction, as if he had felt my jealousy. So did Vidar.

I felt the deep blush of my guilt rise on my neck and dug more zealously into my stew, hoping they would think they'd misinterpreted me. Niero had always seemed to sense me more clearly than I could read him — but Vidar's scowl troubled me more.

As I ate, I told myself that it was just the exhaustion, and the relief of finding Niero alive, but then sorrow that he couldn't be with us, directly, in the face of Kapriel's weakness and more intense need. I told myself that he knew I had Ronan, and Vidar had Bellona, and Tressa had Killian, and therefore, he was concentrating on those who were without guardians. And yet I couldn't deny it. I missed Niero. Missed his attention, his focus, his favor. It had always been mine, it seemed, from the day of our Call.

But maybe those days were over, I brooded.

I, apparently, was only a means to an end. We all were. And apparently, that end was Kapriel.

They'd used me. And now they were tossing me aside.

I swallowed hard, my throat closing around my last bite of meat, making me choke.

Ronan cast me a worried glance, but I shook my head and lifted a hand. "I'm fine," I managed to say, my eyes watering.

"No. You're not," Niero said. He was standing in front of me. "Will you accompany me for a moment, Andriana?"

Ronan began to rise, immediately on defense.

"No," Niero said firmly. "Sit and finish your meal, brother. I need a moment alone with Dri."

My heart skipped a beat when I heard the nickname on his lips, even as cold dread filled me. His black eyes were hard, demanding, searching. And just as much as I'd felt the chasm of missing him, I now fought the urge to flee from him.

"Niero, she's gone through a lot," Ronan tried again, rising with me. "I would like to stay with — "

"We've all gone through a lot," Niero returned. "Just to the edge of the clearing, Ronan. You can keep your eyes on her the whole time." He took hold of my elbow, and I felt a shiver run through me. Because it felt more like the grip of someone who thought I might run than the hold of a friend. Was there a reason to run? Had something changed in him that I should fear?

"Not in me," he said under his breath as he turned me and pulled me along. "In you, Dri. Something's changed in you."

I did a double take and glimpsed Vidar padding behind us. His face was still a mask of concern. I swallowed hard, bile rising in my throat that he was welcome to join this little chat and Ronan wasn't. And why was I in trouble? What had I done besides freeing the prince? Hadn't I given everything I had to the effort? More than almost anyone . . .

The villagers chatted on nervously, but I could feel every pair of dark eyes on us as we passed. I reached out to try and sense their mood, their feelings, but all I could feel was my own gathering dark despair. Separation.

"Niero," Vidar growled.

"I know," he said. He pulled me around a huge pine tree and pushed me back against it.

"What? What are you doing?" It took everything in me not to knee him in the groin for his mistreatment. I was furious. Black with rage.

"Fight it, Dri," he said. "Fight it. I think Sethos must have cast some spell upon you. The darkness of the Sheolites is in your head, in your mind again. In your heart."

"What?" I sputtered. "What're you talking about?"

"The bitterness. The jealousy. If you let it take root, flourish within, they will *sense* you, like one of their own, just as the Ailith sense one another. They will find us."

"I don't understand," I said. Beside me, Vidar put his hand on my shoulder and began to whisper urgent prayers.

And then Niero folded me in his arms. "You're exhausted. Weak. But your dark thoughts have opened the door again, Dri," he whispered. "To the dark ones. Maybe in ways you didn't recognize. But their ways — their dark moods, their dark thoughts — do not belong here. Not in you, Andriana. Not in you. We already draw them, being together in such numbers. Their scouts might sense us. But if you allow the dark to have its way within ..." He put his hands on my shoulders and closed his eyes. I felt my arm cuff kindle with warmth. "In the name of the Maker, be gone from her."

His words seemed to suck the very air from my lungs, and with it came something so big, so vile, so huge, that I choked and fought to breathe, fought to try and remember how to breathe, in the face of something so monumentally frightening.

"You are a daughter of the light," Niero was whispering in my ear, pulling me in and against him, holding me so close that it somehow felt as if he covered every inch of me. His warmth seemed to fill me and spread outward, filter through me, driving out the darkness.

He gripped my shoulders and pulled back, staring at me. But I couldn't take my eyes off of his lips and the words emerging from between them. "This one is a daughter of the light. Darkness, be gone. You have no place here!"

I took a staggering, gasping breath.

And then another.

And in that moment, I felt freedom. Lighter. Warm, for the first time in hours.

And once I was free of it, I realized what my brothers had sensed.

Somehow, I'd brought the darkness of Sheol with me. My time with Sethos ... I hadn't known, hadn't sensed anything creep inside me, or the door I'd learned how to close cracking open. Had I?

"Dri," Ronan growled, standing behind Vidar, his hand on the hilt of his sword.

"It's all right," Niero said, not turning toward my knight, but still concentrating fully on me. His hands moved to my elbows, and he helped me sink to the ground, as if he knew my legs now felt like sludge. And yet even in my weakness, I felt stronger than I'd felt since Keallach had made me his prisoner. *Keallach ... still with Sethos.*

"He likes to weave his way into your mind," Niero said.

Kapriel was there too, then. "They are rather good at it," he muttered. He knelt beside me and put his hand on my shoulder. "Are you all right?"

I managed to nod. I felt empty. But at least I was feeling at peace, too. "Just ... tired. So tired."

"I think we all are," Kapriel said. He looked to Niero. "What if we propose sleep first, to the chief? And all the information she could want, come morning. We'll be much more coherent after some rest."

Niero nodded. "I think we should stay in Aravand for a while, actually. To regain our strength and wait on the Maker's direction. I will stay up and speak with Latonia for a while. But you," he said, looking at me with those dark, intense eyes that missed nothing, then to the rest, "go and claim your rest."

CHAPTER 8

ANDRIANA

I awakened in the morning to the same bird call the captain had made, but recognized these sounds as the real thing. The birds moved overhead and I sat up, wishing I could see them.

The early pink light of dawn illuminated the silhouette of Ronan, asleep on a low palette a few feet from mine. Bellona and Vidar were on the other two in the hut. I eased back the covers and slipped my feet to the dirt floor, shivering in the chill of morning and drawing the brown robe of pelts more closely around me before rising silently. I tiptoed toward the door and glanced back, grimacing a bit at Ronan's swollen and battered face. It looked little different than the night before, when Tressa had tended to all our wounds again before we slept, aided by the Aravander healer. But he had to be seriously weary to not awaken to my movements. As long as we had been on this journey, it seemed all I had to do was breathe differently and he was alerted to the change. I looked at Vidar and Bellona, both still deeply slumbering too.

But as exhausted as I'd felt the night before, I felt wide awake now, and the birds drew me again. I bent low, wincing as I felt my leg wound pull and tear a bit, and pushed through the door and outside, the campfires long cold, the red embers of last night now a cold gray ash. I stared around the clearing of the camp in confusion. Branches had been strewn about. Young saplings, cut and tied together, had been placed here and there beside the huts in haphazard fashion. A method of disguise?

I spotted a flash of blue in the dawning light and my eyes widened in delight. Two massive bluebirds swooped from one tree branch to the next. One chattered at the first, as if in complaint, and the other chattered back, as if telling him to mind his own business. My smile grew and I ambled below them until I'd reached the edge of the last huts. I looked back, and knew I shouldn't go any farther.

There, I knelt and turned toward the eastern horizon, growing a pale yellow with the rising sun. I stretched out my arms above my head and prayed that the Maker would bless our day, praised him for bringing us here, to a forest sanctuary, and thanked him for the gift of Kapriel's freedom and our own.

When I sat up, I glimpsed him, down the path. Niero, moving toward the river.

I hurried forward, feeling a silent permission to leave the village if he was, and yet resisting the urge to call him, knowing I'd likely awaken others. Besides, I coveted this chance to speak to our leader alone. To find out what had happened to him. And what, exactly, might have happened to me.

Niero disappeared over a rise on the path and I doubled my pace. But at the top, I spotted legs dangling from the branch of a tree, and as I came around, saw that it was Chaza'el. He was chattering at the bluebirds, mimicking their call with surprising skill. Perhaps it was a talent cultivated among those of his village too. I remembered the hunters who had found me and Ronan at the mountain's edge and how they had made sounds of the forest.

Chaza'el looked down at me and grinned. "Good morning, sister."

"Good morning," I returned. "I'm surprised you didn't greet me in the language of the bluebirds."

"Give me a few more days with them and I shall." He gripped the branch and swung down and over to the trunk as easily as if it were second nature. Gripping the trunk between the palms of his hands and using his feet, he shimmied down the trunk, slipping in places, but always regaining his hold.

I winced, wondering if he was tearing up his palms, but he leaped the last bit to the ground, crouched and then rose, brushing them off as if there was no pain in them at all.

"So you can see the future, talk to birds, and climb trees as easily as a squirrel," I said to him as he neared. "You might be our most gifted Remnant yet."

He shrugged and tilted his head to one side, grinning as if embarrassed. "Comes with growing up in a bedroom among the redwoods."

I gestured back toward the camp. "Do you know why they cover so much of the camp with branches at night? Anyone who came here would clearly make out their huts."

His smile faded as he glanced back up the path. "They are afraid of the mechanical birds that come, I think." He pointed to the sky. "Not ground troops, but spy birds. They are said to patrol every few days, buzzing past. Tiny mechanical contraptions, disguised as birds."

It was my turn to frown. "What?"

"I don't know what the Pacificans call them. But the villagers call them dark birds. They live in fear of them. But so far, they've been ..." His voice dribbled to a stop as his eyes grew wider and his pupils dilated, so big that his brown irises disappeared.

I swallowed hard and grabbed his arms. He wavered, as if not with me. "Chaza'el? Chaza'el!"

But his mouth dropped open and he stared upward with eerily blank eyes. I noted my cuff warming. It was then that I knew he was having a vision, something of our future.

I grew silent and waited. After several interminable minutes, his mouth shut and he started, looking at me as if he wondered what I was doing there. What he himself was doing there.

"You had a vision?" I asked, giving up on letting him speak first.

He nodded, and I was relieved to see his eyes come back to their reassuring brown.

"What was it?" I pressed.

"I ... I can't share it yet." But I followed his troubled gaze upward to the skies, searching with him, and I had a pretty good idea.

"You're going to speak with Raniero now?" Chaza'el asked me quietly, drawing my attention back to him.

"Yes."

"Ask him how long he intends to stay here," he said.

I narrowed my eyes at him and then scanned the sky around the big trees again. "I will," I said slowly.

He turned and left then. I watched him retreat, debating between chasing him down and forcing him to tell me what he meant and going to speak to Raniero. But Chaza'el had said he wasn't ready to share. Even if I demanded it, would he tell me? I doubted it.

Reluctantly, I turned and padded down the path, thick with needles, toward the river, thinking again of my desire to bathe. But there wasn't any way I was going to strip down to my underclothes and swim in front of Niero. I would have a week ago. But not today. I already felt vulnerable and exposed around him after last night. The thought of that moment in which I'd very nearly betrayed the Ailith just by succumbing to dark thoughts ... I shook my head and bit my lip. I didn't want to be a weakness, a chink in our collective armor.

I saw him up ahead, naked to the waist, his breeches wet and hair dripping down on his brown, broad shoulders. He was sitting on a boulder, staring out to the slow-moving river. He bore none of the green-yellow bruises from our battle at the Wadi Qelt, a week past — those I'd glimpsed yesterday had faded. But wouldn't there be other injuries? I'd seen him take blow after blow myself, to say nothing of what he had to have suffered afterward. He'd moved like he was still hurting a little. And yet now, there was nothing but the ancient scars across his back and a surging strength within him.

"Good morning," I whispered. I settled on the rock beside him, thinking of the grief I'd felt, leaving him behind. The tearing.

"Do not dwell on sorrow, Andriana," he said, still staring forward at the water. "Dwell on things that bring you joy."

I sighed. "You going to tell me how you do that?"

"What?" he asked, breaking up a twig and tossing bits aside.

"Reading my thoughts. All I said was 'good morning.'"

"I didn't read your thoughts," he said, eying me over his shoulder, the hint of a smile at his full lips. "I read your … demeanor. Your tone."

"Hmm," I said, thinking there had to be more to it than that. "What about your wounds? Will you tell me how you heal so fast?"

"By the Maker's grace."

I shifted my neck and moved my leg, which made me wince. For me, yesterday's wounds felt twice as bad today. "Too bad the rest of us don't share that grace."

"We all have our gifts," he said, flashing me a rare, sly grin.

"You're sure you're not Ailith?"

"I'm sure I'm not Ailith."

"Well, you're something, then."

His smile grew at that. "We're all something, Andriana."

"Can you just be straight with me, for once?"

His smile faded. "I don't intend to hide the truth." He pulled his left shoulder toward his head and twitched his lips. "I don't know *how* I heal so fast; I just do. And as to how I know where your heart is, what you might be feeling, it's more of a clear … *understanding* of another and where they are, good or bad. And only on occasion."

I absorbed this and stared with him out at the water for some time. "Maybe the Maker gifted you as such so you could be our leader."

"Undoubtedly," he said. "To each of us, the Maker grants what we need, when we need it."

To the left, in the distance, just as the river bent out of

sight, I saw boys working a line. Fishing, perhaps. I'd seen the racks in the woods, high up, boned fillets drying in the air. Again, it struck me that they would ideally be out in the sun to dry. Maybe it was because they wanted to hide any semblance of civilization …

"How long do you intend for us to stay here, Niero?"

"A few days, at least," he said. "We all need rest. Recovery time, before we wage into further battle. Time to pray and seek the Maker's direction. Time to connect with Kapriel and take him through the armband ceremony. Meld as a group."

A thought startled me. The armbands. "Niero, where are the cuffs? Ronan—"

"Chaza'el knew what was to come. He persuaded Ronan to release the armbands to his safe-keeping."

I breathed a sigh of relief.

I nodded. "Chaza'el had another vision this morning. You'd best speak to him about what he saw. He seemed uneasy."

He rose and turned to face me, fully, for the first time. "I shall. We'll have to pay close attention to his visions as we head back into the Trading Union."

I stiffened. He wasn't speaking of going back to the Valley, but back into places we'd been. Was that truly our call? He picked up another twig and began cracking off bits of it, dropping them in the water, then eyed me. "We must return. We are together now, strong. And there are many, many in need of the hope we can bring them."

"If we can stay alive long enough to bring it," I muttered. I stared at the water again, my mind swirling like the water at the base of the boulder, creating tiny whirlpools, sucking bits of Niero's twig in and then under. Did he speak of the people in the Wadi? Castle Vega? Georgii Post? Places we had so narrowly escaped with our lives? It seemed impossibly daunting. But also irritatingly right. Like I knew, deep within, what he had already seen as truth.

"What happened to you, Niero? Back at the Wadi? What did they do to you?"

"It doesn't matter," he said, rising. "It is in the past."

I reached up and grabbed his hand. "It does matter," I insisted. "You were hurt. You sacrificed yourself in order to distract them from us."

When he said nothing, I dropped his hand. He folded his arms, but he didn't move away. And yet as the silence went on, I knew he wasn't ready to tell me.

"There is much required of all of us, Dri," he said softly. "This is but the beginning of our sacrifices."

I sighed heavily. Already I felt wrung out. Weary of the battle.

"We will rest here for a time. Regain our strength. Our focus. It's important. When we are exhausted, facing foes such as Sethos and Keallach … you've seen for yourself how they use every single crack in our armor to their advantage. Physically, emotionally, spiritually."

The way he said that, I wondered if the two had abused him before they ever reached the coast and ran across me.

"Can I tell you something?" I paused to take a deep breath. "Keallach seemed … *good* to me. As if he only sought to connect with me, not hurt me. I think it's Sethos. Sethos is the one we need to destroy. He is the one who drags Keallach down."

Niero looked me. "Or is that exactly what he wished you to think?" He shook his head dismissively. "No, Keallach is as fallen as his guardian. Only far more clever in disguising his true nature."

I frowned and stared at the water.

"We must become stronger. On our own. And as a collective," he said. "We will need to rely on one another in the days to come." He jumped off the rock and winced, the first sign that he felt any pain at all. Slowly, he straightened, but avoided my gaze.

"Did they hurt you horribly?" I asked softly.

"I've experienced far more horrible things than what they heaped upon me."

I sensed an almost-explanation for some of his scars, tantalizing me, teasing me, but intuitively knew he wouldn't elaborate on the deep past. I only had a chance at what had just occured. "How'd you escape, Niero?" I tried, as he pulled on his dry shirt.

"They grew tired of their efforts, especially once Keallach and Sethos left. I escaped a lazy guard," he said with a shrug, and I knew there was no possible way it had been as easy as he wanted me to believe. But I said nothing more.

We stared at the river together for a long while then. He cast a sidelong glance at me. "Did they hurt you, Dri?" he said. "Aboard the ship?"

"Not in any way you can see," I said. I frowned. "But Niero, Keallach ... I honestly think there is good in him yet," I said, rushing now, feeling the guilt and betrayal of my words in coming to the defense of our supposed enemy. "I think he could be turned. Redeemed. Brought into our circle."

Niero glowered up at me, and for once, I could read him clearly. Frustration and fury. "He is a deceiver, Andriana."

"He has traveled with Sethos for these past seasons. Sethos has influenced him greatly, for certain. Keallach made him his knight after his own died, Niero. There's little wonder how the man has infiltrated his mind and heart. But it doesn't mean that at his core there isn't something worth redeeming."

That brought his head up, and his lips clamped shut. His dark eyes scanned the water, as if trying to see into the world of Pacifica and with it the twins' past.

"There is darkness within him, and it's muddled and bewildering," I went on, shaking my head. "I admit that he might be a master at confusing me, slipping in bits of doubt when I don't see it coming. But there's also good in him. I felt that too, Niero. A longing, a hope. For *us*. For the *Maker*."

"He made his choice," he bit out. "Do you know what happened to his knight? And Kapriel's?"

I tried to swallow, but found my mouth dry. "They died," I whispered.

"They *killed each other*, each fighting to save their Remnant." He closed his eyes and it was a mask of pain. Then he opened them, his brows quirking with urgency. "Do you see what a waste that was? How wrong? It is not the Maker's way. And it was Keallach's decisions that brought them to it."

We stared at each other for a long moment, sharing the pain, the understanding. "He made terrible decisions. Horrific decisions. But Niero, are you certain you are not blocking Keallach's return to us? Stopping him from restoration? Yes, I admit, it sounds like madness. But think of it, Niero. Think of it. You saw for yourself—Kapriel's power, mingled with Keallach's, both in their infancy yet, before the armband ceremony. What if they were working together, instead of battling?"

"It's impossible, Andriana," he said in disgust, turning to go. He paused and said over his stiff shoulder, "Get it out of your mind now. Keallach is using your empathy as a means to infiltrate us and bring us down. He has chosen his lot. He is against us. Lost to the dark."

He left me then, moving down the path, back toward the village as if he feared more that I might say, and I sighed in frustration.

I watched as the boys at the bend in the river moved into the woods too, their nets full of shimmering fish. My mouth watered at the thought of the silver scales, sizzling in pans over the open fire, and the pink flesh below, hot on my fingers, filling my empty belly.

But first I had to wash. My skin felt dry and brittle with the layer of sea salt still covering it. And my mind and heart felt much the same, especially after my tense conversation with Niero. It made me want to cry again.

Without another thought, I disrobed, dropping the heavy pelt to the rock, warming in the morning sun, with nothing on but the Pacifican sheath, still bloody, wishing I could shed it too. Then I dived into the cold, fresh water, staying under, remembering the mountain rivers of my youth.

Of my father, swimming beside me. Of laughter.

And of a time with few tears at all.

RONAN

I awakened with a start and sat up, then clenched my eyes against the pounding ache behind them. Breathing slowly and steadily, I waited for a moment until the pain became a dull throb and I could look again. She was gone, as I knew as soon as I awakened.

I tried to stand using my bad arm and sucked in my breath as stars danced across my vision and I almost blacked out. Once again I paused, calmed my breathing, then rose using my good arm. I shifted slowly, testing my range of motion. I hoped Tressa's prayers and the Aravander healer's herbal poultice would help my wound heal faster. Because the thought of a bum sword arm was enough to make me blind with panic.

Bending low, I exited the warm hut and felt the chill of the morning on my skin. Where had she gone? My eyes searched the huts, but few were up at this hour. There were two young boys hauling jugs of water for their mothers. Another stirring the embers of a small cook fire and placing a small log atop it. Four girls burst through a copse of aspen, giggled and whispered when they saw the boy. They raced off and took to four separate trunks, using a long strap that formed a loop around their narrow backs and the massive girth of the trees. Utilizing it as leverage, they pushed back with bare feet and swiftly rose up and up until they were among the branches. Moments later, four boys descended, their eyes red-rimmed, their skin pale with weariness. Lookouts, I decided. Is this how the Aravanders had survived so long without capture?

Tressa emerged from the hut beside me, Killian right beside her. At least he hadn't let his Remnant slip away while he slumbered. But they didn't pause beside me. Instead, she was moving toward Latonia's hut, right across from ours. It was then that I heard the woman cry from within. A great, wrenching cry that made me wince.

Niero was coming up the river path with Chaza'el, deep in conversation, but both men looked straight at Tressa when we heard Latonia cry again. With one nod, I knew she'd been called to some sort of healing. But what sort of healing did a birthing woman need? I shuddered at the thought.

Now more agitated than ever, I walked over to Niero. "Did either of you see Andriana?"

"She's down at the river," Niero said. There was something guarded in his eyes. Had they been together? A stab of jealousy went through me, but I looked away so he couldn't see it in my eyes.

"She's in labor," the village healer said, emerging from Latonia's hut. He shook his head, and I noticed how wan he was.

"I'll be back with Dri," I muttered over my shoulder and quickly moved toward the path. "If Tressa's called, it's best if you have all the Remnants here, right?"

Niero nodded slowly, looking at me as if trying to figure out what I was hiding. Sometimes I hated that he seemed to know all of us better than we knew ourselves.

A bird called in the far-off distance, and then another a bit away. Chaza'el's head whipped up, looking to the branches. So did a man exiting another hut. Even as a newcomer, I recognized the covert, hushed alarm disguised as birds. The call went from tree to tree, closer and closer, until the four girls I'd seen rise to the canopy were repeating it down to us.

The village erupted in a frenzy of activity. Children emerged from all corners, dragging tree limbs back across the paths that had been cleared, dousing fires with jugs of water, then dirt to smother the smoky telltale tendrils. A woman ran by, hurriedly putting her wailing baby to her breast right in front of me in her desperation to silence him. A small child ran behind her, thumb in his mouth.

My eyes met Niero's, and I could almost hear him say her name, even though his lips did not move.

Dri.

And then I ran.

CHAPTER
9

ANDRIANA

I swam hard, against the slow current, until I spied three tiny, pale lavender flowers of Sweet William among the greenery of the bank. I eased over the slippery rocks and edged aside a thorny brush to grab the treasured leaves that would create a bathing lather. Careful not to drop them, I shivered in the morning shadows, wishing I could swim back out into the sun, but I was intent on not losing the only soap I could find. Later, I'd come back to collect more and boil them to create a proper soap, but it was all I had for now.

I ripped up the tiny leaves and crushed them in one palm until I had the tiniest bit of a lather, then worked that through my long hair. Then I reached up and took the sparse suds from my hair again and again to clean my body. As I did so, I listened to the sounds of the river along the bank, and the birds above me. It was hardly the best bath I'd ever had, I thought, but at least I'd be free of the brine that had made me itch all night.

It was the birds falling silent that drew my attention first.

And then it was the call echoed through the forest, an eruption of bird chatter, from tree to tree. Lookouts. A warning call.

My eyes scanned the length of the river, worried the boys fishing might return to the beach, and then down at my body, my white underdress that would draw undue attention against the dark greenery of the riverbank.

"Dri, that rock, just upstream," urged a man's voice above me, from among the trees.

Ronan. It shouldn't have surprised me that my knight had found me, but it did. And his presence comforted me.

We could hear the whine of a tiny engine, then. And a second.

"My robe," I whispered over my shoulder, anxiety filling me. If they saw the robe of pelts, strewn across the boulder —

"I have it," he growled. "Go now!"

I was already moving, the foreign whining, whirring sound setting my heart to pounding. I couldn't betray the village by letting their enemies find me. I waded back into the water, submerging as fast as I could to my waist, to my shoulders, then under. When I took a breath, still several strokes away from the outcrop of rock that Ronan had seen, I spotted the first mechanical bird round the bend of the river, low above the water and coming fast. I went under and kicked and pulled back my arms as hard as I could, again and again. The current was stronger here, in the deep, and it took everything in me not to rise for a breath. I stroked forward, wondering if the spy bird was above me now, able to somehow see the white of my underclothes beneath the ripples of the green river water, or if it was already past.

I finally reached the boulder and the current released its grip on me. I touched the rock and then willed myself to rise slowly, barely creating a break in the surface, as our trainer had taught us in survival exercises. Back home in the Valley, he had made us submerge in a deep pool for as long as we could, then rise, letting the water fill around our foreheads, eye sockets, nostrils, lips, chin, neck, as if we were a creature of the water rather than of the earth. His lessons rang through my head as I fought to do it again, instead of breaking the surface and gulping in the breath my lungs screamed for.

The outcropping was barely large enough to cover me and it was a struggle to keep my footing, rather than drifting out with the current. It was too deep to stand.

But the spy bird was close. A hovering machine about the size of a small child, covered in faux feathers, but with no wings. It hovered over the boulder on which I'd stood with Raniero, then slowly moved along the bank toward me. A second later it was on the other side of the rock that shielded me. I prayed that there were no footprints visible, no rocks that looked dislodged. I hurriedly inhaled and exhaled, catching my breath in case I needed to submerge again.

The spy bird suddenly banked and moved out to the river, and I drew a sharp breath. As if it had heard me, it paused, and I went under then, all the way under, abandoning my plan to sink my face halfway, allowing my nostrils to remain clear. I dived down and grabbed hold of several huge, rounded rocks, drawing my legs in and trying to stay still, thankful for the anchoring. I prayed to the Maker to shield me and tried to count rather than think about my aching lungs.

When I couldn't stand it any longer, I rose slowly beneath the outcropping and allowed myself to pant for breath when I noted the whine of the small engines were in the distance.

Ronan peeked out from beside a large tree. "Nicely done," he said quietly, his low voice just audible over the river. "Let's give it another minute to make certain they're gone."

I nodded, thankful he was with me. Always with me. So faithful. So true. I studied him freely as he stared upriver. I could see that the swelling had gone down around his eye, though the white of it was still bloodshot and angry, and the skin around it was turning a sickly green-purple. But to me, he was handsome, rugged and strong, even with the bruises.

He gave me a small, tender smile, recognizing the look on my face as clearly as I was reading the love and care in his heart. He loved me as I loved him. But if Raniero discovered the depth of our feelings, what would he do? We were expressly forbidden to have any relationship beyond our Ailith bond. The bond was already intense enough to have such a clear draw to one another, strong enough to sense when others were about. But then to fall in love?

And yet, to me, it seemed like the only possible outcome, if one was physically and emotionally drawn to their knight as I was. Apparently, Vidar wasn't drawn to Bellona—they were more like brother and sister. Killian ... I was certain he loved Tressa beyond kinship. It was she who kept him at arm's length. But with Ronan, well, neither of us could seem to stay away from the other. He drew me as strongly as the moon drew the tide.

"Okay," he said, edging farther out. "You must be like ice, in that water for so long. Come out on the other side of the rock. There's a small path there."

I nodded, my teeth now chattering, my limbs so numb now they felt oddly warm. I swam around the edge of the boulder and then scrambled over the rocks, wincing as their sharp edges dug into my feet.

Ronan was waiting at the top of the hill, his eyes averted, with my robe stretched out and ready to wrap around me. I edged back against the soft hide and pulled it around, then turned to him.

He drew me in close, until my head was nestled beneath his chin, and moved to kiss it. "Dri, that was far too close."

"I know," I said. "I was scared too. Thank you for coming after me. And for thinking to grab my robe."

"You're welcome."

"Chaza'el knew they were coming. I think. Those mechanical birds."

"Drones from Pacifica," he said. "The chief told me they carry small cameras in them. They probably operate off a boat in the ocean. The Pacificans have been scouting every river for decades, trying to find these people. Periodically, they're found, killed, enslaved, or escape."

"But we're here now," I said, my heart picking up its pace. "If they send Sheolite scouts bent on flushing us out, we might expose them. No matter how hard we might try ..."

"Which probably means we can't stay for long. A few days at the most."

I nodded and wrapped my arms around him, relishing this moment alone.

"You smell good," he murmured, pulling me closer too. "You found some Sweet William?"

"A few leaves," I said, happy that he'd noticed.

He looked down at me and I could feel the wave of desire

in him. But it merely echoed my own. He bent his head and kissed me then, slowly, softly. It was our first kiss since the tree village in the mountains, a half of a moon cycle before. And I wanted more. I reached up, tangling my fingers in the back of his dark, shoulder-length hair, for once not tied with its customary leather strap. Had he just awakened?

He moved one arm across my robe, his big hand settling on my lower back, strong and sure, pulling me close, our kiss deepening.

"Stop," said a voice behind him.

We sprang apart, knowing instantly who it was.

Raniero.

He strode through the woods, his face like a visible snarl, and grabbed my hand. With my other, I hurriedly drew the robe tight around me like a shield. I knew I was blushing furiously — was my entire face as red as a berry?

Ronan was rubbing the back of his neck, spots of color spreading across his own cheeks, the other hand reaching out to our leader. "Niero—"

"No," Niero cut him off. "There's nothing to say. You've crossed the line." He dropped my hand and paced a little, hands on hips, then gestured angrily at us. "Don't you see? The Ailith bond is strong enough without this going on," he said, waving between me and Ronan. "Our enemies, given the opportunity, will use the love we share for one another against us. But if you two share the love of a man and a woman..." He shook his head as if in agony and looked to the sky. "It simply cannot happen. You must trust me."

We stared at him. "But what if..." I swallowed, losing my nerve.

"What if it's already happened?" Ronan finished, glaring

at him. "What if I love Dri and she loves me?" The muscles in his jaw clenched and his hands drew into fists. "It's not like we can stop it, Raniero. It's beyond us."

Niero studied him, missing nothing. His brown eyes flicked over to me, then back to my knight. "It's not beyond you. It's a *choice*. It began, fine. Now you must end it. *Now*," he repeated.

"We cannot," I said desperately. "How do you keep the heart from going where it will?"

"By the strength of *decision*," he bit back. "Don't you see?" he said, his voice rising in agitation. "You endanger us all. Our mission."

"Endanger our mission simply because we love? That's ridiculous. How could the love I feel for Ronan be anything but the Maker's way? And if it's his way, how could that impede our mission?"

Niero drew in a long, deep breath. "Andriana," he said slowly. "Already, you've struggled between what you feel and what you know. Our enemy has used your feelings against you. They shall try and use every one of the Remnants' gifts against them, knowing it's your greatest weapon."

"He speaks the truth," Kapriel said, turning miserable eyes on me as he emerged from the forest. I saw the others behind him. All except for Tressa and Killian. My cheeks flamed. How much had they heard? Seen?

"But you are most vulnerable, Dri." Niero took my hand in both of his. "You must trust me on this," he said, looking over to Ronan too. "I know it will hurt, that it will be a struggle. That it is a sacrifice. But you must not give in to this attraction until our last battle has been won."

Ronan ran his hands down his face and then shook them toward Niero. "You ask the impossible," he muttered bitterly.

"You should be used to that by now," Vidar quipped.

But for once, no one laughed.

CHAPTER
10

ANDRIANA

I couldn't bear to walk beside Ronan — our proximity feeling like some sort of odd mocking — so I hurried to catch up to Chaza'el as we returned to the village through the woods.

I touched his arm when he didn't look up, and knew he'd been so lost in thought that he hadn't sensed me approach. "Are you going to tell me what you saw?" I asked. Had he seen us? Had he been the one to betray us to Raniero?

He turned his eyes on me — normally so merry, now filled with angst — and then just shook his head. "It is not for me to share. Not yet."

I frowned. "You must tell me," I urged. "If it concerns Ronan — "

"It wasn't about either of you, sister," he interrupted. "I will tell you when it is right. But Niero ..." He paused and ran his fingers through his jet-black hair. "I know this brings you pain, Andriana. I once loved a girl too. But Niero's right. Your love endangers you both."

We walked for a time in silence. "How do you stop loving once you've begun?" I asked softly. "It's like telling a drowning person to quit reaching for air."

He nodded, chin in hand. "You must reach farther, toward the Maker. For his mission, his call, above all others."

I sighed heavily, hearing the wisdom in his words. What had we been thinking, Ronan and I? Our path wasn't the way of so many others.

I thought back to my own parents, so in love. And murdered because they had dared to raise me … and protect me. It was said that the Sheolites had used their love against them — torturing one and then the other to get information. I tried to swallow, but found my mouth dry when I thought of Ronan held, tortured, in order to get to me. Had it not almost made me crazy aboard the *Far North* just to know he had been taken to the hold?

I pulled aside and waited for Ronan to catch up to me, then for the others to go ahead. They moved on, seeming aware that we needed a moment to talk alone.

I turned to face him, wanting to take his hands, but knew it would make it all the harder. If I touched him, I might not ever let go of him again.

"Don't say it," he said miserably, turning partially away and rubbing the back of his neck. "I know, Dri. I know."

There would be no betrothal ceremony for Ronan and me. No children. No settling into a cozy cottage in the Valley. With a start, I admitted to myself that I'd been fantasizing about all of those things for weeks now. Ever since we'd kissed in the tree house. Maybe even before then, in the Wadi.

No, we would likely give our lives for this cause, to turn the world back toward the Way. To point toward hope. Peace.

"Supreme goals always demand supreme sacrifice," I muttered, repeating a quote my father had often shared with me.

I waited for him to speak. "It's selfish, our love," he whispered slowly, as if each word pained him. "We were born to serve a love even greater than ours."

He turned toward me again, his beautiful river-green eyes searching me, and I watched as the morning sun filtered through the trees and caught the tips of his dark lashes. The longing, the aching within him doubled my own. "We were," I made myself whisper.

Then I couldn't stand it any longer. I pulled him close, resting my cheek against his chest, feeling the comforting *thump* of his heartbeat, the warmth of him as he struggled.

"Dri," he groaned, his voice strangled.

"I know. I know," I said, tears rising. "I just need you to hold me. One more time."

Tentatively, he put his arms around me at last, his hands unmoving. Disappointment sliced through him, and me. A slow, grinding pain, the knowledge of impending division.

"We won't be separate, Ronan. We'll be together more than most married couples are."

"All of the pain, none of the pleasure," he said with a sardonic laugh.

I huffed a laugh with him. "It's a gift to be your best friend, even if I can never have all your love."

When he said nothing, I leaned back to look in his face.

He reached then, to touch my cheek, every bit of his action denoting devotion. "Make no mistake, Andriana," he said fiercely, but softly. "I intend to see this mission through." He put his other hand on my other cheek then. His eyes searched mine, back and forth, and I felt the ferocity of his pledge. "But when it's over, I will not rest until you are completely mine."

With that, he kissed me one final time, just the barest, lightest, slowest touch of our lips.

Then he took my hand and led me back to camp.

■ ■ ■

Ronan dropped my hand as we glimpsed the other Ailith waiting for us, and now I could fully see the village's huts as they were meant to be, camouflaged to meld with the forest.

"They come once, perhaps twice a moon cycle," the chief's husband, Jezre, said as we entered his clearing. People around him were wide-eyed, still hyper alert. Several searched the sky, as if expecting the spy birds to return. Others were shimmying up or down trees — probably those who had alerted the camp to hide.

A clenched-teeth wail from his hut made all of us flinch. Jezre stared back at the hut for a moment, then sank wearily to the ground, and I could feel the heavy mantle of responsibility he carried. We sat down with him.

"So you don't believe our presence brought them upon you?" Niero said carefully.

Jezre moved his head back and forth as if weighing that idea. "It could be. Kapriel's escape will chafe our enemy, and they'll likely suspect us. They will double or triple their efforts to find us. They know we travel by boat. So they search and search the rivers and streams. But never have they come inland, thank the Maker. Despite our efforts to disguise them, they may see our huts and fires and paths between the trees."

I could see the fear lurking behind his eyes, even as he tried to hide it. Slowly, he looked around his village.

"Two seasons ago, we thought all was lost," he went on. "We'd been living far nearer the coast, just up the mouth of another river, about three days' journey from this river. More than half of our village was either taken prisoner or killed on sight."

"By the Pacificans?" Niero said. "For what purpose?"

Jezre shook his head, and I noticed his long, graying-black hair shimmering in the sun. He had to be past his fourth decade, old for a father. "They called us rebels."

"You *are* rebels, are you not?" Niero returned gently.

He lifted his thin chin, each motion regal. "We are ... separatists by necessity. Followers of the old ways. We have not wished to swear fealty to Pacifica, especially as we learned more and more of them."

"What do you mean?" I asked.

"They are difficult to discern without time among them, but once you are a part of their social order, you recognize the deep illness that permeates them. They are of the dark. We have been waiting for ... you Remnants, really. I believe we've been waiting all along, through the generations. We'd heard the foretelling. We knew of your coming, even if we didn't know your exact shape," he said, waving over us. "And we hoped. Hoped there would be an alternative. And now here you are." He swept a gentle smile over the group, but I felt his confidence waver, even as he kept his face steady as his wife screamed in the hut behind him. He grimaced and looked down. When she was silent he said, "We shall aid you in any way possible."

"But we are not as you expected," I said.

His brown eyes shifted to meet mine. "No. My father … He always thought you would bring an army. Weapons. And many behind you to fight."

"There are many behind us," Kapriel said. Bellona shifted to allow him better access to our circle.

"More than even you might realize," Niero said, nodding to the prince. "And many ahead. Everywhere we go, we will gather momentum now, find people who support our cause and will rise to our defense. Beyond the Wall, there are many who don't yet see that Pacifica is using them, sucking their resources dry and leaving them to the ways that continue to eat away at their foundations. But the Remnants are here to change that."

Jezre took a deep breath, tapping his steepled fingers together. "How can we assist you?"

Niero glanced around. "For now, serving as a safe haven as we regain our strength is a tremendous gift."

"And you have a good knowledge of healing herbs in these woods," Chaza'el said. "Tressa would do well to spend more time learning of them."

Kapriel nodded. "Pacifica hordes their medicine to fight the Cancer. If we could make medicine available to the Trading Union—"

"That'd buy further support," Killian put in. He pushed an errant blond dreadlock over his shoulder. The rest were tied with a leather strap at the back of his neck. "You also have salt."

"Salt would be of excellent value too," Vidar said.

"Though it's more challenging for us to harvest," Jezre said, "without being seen. It's best to have wide places, open to the sun, and better farther south, where the sun is more plentiful. Hiding from Pacifica—well, it limits our productivity."

"The fish," Niero said. "There are many?"

"More than we can harvest," Jezre said.

"We need every man, woman, and child on the task," Niero said. "Dried fish would be welcome in trade. And these pelts," he said, running his hands over the brown fur across his chest.

"Beaver," Jezre said. "They're farther inland, up higher on the rivers, but they are making a good comeback to these streams."

"Trap as many as you can without endangering their return," Niero said.

"We'll need to take a great number of them with us as we travel north," Kapriel said. "To keep us warm."

We all looked at him in confusion.

"In time," he said, nodding once, slowly, as if this should be obvious to everyone. "We shall go everywhere we've already been . . . and beyond. Building support. Destabilizing Pacifica's strength."

"But not Zanzibar," Killian said.

His mouth dropped open as Niero met his gaze.

"Everywhere we've been, and beyond," Niero repeated.

Killian cocked his head and folded his arms. "Everywhere we've been, we've left some serious enemies behind us. And *Zanzibar*." He leaned forward. "There is no way I'm taking Tressa back there."

"If the Maker calls us, we shall go," Niero said calmly.

"Do you not remember where Tressa was when we freed her?" Killian spat. "How close she was to being hanged?"

"If the Maker calls us, we shall go," Niero said again, staring Killian down.

They were silent for several seconds, before Killian broke

first, shaking his head. "You're mad! Did they strike you a few too many times across the skull back in Wadi Qelt?"

"Sometimes the right path looks wrong from afar. We will not go anywhere the Maker does not send us. We must trust, Killian. Not in our own strength, but the Maker's."

Ronan let out a mirthless laugh and turned away, lifting his face to the sky. He was as stunned as Killian. He turned back, and I could see the agitation within him. "Our enemy actively hunts us," he said, lifting a hand toward Niero. "Now more than ever, with Kapriel in our fold! And you want to go back to cities they have easy access to?"

"If we follow the Maker's lead, those cities might become Community strongholds. And not all of our time shall be spent in the cities," Niero said, his gaze clear-eyed and assured. "There are many communities like this one and the Hoodites. We will sojourn there too."

I tried to swallow, but found my throat terribly dry. Thoughts of our narrow escapes in one city after another— even from the Drifters. "Why?" I sputtered. "Why must we return to those places? Why not edge around them?"

"Because the people in each of those places are speaking of you, even now," Niero said quietly. "Don't you see?" he asked, looking around at each of us. "Hearts are softening. People whisper of the miracles we've left in our wake. It's clear to them that the Maker travels by our side. They are ripe for the Truth. We can turn them, prepare them to take up arms against Pacifica."

"If Pacifica doesn't kill us first," Ronan said bitterly.

"Death does have a way of slowing a man down," Vidar said, laughing a little at his own joke. Bellona shook her head, clearly not amused.

Latonia cried out from inside the hut, and we all held our breath.

Tressa came out a moment later, her ivory skin covered by a sheen of sweat. We waited for her to come near. "It appears we have a long day before us. Can you come and pray over her?"

As one, we rose, immediately moved by her suggestion. It felt more like a command, like the Call.

Jezre grabbed Chaza'el's arm as he turned, and shook his head slowly, sorrowfully. "We've never had a babe born alive. Latonia ..." His words trickled away as he looked to the trees, his eyes bright with tears. He turned away, and I felt the shame within him. "She can't survive many more losses."

Chaza'el turned and put a hand on his shoulder, as his wife cried out again from the hut. "Today, Jezre, you will greet your son."

Jezre glanced at him, hope and disbelief warring within him.

"But we must pray, brother," Chaza'el said. "*Pray.*"

CHAPTER
11

ANDRIANA

Niero insisted we pause to give Kapriel his armband first. "Whatever's about to happen in there," he said, gesturing to Latonia's hut, "I think we need all Remnants with every bit of the gifting the Maker has granted them. Agreed?"

We readily nodded, none of us in a hurry to face the laboring chief, except for Tressa, who had probably already witnessed a hundred births as a healer. So we quickly gathered, with many of the Aravanders around us, and Kapriel pulled off his shirt. I swallowed hard when I saw Kapriel's back, crisscrossed with long, red, angry scars, evidence of a whipping. It made me grieve what he'd been through and feel guilty over defending Keallach. But I put his brother firmly out of my mind as he placed his right hand on my shoulder, preparing himself, as Chaza'el knelt at his other side.

My skin tingled with anticipation of what was to come, the

most vivid visitation from the Maker I'd ever experienced. But Niero was moving quickly, reciting ancient words that we were coming to know well, words we loved. And then there was fire, and a rush of wind, and we were done, Kapriel crumpling forward, gripping his arm, face full of wonder.

Niero gave him only a couple of moments to gather himself. Then, as one, we entered the chief's hut, and the smell of blood and sweat was nearly overpowering. We crowded in, shoulder to shoulder. Two women supported Latonia from behind, a blanket draped over her legs. I braced for a funny comment from Vidar, but for once, his eyes were wide and his lips were clenched shut. Chaza'el, Kapriel, Vidar, and I gathered around the laboring chief's back.

"The babe is breech," Tressa said lowly, as Latonia cried out again and panted through a contraction.

"How can we help you?" Kapriel asked.

"Pray with me as I turn him. Latonia is terribly weak, but if we don't do this, the babe will not survive. She might not either." Her last words were in a whisper, and I wondered if I'd imagined she'd even said it.

"Save him," Latonia said, reaching out and grabbing Tressa's arm with such force, the skin turned white around her fingers. "Even at the cost of my life. Please," she said, and then her voice softened, weary tears slipping down her face. "Please."

Chaza'el came closer and took the woman's hand from Tressa and held it in his own. "Latonia, I have seen it. You will be holding this baby by noon. And he will be a great leader for your tribe. Just as you helped to deliver us, we shall help deliver you."

"Literally," Vidar said.

"*Vidar,*" Bellona and I said together.

Latonia clenched his hand and screamed through a contraction.

All trace of frivolity drained from Vidar's face, but his fear wasn't over this laboring woman, it was something else. I followed his gaze to the door. It was then that I felt my armband move from a chill to a pulsing warmth and then back again. That chill ... His eyes met mine as I fought panic.

"They're coming," he whispered. "They know we're here."

Bellona knew it too, her hand on her cuff as she edged past Vidar and opened the door to Niero, who was just on his way in.

Latonia cried out again and lifted her face upward, as if beseeching the Maker for relief, but my eyes stayed on Niero.

He nodded grimly, looking only to me and Vidar. "The knights and I will keep you safe. Trust us to do our work and you do yours."

"We will," I said. I didn't know if he could hear me over the moans and cries of Latonia between us, but I believed he knew what I had said.

"It is not us that may have brought them here. They want this one," Vidar said, his dark brows knit in consternation as he turned back to Latonia and stared at her midsection.

I frowned. The baby within the village chief.

It made sense.

The Maker wanted this child to live.

And therefore, Sheol wanted the child to die.

Die. Dying. Death. Dead ...

A chill ran down my neck and I felt the cold chasm of death tear at me from within.

Vidar reached out to grip my arm, his fingers like a vise.

"Andriana. Remember who you are. Who you have always been. And who created you as such."

I nodded. And with his urgent words, at the remembrance of my Maker, and with the overwhelming love and care within him, the chasm closed and warmth of the Spirit sealed it.

Outside, we heard our knights shout and the sound of swords drawn, but inside all I could feel was a sort of protective cocoon. It was as if a physical wall had been erected between us and the dark ones I knew approached. Was that Kapriel's doing? Some sort of storm? I thought briefly of the villagers, the children, the old ones who wandered from hut to hut, but it was only a fleeting thought.

I glanced at Vidar. Sweat poured off his face and beneath his hairline as quickly as it did from Latonia. He could feel our enemies approach, just as I did. Were they Pacifican soldiers or worse, the dark ones we'd encountered beside the Hoodites?

He hurriedly wiped the sweat from his eyes, but I noted his attention was on the swollen mound of the chief's belly. I, too, focused there. The Aravanders had saved us. Now we were to save the tiniest of them all.

As Kapriel prayed, and we silently echoed him, I became more and more tense. Sweat ran down Tressa's red face, dripping on to her hands, which were working and working over Latonia's taut belly.

"Come," Tressa said to all of us, and climbed up on the bed above Latonia. "Place your hands on Latonia and pray as I turn this child ..."

The women let Latonia lay flat again, and each took one of her hands, murmuring to her, wiping her face.

Tressa did not wait. After briefly tracing the child's shape as if visualizing where he was — she pressed down, hard, with the heels of her hands.

Latonia screamed, long and hard as she worked, her cries so pitiful, her pain and fear so immense, that I wept with her.

Dimly, as if from far away, I heard other cries. Shouts. But we remained in prayer for this child, this precious child, that for whatever reason the Maker had ordained would live. Thrive.

"There," Tressa muttered, her auburn brows lifting in hope. "There!" she cried in triumph.

We could all see the mound of the child shift beneath Latonia's taut skin, and her cry turned to the silent weeping of relief rather than pain.

"Now you can push," Tressa said. "At the next contraction..."

And then it was upon her. The chief's face became red and her friends helped to lift her up. Vidar, Kapriel, and Chaza'el turned slightly to the side, giving her some bit of modesty, but I could not look away as the babe's head crested and emerged after just two rounds of pushing. Tressa caught him as he slid out, the shoulders and the rest of his body following easily.

Tressa wiped the babe with a bit of cloth, grinning so widely that I never thought her more beautiful. But it was because I knew the joy within her. It bubbled up inside me, around me, making me grin too. *Maker, Maker,* I prayed. *We have heard you. And we have answered. Save us. Save us all.*

CHAPTER 12

RONAN

The last time I'd felt such foreboding was outside the Hoodites.

Killian and I shared a look as Niero drew his crescent-shaped blades and looked at each of us fiercely, then over to Bellona. "Whatever you do, do not leave the Remnants unguarded," he grit out. "I shall return."

But even as I agreed, Raniero had shoved off, the toe of his boots creating divots in the loamy soil. He dashed head-long into the thick of the trees, and I felt a wave of warmth wash over my arm cuff then. Somehow, some way, he was not alone. There were unseen warriors with him.

But my eyes narrowed in on those we could see, emerging through the trees. Sheolites, caped in red. I glanced over at my fellow Knights of the Last Order, wondering how we were to defend ourselves, just three against what looked like twenty, no, thirty warriors emerging from the trees.

We heard the mewling cry of a newborn inside, and shared a grim smile. So the child was born — the newest, tiniest victory.

"Ronan," Bellona said, gesturing with her head toward thirty or so Aravander warriors gathering behind us, all armed with bows and arrows and led by Jezre, the chief's husband. They ranged from young boys to old women, but each carried a determined look. I supposed if my tribe had been hunted for decades, I, too, would be ready for a battle at last. And with their chief in the birthing hut behind us, the cry of the long-awaited child in their ears, I figured they'd never be in fiercer fighting form.

"Take a knee here!" I cried. "Ten of you! And ten more above them, on their feet! Two lines! Quickly!"

The Sheolites were running toward us, abandoning any last semblance of covert approach.

I wondered if I'd made a fatal error, forming them in lines before asking them to fire. If there'd be time to let loose their arrows at all. But they were children of the forest and moved lithely, assuredly, as if they'd trained for this very event all their lives.

"Fire!" I cried, before the last few were even in place.

The arrows arose like a flock of long, deadly birds. Some of the Sheolites gathered together, raising shields to form a combined barrier. Others dodged behind trees. A few took arrows to shoulders, guts, legs.

"Fire again!" I cried.

As soon as that volley of arrows was aloft, Jezre called, "Young and old, retreat! Hide! Those able, aid us!"

They scattered, some quickly, and some ambling at a painfully slow pace. Jezre and three other men, as well as two women, stayed behind with us but withdrew ten paces in order to get a better vantage point at the warriors almost upon us.

Vidar and Kapriel emerged then, Vidar taking up his halberd and Kapriel a lance. But as we faced our enemy, each of us knew that there were still far too many.

Far, far too many.

ANDRIANA

The sounds of battle were all around us. They seemed to surround the hut and almost go over us as the tiny boy took to his mother's breast and Latonia stroked his tiny cheek. "Long have I awaited you, sweet child," she said, seemingly oblivious to all that was happening. Perhaps she feared that we would die this day. Perhaps she thought she must take every second she could with him.

Latonia raised her head and looked to a young maid. "You must take him," she said. "Into the woods and hide." She hurriedly wiped the tears from her cheeks and set to swaddling her child.

I couldn't breathe. The wrenching pain of Latonia sending her baby away was reminiscent of the same tearing I'd experienced with Ronan.

But the girl grimly agreed with the queen. "I will guard him with my life."

Latonia turned to the others. "Quickly. Bring me my bow and my sword. I will relish taking down my enemy on this day of days. My sisters," she said, looking to the village women who attended her, "I need you to show each of these new friends to the longboats. Please. For me?"

I stared at her, wondering about the strength of a mother,

remembering my own. Sending me off, serving a greater cause, no matter the cost.

The younger woman bound the child next to her chest, then wrapped an animal-skin cape around her shoulders. The baby was quiet, already asleep, seemingly unaware of the crisis around us. I envied him.

I moved out of the hut, tentatively peering around to make certain I had room to exit without being eviscerated as soon as I was erect. Outside, Ronan and Killian were each battling two men. Many had fallen, either wounded or dead, both Sheolite and Aravander. Arrows sang through the air, some so close I swore I could feel the *whoosh* of their passing. More Sheolites fell, one right beside Ronan.

I saw Kapriel, then, a distance off, holding his own despite his weariness, testimony to his skill with the double-pointed lance he fought with. Chaza'el fought beside him. It was clear they'd been trained as children to use their weapons, Kapriel easily parrying thrusts and strikes and dodging others. But at one point, he stood back, closed his eyes a moment, then with a wave of his hand, sent a great gust of wind through a stand of trees, crushing ten Sheolites at once.

Chaza'el used both a whip and a small shield, unbalancing and striking one after another, on occasion pulling out a long dagger from his belt. He struck down his assailant and looked to me then, panting, wiping his lip of sweat, and his eyes swept across the forest floor and then back, full of understanding.

It had to be a boon, I thought, *to have the gift of foretelling.* Perhaps he'd seen every one he would come against this day.

Still, they poured toward us. Far more than we could fight off.

I gripped my sword and waited for Ronan to turn and see

me. I felt Latonia's young maid behind me, heard her frightened gasps. An arrow came from behind us then and struck the man who rose from the ground, intent on coming back after Ronan again. It pierced his neck and the man reached toward it, a terrible gurgling sound emerging from his mouth. Then his eyes went blank and he fell backward.

I looked to the archer. *Jezre*. He nodded once to me, notching another arrow even as he did so.

Another maid came through the doorway and immediately turned and ran with the baby into the woods. Latonia had chosen well—the girl was swift and sure on her feet. The first still cowered behind me and I could feel her panic, so strong I had to concentrate on not making it my own. A boy arrived, carrying the queen's bow and a quiver of arrows, as well as her sword.

"Ronan," I said, quietly, trying not to draw any undue attention. The first maid was already shifting behind me, clearly intent on escape. If we lost her, we'd be unlikely to find our way to the longboats. "We must be away."

Ronan's eyes met mine, then moved past me to the girl.

Grim, he took a breath, ignoring the battle going on all about us, trying to sort out the best way. Killian moved away to take on another opponent, a fearsomely tall scout who grinned in anticipation.

I knew the tearing within Ronan. Everything in him had been trained to protect me. And we were definitely safer with the rest of the Ailith beside us.

"We have no time," I said urgently, as Tressa edged up beside me. I thrust a fallen Aravander's shield in her hand. "Today, no matter how we *feel*, we protect ourselves," I hissed. "Our knights have enough to handle."

Vidar and Bellona neared us, and Niero hurriedly came

toward us. "We must divide." He nodded toward Vidar and Bellona. "You two get Chaza'el and Kapriel to the longboats and away," he said urgently. "It is vital we protect the prince. The rest of us will hold them off as long as we can."

Alarm and dismay filled them all, but we had no time to assuage their fears or convince them.

"Go! You waste any edge we might give you," Ronan ground out, then turned to fight off a Sheolite scout who was barreling toward us with an eerie scream. I felt Ronan's protection as a shield and it strengthened me. So did the hope I felt in the other Ailith disappearing into the wood, Kapriel giving me one last sad and yet thankful glance over his shoulder.

Protect them, Maker. And give me the strength to not only protect myself, but to fight.

CHAPTER
13

ANDRIANA

With the help of a line of brave Aravanders, led by their chief and her husband, we managed to hold our enemies off for some time — the Sheolites, and behind them Pacifican soldiers. But when it became clear that we would be soon overcome, Niero turned to Ronan and Killian. "Time to go," he said.

"This boy will lead you to a longboat," Latonia said, letting a quick succession of arrows fly and accepting a new quiver from a child about a decade old. She looked to Niero. "We shall make our way to Chaza'el's village. Summon us when it is time. We will come to you. And bring others."

Niero nodded, put a hand briefly on her shoulder and then looked to the child. "Lead us," he said.

The boy's eyes widened as he glimpsed a mass of warriors behind him in a dead run toward us, then turned and yelled, "This way!"

We followed him then — Niero, Killian, Tressa, Ronan, and I.

The Sheolites behind us hooted and laughed, closing in, reminding me of a pack of wolves from the stories of old. I had no idea how many we'd managed to hold back from chasing the rest of our companions and the Aravanders who were running north into the hills. All I knew is that there were too many for us to fight off alone. With twenty or more behind us, it was clear they'd take us in time, dead or alive.

They seemed to sense our fear and grew louder. I could hear dead branches cracking beneath their feet, so close that I worried they could reach out and strike Ronan dead behind me. In my peripheral vision I saw that they attempted to flank us. "Faster!" I urged our guide.

He didn't look back, and I could tell he was running as fast as he could. I fought the urge to pass him up, to save ourselves, even if we couldn't save him, but I knew I couldn't do it. *But were we all to be —*

The forest broke in a burst of open space and sky and I only barely swallowed a scream. Our guide was running across an old rope bridge, the planks few and far between.

"Go, Dri, go!" Ronan roared when I hesitated, my eyes wide, my heart in a panicked pace at the view of the drop to the bottom of the canyon, the rushing river a couple hundred feet below us.

"I-I can't!" I said, my feet as rooted to the ground as the trees around me.

"You must! I can't carry you across that! Our combined weight will — "

Killian and Tressa tore across the bridge, leaving only Niero panting beside us. We could all hear the shouts and sounds of our enemies in pursuit. Perilously close now. But I couldn't take my eyes off the planks beneath Tressa and Killian's feet, cracking, falling away in places. The ropes swinging precariously ...

"Go! Leave me here!"

Niero grabbed hold of my arm. "Andriana! Dig deep! This fear ... it isn't something the Maker has given you. It is the enemy's tool!"

"Stop!" Ronan cried, pulling away his hand. "Let me talk her through!"

Niero let out an exasperated breath and turned to the woods. "Get her across," he grunted toward Ronan, and then with weapons in both hands, ran *toward* our enemy, disappearing among the trees.

"Niero!" I cried in terror.

Ronan let out a frustrated growl, picked me up with such force it took the wind from my lungs, and set off running across the bridge. I closed my eyes and wept, feeling the uncertain sway of the ropes, hearing the cracking of ancient, sun-dried planks giving way beneath our combined weight ... and cursing my weakness. My fear that endangered us all. That had sent Niero to ... his death?

I lifted my face, aware that the Sheolites and Pacifican soldiers had emerged. A good fifteen were on the ropes behind us, picking their way across the battered bridge, with five more on the bank at the end, clearly waiting to see if their companions made it first.

There was no sign of Niero.

The nearest was soon only a few leaps behind us, his teeth bared in fierce determination. We were moving faster now, the ropes growing tauter and not giving so much sway.

Nearing the end? The thought of it made me almost delirious with hope. And then I felt the surety of rock and soil as I was unceremoniously tossed to the ground. Ronan turned to meet our pursuer, drawing his sword in one fluid movement.

Guilt flooded me. The Sheolite lashed out savagely and very nearly struck Ronan. He lashed again and Ronan leaped backward. The man reached firm ground and formed a barrier to allow the next to draw closer. Killian was there fighting beside Ronan, and I sensed Tressa behind me. My eyes trailed along the rope bridge and I knew what I had to do.

I reached for my sword, and rammed it down on the nearest rope, right behind the second man after he charged toward Killian. More of our enemy were getting closer, emboldened by the sight of the far bank. My sword slammed against the old rope, about the width of my forearm, and a third of the brown strands sprung apart.

I wasn't so lucky with my second strike. Ronan, tumbling with the first man, on top of him for a moment, choking him, then under him, distracted me from a good aim. But I knew if I didn't stem this flow of our enemies, we'd all be captured within minutes. The third man, nearing us on the bridge, grit his teeth as he saw me raise my sword again, and managed to block my strike as I brought it down. Then he was up and over the last few steps of the bridge, coming after me with a ferocity I hadn't seen since I battled Sethos himself.

The thought of our adversary made me thank the Maker that the sorcerer was absent. We were weary and too few to take on his power as well. Ronan was on his feet again, but still battling his opponent.

The Sheolite rammed at me with his sword and I parried,

the clang of our swords sending a teeth-jarring reverberation through me. And then again.

I jutted my sword toward him, intending on stabbing him, but he dodged my move, grabbed hold of my arm, and smashed it down on his knee.

I cried out and the sword dropped. My arm wasn't broken, but it had been close, and I held it against my torso, backing away.

He smiled, and I saw gaps between his teeth. "It is fortunate for you that we are to bring back alive as many Remnants as possible. You fight for no reason. Surrender, show your mark, and you shall be saved." He advanced on me, whipping his sword back and forth. Behind him, I saw our Aravander guide desperately bring my sword down on the rope where I had managed to partially cut it, just as the next group of Sheolites neared the end. If nothing else, if I could continue to distract this one, the boy would have a chance ...

My attacker tossed his sword aside and tackled me, apparently honest in his intent to return with me alive. I hit the ground and felt the wind knocked from me under his weight, but forced myself to twist and elbow him in the face, as our trainer had taught us. I gasped for breath, willing air back into my lungs and glimpsed Ronan driving back the next of the Sheolites as the guide hacked at the rope again and again. Trapped by those before them, the Sheolites could only watch in horror as the rope sprung loose, one strand at a time, gravity now taking its course.

Two more managed to make it to the end before the rope, with a great *thrum*, broke apart. The men still on the bridge cried out, grasping for a hold, or pressed toward either end in a last, mad gambit to reach safety. The majority sank out of sight or screamed as they fell down the canyon. I winced and squeezed my eyes tightly, sickened by the sounds of terror. Even if they were my enemies, I thought it the worst possible way to die.

Falling...

My attacker leaped to his feet, enraged by the sight of his comrades dying, and whipped around toward me, clearly holding me responsible for his friends' deaths. I managed to stand again, but viewed my trembling legs and hands with consternation as if they belonged to another. I was absorbing all their fear, feeling it with them. Despite the Sheolite closing in on me, I shut my eyes tightly, seeking to grab hold of truth, of the memory of some feeling that would bolster me and give me courage in the midst of this cacophony of panic and despair and furry.

Love, I thought, remembering what it was to be in Ronan's arms. To look around at my brothers and sisters, all in one circle. Mom and Dad, holding me close.

Faith, I thought, remembering what it was like to see each of the Remnant's gifts unveiled.

Hope, I thought, remembering the Maker's promises, and finishing the circle of protection in my mind.

I concentrated on all three of these, remembering my father quoting the ancient sacred words. "But the greatest of these is love." *Love, love, love*, I repeated silently, looking toward my attacker. I scrambled to hold on to some part of the feeling while I looked at him — even the scarcest measure — casting it toward him as he reached me, his fingers encircling my neck. But when he touched me, his fingers sprang backward, as if burned.

His brown eyes narrowed in confusion. "H-how? *What*?" He reached for me again, but once more, he couldn't hold on to me. His face softened, as if he wanted to hug me instead, as if we were friends, but I scrambled away. He took his head in his hands, as if intent on squeezing out the madness.

A scream brought my head up and around. *Tressa.*

The guide gestured toward me. "Come! We must be away!"

But Tressa cried out Killian's name, her tone desperate.

They were both in trouble. If Killian was down …

While I hated fighting and struggled to bring myself to bear arms, Tressa outright refused.

We heard a desperate, guttural roar from Killian then. That was it. I set out running, passing Ronan, who had wounded one Pacifican soldier — now writhing on the ground — and struggled to keep another pinned to a tree. "Stay here, Dri!" he grit out, sweat pouring from his brow.

But I ignored him.

I broke free of the woods and was back in the clearing beside the bridge before I recognized the chill in my armband. I stopped short, realizing my folly of running toward the fight without my knight. Our enemy was here — Sheolites. Not just those who had managed to cross the bridge. Somehow, some way they'd gotten around. Maybe even before I cut the bridge down. Maybe even before we'd reached this side.

Killian was down and yet struggling to rise, blood flowing up and around his fingers, covering a horrible abdominal wound. "Killian!" I knelt beside him and cradled his torso in my arms, urging him to settle back.

His emotions flooded me.

First panic. Heart-stopping, breath-stealing.

Then the desperation — to get to Tressa? — chilled me more than the Sheolites' presence.

Then such sheer pain, making me suck in my breath.

And yet still, Tressa's knight tried to rise, looking to the far side of the clearing. "There," he gasped, and I followed his gaze.

I just caught a glimpse of the swirling red robes of two Sheolite scouts and Tressa's boots dragging between them as they disappeared through the trees. "I know," I whispered in his ear, "I know. We'll get her. It's all right, Killian. Right now, you just have to focus on staying still."

I put my hand atop his on his belly, and swallowed back a wave of bile when I felt the sickening, loose sensation, in a place that should be sheer muscle, strength.

Maker.

My breathing became shallow, panicked. We needed Tressa back. We needed her if we were to save Killian.

Ronan burst into the clearing, then. His chest heaved and sweat dripped down his cheeks, creating rivulets through the blood spatters. "Are you all right?" he asked me.

"I'm fine! They have Tressa! Two Sheolites!" I nodded toward where they'd disappeared. "Go!" I added, when he hesitated.

He swiftly looked about, and touched his arm cuff.

"It's just those scouts we sense!" I insisted.

Scowling and slowly shaking his head, Ronan stubbornly remained.

"Ronan. If you don't go after her, we'll—" I began.

"Lose us both," Killian grit out, grimacing.

It was an impossible decision for my knight. I knew that. But there was only one thing I wanted — Tressa back — and if he hesitated any longer ...

He let out a sound of exasperation and shook a hand toward us. "Stay right here."

Killian let out a wry laugh. "Hard for me to go very far."

"Dri?" Ronan insisted.

"Yes! *Yes!* Go!"

He turned on his heel and ran, sword in hand.

I patted Killian's shoulder. "I think it's best if we get you flat. I'll help you put some pressure on that wound."

He agreed, and as gently as I could, I moved out from behind him and helped him settle back, his dreadlocks snaking out among the pine needles. Ten paces away was a dead Pacifican soldier. I could see another's boots around the corner of a boulder. Every enemy was dead, the Sheolites gone with Tressa, right? Why, then, did the chill remain in my cuff?

"Dri," Killian said, his forehead a mass of wrinkles from the pain. He gestured toward my cuff, warning me.

"Shh, I know." I set his fingers on top of his wound, which was still bleeding profusely. I strained to listen for some hint of an enemy's approach, but heard nothing. "It's just the lingering stink of their presence," I whispered, shrugging out of my coat and pulling off my sweater, then my T-shirt, leaving only my camisole and bra.

"Dri, please," he said, "I'm taken."

"Shut up," I said, shaking my head and using my knife to begin tearing a strip off my T-shirt, creating a long bandage as I tore around the bodice. His uncommon wisecrack made me long for Vidar and Bellona, who were now on the far side of the canyon. How I wished they — and Niero, and the rest of the Ailith — were with us. Once again, I paused, the hairs of my neck pricking up. I listened but heard nothing, so I resumed my work.

When I'd ripped all the way to the neck of the T-shirt, I cut it off, then folded the remains into a thick square about the size of Killian's wound. I thought about gathering some sort of poultice from the woods, but gave it up in favor of just staunching the blood flow. Already, there was a small pool by his waist and his skin was growing ghastly pale. "Here," I said, gently pulling his long fingers away from the wound. I tried to bring either side of his skin together — ignoring his gasp — and quickly placed my square atop it. I frowned as it almost immediately soaked through. But it was the best I could do.

I'd planned to wrap the long bandage around his torso, securing the square, but I saw the folly of that. Moving him to a sitting position would just increase the blood flow. I looked up toward where Ronan had disappeared after Tressa, willing them to return on the run.

I felt my lips part in horrified surprise.

Because there, not ten paces from us, was Sethos.

And on either side of him, a Sheolite.

RONAN

I ran through the trees, ignoring the bushy needles and branches scratching and tearing at my sleeves. I swore under my breath, feeling as if I'd been ripped in two — wanting to run back to Dri, and yet aware that if I didn't take this path and free Tressa, we'd lose two Ailith this day.

How far could they have gotten, dragging her? I could see signs of her struggle, deep trenches from where her boots had connected with the loose soil of the forest or piles of pine needles, deeper pits where she'd clearly wrenched away and then been pulled to her feet again. *Good girl,* I thought. *Fight them. With everything in you, Remnant.*

After a few more minutes my armband fairly hummed

with cold warning, telling me that at last I was getting closer. I paused to catch my breath so I might steal up on them. Taking on two Sheolites was infinitely harder than Pacificans, as it seemed their training had been nearly as good as our own.

I heard the sounds of scuffling and stole closer, slowly peeking around the trunk of a broad tree. One of the Sheolites wrenched Tressa up to her feet and shook her, then slapped her across the face. Inwardly, I seethed, but I held back, considering my options. I figured I'd follow along for a bit, and next time Tressa fought or they paused to rest, I'd take down the other man and then turn on the second. I knew that Tressa couldn't bear to kill another, but in times like this, she'd been known to at least try and waylay our enemy. If she could keep the second man occupied until I was free we'd have a chance. I just prayed we wouldn't run into any other Sheolites before that was done.

They took off again, mostly lifting Tressa between them. She didn't help them, despite their threats, and was obviously a dead weight. When the weary men again stopped, and the leader raised a hand to strike her, I charged. I barreled into the first man, ramming him against a boulder and hearing the satisfying crack of breaking bone. He cried out.

I rolled over and off of him and was immediately after the second man, who tried to grab Tressa. She ducked and rolled, evading him by inches, and he turned and pulled out two daggers, awaiting me.

I brought my sword down toward him, but he leaned back and I missed him. As I was coming around, he pounced, plunging a dagger into my shoulder. Thankfully, my leather chest armor — a gift from the Aravanders — deflected his strike. We grappled, fell, rolled, and I lost my grip on my sword but ended on top of him. I concentrated on holding his other hand, still gripping a dagger, away from my throat as I choked him. I ignored his steady pummeling of my neck, my cheek, recognizing he grew more faint by the moment.

Tressa moved to my sword and lifted it, ready to hand it to me the moment I asked. Finally, the man beneath me passed out. Ten paces away, the other Sheolite was fighting to rise, glaring at me with intense hatred. I rose, took the sword from Tressa, then whirled and cut his head off, so that he might never rise again. Niero had told us — piercing the heart or decapitation was the only way to be assured we wouldn't fight the same Sheolite again.

The other hobbled toward me, his leg clearly broken, nothing but murderous rage in his eyes. He wielded a sword as large as mine, and we circled, sizing each other up. "Run, Tressa," I growled over my shoulder, as I came between her and the Sheolite. "Killian has need of your touch."

I smiled as I heard her turn and do as I'd asked. The man before me scowled, hatred practically seething from his pores. "What is it?" I asked. "Have I interfered with your mission? You shall never succeed in taking a Remnant while a Knight of the Last Order yet lives."

The man let out a scoffing sound and glanced to where Tressa had disappeared behind me. "We may have lost that one," he said, spitting blood from his mouth as a slow smile crossed his face. "But the master shall have another this day."

A chill ran down my neck. Who did he speak of? Surely not —

I charged him, ramming my sword down again and again, but he deflected each blow. If he'd had two good legs, I would've had a serious fight on my hands. Unfortunately his defense was formidable.

It took until I was well winded myself, my arm trembling with the effort to raise my sword again, before I was at last able to take his good leg out from under him and then send him from this world.

Panting, I turned to eye the path that would lead me back to Andriana.

It was then that I realized my armband was still ice-cold, even after this last Sheolite had been dispatched. I rubbed it, thinking how it should be getting warmer now, or at least neutral, if our enemies had truly been driven away or killed.

But it was the very semblance of winter about my skin.

CHAPTER 14

ANDRIANA

I rose slowly and casually swung my sword in a circle before passing it to my other hand for another circle. Sethos eyed me as if I were idle entertainment.

I itched for the chance to take him down. Could I not summon the strength within me for this, the greatest opportunity I'd ever had to free Keallach from whatever evil hold his "guardian" had over him?

And yet as soon as I began pleading with the Maker to steel me for the task, other Sheolites emerged from the trees, surrounding me.

Sethos gave me a thin-lipped smile. "Fight or come peacefully, but you shall accompany me, Andriana." He bowed his head and steepled his fingers, staring at me. "The emperor demands it."

I gasped for air as his look seemed to translate into a

physical clamping around my neck. *It's a trick,* I told myself. *A sorcerer's trick.*

I swallowed hard, planted my sword in the soil at my feet and rested my hands on the hilt of it, then returned his gaze. *Maker, bind your enemy. Banish him from my heart and mind.*

Immediately Sethos lifted his head, his lips parting in surprise. He let out a laugh. "Well done, Remnant," he said, striding toward me slowly, his hands outstretched to show me he was unarmed. But well I knew that his most powerful weapons were not of iron, but of the spirit. He thought himself invincible. That I wouldn't dare to strike at him while I was surrounded by his men.

It would be folly.

It would be the doorway to my own death.

It would be an honor, I thought. Without Sethos in the way, poisoning Keallach and many others in Pacifica, what headway could the Remnants make in securing a future freedom and peace? *I was created for this moment*, I told myself, my grip tightening on the hilt of the sword. *I can do this.* Strike down my enemy, endure the onslaught of emotional pain, with such a distinct reward in the end.

He stopped in front of me. "The emperor would like me to bring you back whole, but he said nothing against beating you into submission."

"I'd like to see you try that," I said. I visualized myself lifting the sword, the turn of my wrist, the muscles it would take to bring it up and through his neck.

"Brave words for a Remnant without her knight." He sniffed, looking over to Killian who had faded into unconsciousness. How many minutes did Killian have left? Where was Ronan? And Tressa?

"Remnants trained alongside their knights," I said. "But then, you know that. Because it was you who saw to it that both Keallach and Kapriel's knights were pitted against each other, didn't you? Conveniently removing them both and opening up the path for you to fully infiltrate."

A smile tugged at the corners of his lips. "I know nothing of what you speak," he said, an obvious lie. It enraged me that he could find amusement in the memory of the day two of my unmet brothers died. With a cry of fury, I lifted my sword and turned to give weight to the momentum of my strike, bringing it toward his neck.

With casual elegance, he reached out and grabbed my arm, staying me.

Without pause, I turned the other way, wrenching my arm free of his grip and coming around — hoping to at least wound him in the torso or leg if I couldn't kill him.

But he wasn't where I expected him to be. He moved so swiftly … one moment on one side of me, the next, the other. He kicked the back of my thigh, making my leg buckle, then rammed an elbow between my shoulder blades. I went down hard, pain shooting up and over my head and down my spine. I tried to rise, but he put a boot on my back and shoved me to the ground again. "Bring her," he said to the others. "Leave the knight to die."

I was up on my feet as soon as he'd taken a step, but the Sheolite guards were too, one taking each arm. I tried to wrench away, but a third faced me and rammed his fist into my belly. I gasped for breath and crumpled, my vision swimming, and felt the men dragging me forward, just as they had done to Tressa …

Gradually, my breath returned, and when we entered a

boulder field, I tried to use the varying heights of rocks we were crossing to pull away from the iron grip of my enemies.

"Cease your struggle," Sethos said, suddenly at my side again and grabbing hold of my hair. He forced me onward, pulling me upward again by the hair when I fell painfully to my knees. At last I saw that we were beside a cliff again. He pressed me forward until the tips of my boots were over the edge, pebbles around them tumbling downward. "Do you really wish to press me?" he hissed.

My heart pounded. "No," I grit out, giving in. What good would I do the Ailith if I ended up dead?

He turned and fairly tossed me back to the two guards, who were looking both sheepish and furious that I'd made them appear incapable. We took a steep path down toward the river, and soon I could smell the water, we were so close. It made me both desperate for a drink and panicked that we'd reached a boat that might separate me from the rest of the Ailith in swift order. I prayed that Ronan would find us and somehow help me to escape.

I prayed that the Aravanders would rise from the cattails and shoot all the Sheolites dead.

I prayed that Sethos would stumble and fall off the narrow trail, his head cracking upon the rocks beneath us.

But none of that happened.

RONAN

I knew she was gone before I reached the clearing.

And as much as I wanted to go after her, I could not turn away from Tressa and Killian. Tressa reached for me, tears streaming down her face. "I know where you belong, Ronan," she pleaded. "But I need you here. I cannot do this alone."

Stifling a mangled cry that gathered in my throat, I hurried over to them and crouched down by my brother. He looked ghastly. Gray skin, unresponsive. I lifted an eyelid. "Tressa …"

"No," she bit out. "Don't say it, Ronan." She caught herself, faltered, swallowed hard and reached for my hand. "Please. I need you with me in this. We've seen the Maker's miracles unfold already. Those with the Cancer in Zanzibar. The goatherd's foot in the desert. Please … He can heal Killian too. Can you …" She paused and took a deep breath, as if willing herself to do this task too. "Can you believe with me?"

"I'm with you sister," I said, covering her hand with my other one. I swallowed my desire to add *Let's do this fast* …

She began praying, closing her eyes. Her hands hovered inches over Killian's wound as she begged the Maker to create anew what had been unmade. To save our brother. To bind his wound from the inside out. To steady his heart. To give him breath and blood to spare.

Holding on to Killian's arm, I repeated every word she said in a whisper, and then again, and then again. And as we prayed, my armband began to warm, the dreadful chill at last dispersing. I told myself it wasn't that I was getting so far behind Dri and the Sheolites who chased her. It was because the Maker was present, doing as we pleaded with him to do, healing our brother. I opened my eyes and stared for several long seconds before I admitted to myself that it was truly happening.

The hair on my head and neck and arms all stood on end. We were not alone. We were in the Presence. Here in this forgotten land, so recently trod by our enemies.

While still praying, Tressa carefully pressed the ragged edges of skin together, her fingers and nails eerily red with her knight's blood. But my eyes were on the wound itself; just as we'd watched the goatherd's foot straighten, I saw Killian's cut begin to seal together from one end to the other. Still red and angry. But *together*, as if knit together by the nimble fingers of unseen angels. Tears welled in my eyes as his skin began to turn from gray to his normal ruddy tone. Then his chest lifted and fell with deep breathing — not the shallow breaths that I'd feared would soon stop forever.

Tressa laughed through her own tears and bowed her head to Killian's chest, sobbing and thanking the Maker again and again.

I laughed through my tears with her. But then I knew that we weren't alone.

I wrenched my head left, immediately on my feet, hand on the hilt of my sword. But when I saw who it was, I took a staggering step backward. "Niero! You spooked me, man."

"Well done, Remnant," he said, passing me, looking solely at Tressa. He crouched and leaned down, touching Killian's shoulder. And at that moment, my brother stirred and opened his eyes, looking confused.

"He will be on his feet soon," Niero said to me. "But now, I have need of you, Knight. Your own has been captured."

ANDRIANA

Hands bound, the guard behind me prodding me with the tip of his sword, the one in front of me keeping enough distance to avoid any attempt to shove him off the trail, I felt despair swallowing me.

Twenty paces away, Sethos reached the bottom of the trail just as a boat rounded the bend of the river. White steam billowed from a smokestack at its center. And at the rail was Keallach. The engine was idled and the boat slowed moving against the current, it soon came to a standstill. A soldier in gray tossed out a heavy anchor.

I tried to swallow, but my mouth was dry. Keallach looked pensive. Sethos was coming toward me. I had to make my move.

"Keallach!" I cried, pretending to greet him as my savior. "I'll come to you!" And then I trudged toward the boat and dived into the water when I was only waist-deep, as if solely intent on reaching him. But instead of rising, I went as deep as I could, kicking hard until I was into the current, riding it downward.

I let out my breath as slowly as I could, realizing it might give away my path, and yet battling to stay deep and not bob to the surface. There had been that patch of reeds along the bank. Could I reach it?

My lungs screamed for air. Ached for it. But with the oxygen gone, I remained down on the muddy bottom. I didn't have much time left. I'd either pass out and drown or survival instinct would kick in and I'd scramble for the surface. I grabbed hold of one mossy boulder, but couldn't hold on for long. The next was more ragged, and my legs turned down-current. I let go of it and angled for another, and felt the blessed, welcome, slimy sensation of the first reed. Knowing I only had seconds remaining, I pushed my left leg against a rock, bent my knees, and then propelled myself deeper into the reeds.

It was all I could do. I rose, as quietly as I could, but I knew my emergence would have made my trainer shake his head in disgust. I panted for breath, mouth open wide, praying that the sounds of the river's rush would keep my presence a secret. But had they seen the reeds moving around me? What did it look like from the river bank?

I dared to turn my head, slowly one way, and then the other. I could hear the shouts of the Sheolites as they searched for me, the sounds of men diving and rising, again and again. And then, moments later, utter silence. That spooked me more than anything.

I couldn't make sense of it. Had they ... gone?

And then there were arrows slicing through the air. Sheolites and Pacificans crying out, wounded. Sethos's roar of rage, then urgent shouts of direction. *Yes*, I cheered inwardly. *Yes*.

I dared to peek out higher, hoping that I wouldn't be pierced by an Aravander arrow. Did they know I was here? Had they seen me being dragged toward the river boat?

It was just at that moment that Sethos's gaze swept about and passed over me. I thought he'd missed me, and I immediately ducked lower in the reeds, but then he paused and backtracked. His dark eyes rested squarely on me and his brows lifted.

I rose and tried to run in the opposite direction, but the mud that made for such fertile growing ground for the reeds and cattails also created a horrifying trap for me. I struggled to lift each leg, losing my boots in the process, as well as precious seconds until I finally, finally made shore.

I chanced a look back. He was almost upon me, terrifying with the robe flying behind him, face alight with rage, arrows missing him by inches.

I continued to run, but the river rock dug into the arches and heels of my feet like demon children, slowing my pace nearly as much as the mud had. I steeled myself for the moment when Sethos's wretched hand clamped down on my shoulder and mentally planned my response.

When it happened, I fell back at once — deadweight hurtling toward him — hoping my skull would catch his chin or nose, but instead I hit his chest. He let out a low grunt, but I didn't hesitate, gathering my feet beneath me and launching forward again. I felt the brush of his fingertips at my back. Heard his low curse.

But again, the rocks proved my enemy. I tried to step toward bits of grass or sand, but missed here and there, wincing from the pain. And then, up ahead, near the woods that had beckoned me moments before, was something that made me come to an abrupt stop.

Wraiths.

My breathing came in alarmed pants from my nostrils as I stood there, frozen, facing a smoke-like enemy that I hadn't seen since I faced them alongside my brothers and sisters on that field near the Hoodites. It was only weeks ago, and yet it seemed like days …

They swooped up and down, like light garments on the arms of dancers. They surrounded me in a swirl, sang to me like spirits of the deep. And I stood there, unable to move, until Sethos snapped his fingers and they made way for their dark prince.

I whirled, but his hand was at my throat, driving me backward to the cliff. He rammed me against it and I gasped. But he only smiled, eyes narrowing, and lifted me higher to my tiptoes.

"You think you are so clever, Remnant," he said, easing closer to whisper into my ear. "You think you are my equal?"

"No," I said, waiting until he eased back to meet my gaze. "I am your superior."

He let out a breath that sounded like a sigh from hell, and that was when I realized he'd brought a knife to my neck. "Time for our acquaintance to end, Remnant."

His fingers tightened around the dagger.

I steeled myself for the coming pain, only sorry that my battle would end now, before I could take this one down.

"Sethos, *stop*."

The voice made us both freeze in surprise.

Me with hope. *Keallach*.

Sethos with deadly frustration.

"Allow me to dispatch this one, Highness," Sethos said, not lifting his eyes from me. "She is a distraction. There are other ways toward our goals." His words were light, but his gaze upon me was sheer darkness.

"No, Sethos. Step away from her. I shall see to her future."

Hatred seeped from my enemy and into me in a dark wave.

And I returned it.

He lifted his chin, and once more, a smile tugged at the corners of his lips. "She is all yours, Highness," he said a breath too late for true respect. But as he pulled me around him to hand me off, he whispered, "But mark this moment, Remnant. Someday you shall be all *mine*."

RONAN

We ran for a time, up one hill and down another. "Are the others all right?" I asked Niero.

"They are well. I ... sensed that you four were in trouble. So I set off to find you."

"And the child? Latonia's child?"

"With them as well?"

His words came as a relief, and I thanked the Maker for sparing them all as well as bringing Niero to us. With him by our side, I felt stronger, more capable. As if — even though we Ailith were but five — we were more like fifty. Like the fight was fierce ahead, but we were not without ample weapons. *His mere presence makes me bold,* I decided.

We reached the cliff — edging closer on our bellies — just in time to see Keallach lift a soaked Andriana aboard the ship and then escort her inside a cabin, just like when we were aboard the *Far North.*

I opened my mouth to call to her, wanting her to know she wasn't alone, but Raniero huffed a quick *no,* and put a firm hand on my shoulder, keeping me down.

I frowned at him, wondering what his plan was. He gestured toward the boat with his chin and I looked again. A soldier had rounded the end, holding a machine gun. Had I taken off down the path, he would've simply cut me down. A second one appeared on the bow, and a third atop the roof of the steamship, just as plumes of white came billowing out the tube.

"Niero …" I growled, watching in horror as a sailor hauled in the anchor and the ship turned to enter the central current of the river.

"Stay where you are," he said, reaching out to grasp my forearm when I moved to rise. "You do your Remnant no good by getting shot now."

"I do no good for her now," I retorted, shaking off his hand and leaping to my feet, "watching her get carried off by *Keallach.*" I moved toward the path.

Niero snaked his arm under my chin and hauled me

backward until we were under a tree. I writhed and elbowed him, trying to get free, but he held me in a headlock until I glimpsed the rising steam of the boat in the distance — too far away to catch. Panting, I cried, *"Why? Why? Why would you let them take her?"*

He tossed me aside. "I didn't let them take her," he said in disgust. "They already had her. I was saving you, so that one day you might rescue her."

"One day?" I ranted, pacing back and forth. *"One day?* After Keallach takes her back to his palace in Pacifica? Have you seen how he looks at Dri, Niero? It is hardly *brotherly,"* I spat, clenching and unclenching my hands, itching to take out all my fear and frustration on him. "Do you remember how Maximillian looked at her? What will become of her there, alone? Surrounded by them all?"

"It is as the Maker has seen. *He* will sustain Andriana, just as he will sustain you."

"But he put us together as Knight and Remnant for a purpose." I stepped toward him, until our noses were just an inch apart. "Why would he tear us apart now?"

"He did not tear you apart," Niero calmly said. "The enemy did. But that does not take either of you out of his reach."

I let out a humorless laugh, shaking my head and lifting my hand in the direction the boat had gone. "If that ship reaches the sea, we shall never see Andriana again."

"You do not know that."

"No. But I do know I have to try and intercept it. If something happens to her …" I was already turning, digging my toe in to begin running. But as I stepped into my stride, Niero barreled into me, taking me down again. I let loose then, pummeling him with my fists, tearing away from his fierce grip, again and again. We rolled, and he was atop of me, straining to pin my arms and legs, and then we rolled again. I struck him across the face once, twice, before he managed to grab my head, twist it and roll with me. It took several long minutes for me to realize he wasn't striking me back, only trying to contain me like some sort of aggravating octopus. Dragging me back. Dragging me deep. Dragging me away from Dri.

But not trying to harm me.

I let out a guttural cry of frustration, holding my head and slumping off of him, feeling grief swallow me.

Niero rose slowly, hands on hips, head hung low. "I love her too," he said softly. "Not as you do, brother. But I love her. And it pains me to let her slip away. But trust me, trust me. It's the only way. Dri's best chance is if you stay alive." He moved over to me and crouched down, cradling the back of my head and pulling my forehead forward to meet his. "You shall see your Remnant again."

"Will I?" I asked, looking into his jet-black eyes, eyes that always felt so old to me.

"Look at Kapriel! Free and with his fellow Remnants. Despite the odds."

"Kapriel," I returned dully. "Our brother who languished in prison so many seasons before we freed him. Are you saying that Dri might be away from us that long?"

Niero didn't flinch under my angry gaze, but he released me and lifted his head. "I pray it will be days, not months or years of captivity for Andriana. Maybe the Maker has a task for Andriana within Keallach's palace. Let us trust him — and her — to see it through. And wait for the opportune moment we need to free her."

"You're saying that you would let her stay in Keallach's

care for *multiple* seasons?" I said. The idea of being apart from Dri more than a few days made me nearly frantic.

"I'm saying I hope it will not be that long," he said, rising, brushing his hands off against his pants. He paused and leaned toward me, shaking a finger. "But our mission has always been to see through the Call upon all our lives. I know it's inborn for you, Ronan. To protect her. With your very life, if necessary. But right now, Knight, the Call upon your life is to serve where you find yourself, and serve that Call above your call to protect Dri. Understood?"

I rose, feeling sick to my stomach. "Niero, she's not strong enough ..."

Niero grabbed hold of my shirt in a savage grip and pulled me close. "Never say that again. Never. She has learned much in these last months. The Maker will use those lessons to sustain her now. And he shall sustain her. Do not bring dishonor upon him or us now, Knight, with your distrust. Are you with me?"

I hesitated.

"Are you with me?" he demanded, his lips in a firm line.

"I am with you," I agreed reluctantly.

CHAPTER
15

ANDRIANA

When we reached the end of the river, Keallach led me to a small boat tied to the end of the steamship. Once we were on board, the soldier at the tiller roared the engine to life and we took off for the larger ship bobbing atop the ocean's waves. I settled beneath Keallach's arm, reassured that on this boat, despite what I'd done, he still seemed dedicated to the idea that I was his sister, and he my protective brother. *It's the Call,* I thought. That familial pull we Ailith all felt between one another. The Maker had made a way for us, even when one had fallen so desperately off the path. Again, hope surged within me. Maybe this was all part of the plan. For me to save Keallach. Bring him back to the fold.

Once onboard, Keallach took my hand through the narrow doorway and led me down the tight hall to a room on the far right. He opened the door and gestured for me to go in. Behind me, he whispered to a servant, waited, and then brought in a blanket, which he wrapped around me. Oddly, I felt the gesture protective, caring. Something Ronan might do. Then he knelt in front of me, taking my hands.

"I pledge to you, Andriana of the Valley, that I, Keallach, shall never harm you. You are my sacred sister. And soon I hope that you will count me as friend, if not brother. I know that I've made decisions that you do not yet understand. But in time ..." He paused, looked to the window and sighed. Then back to me. "In time, I hope you shall. Will you give me a chance?"

"Do I have a choice in the matter?" I asked.

He held my gaze and stiffened. "Yes. Since you've given *me* little choice." His smile was back, then. "But it won't be forever."

"You shall free me," I said dully, disbelieving. "To leave Pacifica."

"If you choose to do so. Yes." But I noted the hollow look in his eye. Because he feared being left? Being cut off forever from the Remnants? Or ...

He rose and went to the small desk in the corner that held a crystal decanter. He poured two small glasses full of an amber liquid, returned to my side, and offered one to me. I shook my head.

"Take it," he insisted.

"The last time you gave me wine, I didn't wake until morning. And without my own clothes."

"As I've said before, I did not consider that you might not be accustomed to evening wine," he said, raising his chin. "Truly. Will you not forgive me that oversight? Besides, this isn't evening wine. It's port."

I studied him, reluctantly nodded, then took the tiny crystal goblet. After he sipped from his, I took a sip of the raisin-flavored liqueur too. The boat leaned one way and then the other, following the curve of the river. Keallach put a hand across a beam above him and stared at me, sipping again from his goblet.

I was irritated by the sudden self-consciousness that flooded through me. It was clear I was drawn to him, just as I was drawn to all my Ailith kin. But there was a surge of man-woman heat that brought a blush to my cheeks.

He grinned, still staring at me. "The heavens would attest, Andriana, that you are beautiful. A constellation should be named after you." His smile widened. "I shall see to it. As an official act of the Emperor of Pacifica."

"What? No," I said, embarrassed. I rose, needing to put some space between us. His words reminded me of something Ronan has said to me once — it seemed odd that he would be that intimate. I dropped the blanket behind me, feeling no need for added warmth at the moment. As he joined me at the small window, I belatedly realized I wore only the damp leather of the Aravanders' sleeveless tunic, that covered me from shoulder to thigh, and it left my armband exposed. Not that Keallach wasn't already completely aware of my cuff. But leaving it so open made me feel ... vulnerable. It practically gleamed in the candlelight.

He glanced down at it and then let his sultry eyes drift up my arm and face like a caress. Was that part of his gifting? That gaze that felt like a physical force?

But instead of asking me about the armband, about the others, he simply stood beside me and sipped from his crystal goblet.

I wondered why Keallach hadn't used his gifting against the Aravanders, as he had his brother. Was that because he'd used it up, in a sense, for a time? Without the armband, without the ceremony, he would not receive his gifting in full. And yet what I'd witnessed on the Isle of Catal had been significant. What would Keallach be like if he was given the full might of his gifting? Keallach with his power to move inanimate objects?

The thought overwhelmed me.

"What is it?" Keallach asked, shaking me from my reverie.

"Ahh," I said, turning away from the window and returning to a sitting chair. "Where should I begin?"

He chuckled lowly and settled in a chair across from me, leaning over his knees, goblet balanced between his hands. "You are weary," he said. "I should leave you to rest."

"No," I protested automatically, and then, realizing that I merely drew comfort in his Ailith presence, quickly amended — "No, you're right. It'd be good to get a good night's rest." I leaned forward, rubbing my forehead. It had been what? A week? Two? Since Wadi Qelt that I'd slept — really slept?

He remained where he was. "You feel it, then too. My presence. As comfort."

I rose quickly. "As surely as I feel Sethos's presence as danger."

Keallach stood and set his empty goblet down beside mine, which was still half-full. He started to reach toward me, caught himself, and then clasped his hands before his chest. "I will hope that in time you and Sethos find your way."

I stared at him. "Keallach. Never, ever, will Sethos and I 'find our way.' Only when one of us dies will that way be found."

His brow lowered, as if he was confused. His lips clamped together. "So say you. But I believe in an alternate ending. Perhaps one that you cannot yet see." His eyes slid down my damp clothing. "I've been remiss, keeping you up. I'll send a servant straightaway with a change of clothes. There will be two guards at your door, with my strict instructions that no one — not even Sethos — shall enter before morning. Can you trust me that far, Andriana? Until morning, at least?"

He lifted his palms to me, an offering.

"Tell me one thing," I said, crossing my arms.

He folded his own arms. "Anything."

"Did you kill or capture any of my Ailith kin? Either Remnant or Knight?"

He swallowed, but I sensed no duplicity in him. "No. We tried to *capture* them," he said, lifting one hand, "because I'd very much like to speak to them as well. But we did not succeed."

"Thank you," I whispered.

"Andriana," he began, remorse etching his brow. "About your knight ... Ronan. Forgive me for injuring him. I only sought to keep Kapriel with me."

I held my breath for a moment. Ronan would've killed Keallach had he had the chance. It had been battle. "I understand. But if you ever hurt him again, I will try and inflict the same wound upon you." Let him think I could. I'd certainly be willing ...

"The feelings between you two run deep."

"As they do between all Remnants and Knights."

He gave me a funny smile. "Not quite like what runs between you and that one."

165

I felt the heat rising in my cheeks and turned slightly away. "Until morning, then?"

He nodded. "Until morning." I felt the hope, the glimmer of glee within him. He sensed our connection, and took my acquiescence as trust.

I saw him to the door, then closed and latched it behind him. A moment later, a soft knock made me open it again. Two male servants delivered fresh linens, a bucket of hot water, soap, and a change of clothes. They exited without ever looking me in the eye. Again, I latched the door and laid my forehead against it, feeling the rhythmic stroke of the steam engine escorting us back to Pacifica.

Would we return by daybreak? Tomorrow afternoon? All I knew was that sometime soon, I'd be in Keallach's realm.

And never farther from my own.

CHAPTER 16

ANDRIANA

In the morning, after a surprisingly decent night's sleep, I dressed in the Aravander leathers. I had reluctantly changed into the white Pacifican gown that had been laid out for me but had hung up the leathers to dry overnight. It was a small act of defiance, but it made me feel less the conquered prisoner and more myself.

Keallach came to my door with two guards a respectful distance behind him. His green eyes flicked down to my bare toes and back up, but he said nothing about the rejected gown. "Hungry?" he asked.

"I could eat," I admitted, while inside my stomach screamed *famished*.

He offered his arm but I elected to walk beside him, hands clasped behind my back. We strolled to the back of the ship where a table for two had been set up. Keallach pulled out a chair for me and gestured to it. I sat, my eyes hungrily taking in the bounty before me. An egg dish of some sort. Delicious baked goods, golden and laden with fat. Fruit, like I'd mostly seen in books. Berries, grapes, melons. I didn't wait for him to offer — I loaded my plate with some of everything, my mouth watering. It had been a day and a half since I'd eaten with the Aravanders.

Keallach slowly took his own much smaller portion, watching me with delight as I shoved one forkful after another in my mouth. "Easy, Andriana. We can always order more if we run out."

I considered him. Nowhere, even at the Citadel, was food in such ready supply that one of us might say the same thing. Obviously there were additional stores in places where the Community resided, but no one would be so cavalier in referring to food. It was a commodity. Every village and city carefully monitored their foodstores. But apparently this wasn't the way in Pacifica.

I gasped as I bit into a piece of fruit, its tart-sweet glory sliding over my tongue. "What is this?" I asked, mouth full, lifting the fork.

Keallach smiled and leaned forward on the table and casually picked up a cup full of steaming hot coffee. "Pineapple," he said, a gleam in his eyes. "We just established a trade route out to the islands. And down south. Both are eager to trade pineapple for grain."

I lifted one of the light and flaky baked pastries. "Pacifica has been successful in harvesting grain?"

"In certain sectors," he said, taking one himself. "If our weather trends keep on the same track, we'll do even better next harvest. We may have enough for trade with the Union."

I ignored the fact that they'd traded with foreign lands rather than us this harvest and bit into the pastry. Again, it was a taste explosion. Rich and yet light at the same time. After months of camp and trail food—porridge, soup, unleavened bread—I thought maybe I'd want to stay at this table forever. And then I had a hard time swallowing, feeling guilty and traitorous as I thought of the other Remnants and Knights out there somewhere, probably hunting or fishing for their food this morning. I reached for the glass and took a quick swallow of clean, fresh water.

We were heading south, it appeared, following the coastline just outside of the waves crashing toward shore. I considered a dive off the deck—an attempt to make it to shore—but here, there was nothing but wild hills and scrubby trees and brush. Keallach's men would easily find and recapture me, even if I made it to shore.

"After the Great War, when so much was flooded," Keallach said, following my gaze, "many of the old cities were lost to the sea, and what had once been desert became farmable land. In a way, it worked to our advantage, as we began to irrigate and sow seeds." He gave me a wry smile. "No buildings to remove in order to plant the crops."

I frowned, thinking of the millions of people who had lost their lives during those harshest of years.

"Forgive me," he said, wiping his mouth with a thick napkin, like one I belatedly saw beside my own plate. "That sounded cavalier. I suppose I feel that we have to see blessings wherever we can find them in this day and age."

"That's true," I allowed, taking another bite of the pastry.

He sat back in his chair. "So tell me, Andriana. What will it take for me to obtain an armband?"

I gave him a small smile. "Leave Pacifica, pledge your loyalty to the Maker, and join us."

"Ahh," he said, sipping his coffee. "Such minor demands."

I started to reach up to touch my cuff, conscious of it now. It was neutral. "The Sheolites are gone?"

"Who?"

"Sethos and his men. Are they traveling by separate boat or something?"

"Actually," he said, eyes narrowing, "they are. They are in search of any remaining Ailith or Aravander."

"To kill them?"

"To capture them."

I popped two berries in my mouth and reached out to try and search him. There was only a sense of ease, as well as curiosity, within him. He wasn't lying to me. In fact, he'd given me a very direct answer.

He stretched out his arms. "Find anything objectionable within me, Empath?"

"Not at the moment," I said, barely covering my surprise. I put two more small blueberries in my mouth. "Is it that obvious?"

"No," he said, with an easy smile. "You simply get a very intent look in your eye. Your pupils dilate a bit."

"Truly?" I remembered Chaza'el, when he was receiving a vision, and how his irises disappeared.

"Truly."

I shifted my eyes from him, feeling somehow exposed. "So …" I said, taking a forkful of the egg dish. "What about your gifting?"

He considered me. Then he lifted his hand, concentrated

on the table, and swished his fingers to one side. My napkin fell to the floor.

"So it's true. You can move inanimate objects." I bent down and retrieved the napkin.

"As well as the animate," he said, looking again at the table. Without touching it, he slid the basket of pastry toward me and then shrugged. "Not quite as impressive as a command of the weather, right?"

"I don't know," I said. "Moving objects is pretty amazing."

He gave me a catlike smile and leaned back in his chair again. "It does help keep my men in line, on occasion." He gestured to my cuff. "But I'd like to see what I could do with one of those."

"It's not only the armband," I said. "It's the ceremony. You don't get one without the other. And I've already told you what it will take to get either."

He smiled and lifted his hands. "Right. Just give up being emperor."

"No," I said, leaning forward and dropping the pastry on my plate. "Give up a role that wasn't ever yours alone and rejoin the Community you were born for."

He let out a huff of a laugh. "Such easy words of treason you drop, friend. Just wait until you see what Pacifica has to offer. It may change your perspective."

"That's unlikely."

"Give me a few weeks, Andriana. I think you'll be surprised."

I tried to absorb his reference to "a few weeks" without reacting. "And then?" I asked casually. "You'll let me go?"

His lips closed and he studied me a moment, then fiddled with his knife. "That remains to be seen."

"Why?"

"Because you and yours pose a certain threat to my goals."

"So I am to be your prisoner."

"My *guest*," he said.

It was my turn to laugh. "Are you truly that delusional?"

"It's not delusion," he said, and I felt a wave of irritation from him, then a darkness that made my mouth go dry. "It's perspective. I could've taken you prisoner, Andriana. I could be bringing you to Pacifica in chains. Utilized your presence in far more nefarious ways. But you are my friend." His face softened, the longing and loneliness within surfacing. "At least I hope you shall be."

"I am your friend, Keallach. Your sister," I added. "And I will give you the chance to show me the glories of Pacifica if you give me the chance to convince you that you are far from home."

He rose, slowly, and so did I. "So we have a deal? We each have a few weeks to convince each other of what we hold as truth?" He reached out a hand.

"We have a deal," I said, taking his hand in mine. And as he touched me, I pushed feelings of connection and conviction.

He dropped my hand as if it was hot, and then smiled. "Oh, that is not fair, Remnant. Not fair at all."

■ ■ ■

It felt odd to enter the harbor again and tie up alongside the weathered planks of the pier — the same pier where the Ailith had stolen aboard the *Far North*. Pangs of longing for them swept through me, and I actually paused a moment, trying to catch my breath. Where were they? Were they all well? Killian had taken a terrible blow in that fight. What if — ? I forced myself to continue on, pushing away the awful thought of Killian dying.

I was escorted off the ship, but not in chains. Keallach again offered his arm, at the bottom of the gangplank. I cast him a curious look. "I'm more than capable, Keallach, you know, of *walking.*"

He rolled his eyes and lifted his hands. "Is it so awful? To bring back some formal traditions? I think you'll see that it's a benefit of Pacifica. In a world gone mad, often degraded to its worst possible common denominator, you'll find that Pacifica is remarkably genteel."

He again offered his arm, and with a sigh, I slipped a hand through the crook of it. I wasn't entirely certain of all he'd just said or meant, but I got the gist. He thought a lot of his country; he was proud of it.

We'll see.

But I'd promised Keallach I'd give him the chance to show me the golden side of Pacifica. Perhaps I was making all my decisions based on preconceived ideas. I'd give him a chance, just as I hoped he would give me the same. If we could somehow meet in the middle, if I could bring him back to the Remnants, see his complete gifting unfold, who could stop us?

I was not outside of the reach of the Maker. He was here, with me, just as he was with me in Wadi Qelt, or Castle Vega, or Georgii Post, or with the Drifters, or back home in the Valley. I either believed it or I didn't.

And I believed.

My pulse picked up. Had the Maker brought me here, into Keallach's confidence and inner circle, so that I might bring my lost brother home? Bring him to a point of reconciliation and wholeness?

"What is it?" Keallach asked, looking at me with a secretive smile.

I realized I had to be casting hope and joy toward him, without even meaning to. "Oh! Sorry!"

"For what?" he said, putting his other hand over mine. "Don't apologize for that. You can send me those feelings all day long."

We kept walking away from the wharf to a nearby street, where five identical, sleek black cars were waiting. But I slowed as I sensed who was waiting for us even before I could make out who it was. *Sethos.*

Keallach's smile faded as he felt my reluctant pace. "It'll be all right. I shall see you are safe, Andriana."

But it didn't matter what he said. Around the Sheolites, I felt nothing but cold dread, in tandem with my armband. I longed for my lost sword or my confiscated daggers. To be armed around men such as these left me feeling more than a little wary.

We stopped a few steps away from Sethos and four Sheolite guards.

"Highness," he began. "I'm afraid I have distressing news. May I have a word with you?"

Keallach gestured toward a car, and one of the Sheolites obediently opened the door. "Wait for me in here," he said to me. "I'll be only a minute."

I had little choice. I stepped inside and slipped back into the wide seat. The guard closed the door, and all sound from outside was blocked, keeping me from eavesdropping. I looked around.

The fabric of the seat beneath me was smooth and cool to touch. I realized the engine was running and frigid air was emerging from tiny vents alongside me. I lifted a hand to it, wondering over the coolness. The windows were dark, shielding me from the sun, and ahead I could see the silhouette of a driver behind another dark glass. So much shading ... because Pacifica had so much sun? Truly, I doubted I'd experienced as much sun in all my collective Harvest seasons. Did this place even experience Hoarfrost? I knew Keallach had his Winter Palace, but was that a nod to tradition or born out of a true need?

Just the thought of all the sun made me thirsty. To my left was a crystal decanter, full of amber liquid, and glasses. To my right was a matching pitcher, full of water so cool it was sweating on the outside, sending droplets sliding down its smooth face. I eagerly poured a goblet full, drank it down, and then another.

I looked outside to where Keallach was talking to Sethos. Keallach had his hands on his hips, head down, listening as Sethos continued to talk, gesturing with one hand, palm half up. So he wasn't demanding something of Keallach, he was asking. *Interesting* ...

Keallach turned to look at me, then back to Sethos. I sank down in my seat, feeling embarrassed that he'd caught me watching. It made me feel childish. A moment later he came over, opened the door and peered in. "Listen, I have to go away for a few days. I know it's poor timing, but there are some things that only I can resolve. You'll be taken to my palace and shown to your guest quarters. Every need will be met. Rest. Eat. I'll join you as soon as I can."

"No, Keallach!" I cried, but he was already shutting the door. A Sheolite leaned down and talked through an open window to my driver and glanced back at me, a small smile tugging at his lips. Cold fear rippled through me.

The car pulled out, with another behind it. Guards? I couldn't see anyone but the driver, but I doubted they'd send a Remnant to Keallach's palace without a good number of guards.

Keallach moved toward the third vehicle, but he watched as we drove away.

Sethos was no longer in view.

And I realized that if I'd ever felt alone before, I'd been mistaken.

CHAPTER
17

ANDRIANA

I exited the car, ignoring the driver's offered hand, and glanced around. We were in a clean courtyard with a luxurious building rising eight stories all around me. Everything was pristine, white marble and lush, flowering vines ... oddly screaming *life* while my armband was tolling *death*.

I turned to face the sorcerer. "So you managed to separate me from Keallach. Do you think you can do that forever?"

His full lips curved up in pleasure. "Ah, there is the fight in you I so enjoy. We shall have such a lovely few days together before the emperor returns to us." He reached out as if to caress my cheek, and without thinking, I bit him. But I didn't just bite down and release him; I bit down and held until I tasted blood in my mouth, choking on it, but refusing to let go as he shrieked. I pummeled him with my fists, going for his kidneys.

He bashed at me with his left hand in a frenzy, striking my jaw, my eye, the edge of my nose, but still I stubbornly held on.

And then someone rammed me on the back of the head.

My vision swam. My jaw grew slack. Then … nothing.

■ ■ ■

I awakened in a bedroom. To my relief, I could tell that for once I'd been left in the clothes in which I'd arrived.

I sat up, looking around, straining my good eye in the dark to see where I was, who was with me. "H-hello?" I called out. But no one responded. I heard nothing but the feel of yawning, cold space all around me. No other person breathing. After months in the constant company of others—and always with Ronan—the silence unnerved me as nothing else might. I pushed back and back until I leaned against the headboard, comforted by the knowledge that at least no one was behind me.

My head ached. It throbbed in back from where I'd been struck and from the front where Sethos had beaten me. My left eye was swollen, and I realized it hurt too. I let my head lean backward until it pressed against carved wood and reached up to gently probe my face.

A split at my lip and the edge of my eye, wounds that would likely leave scars if left untreated. I wished Tressa was here, tending to me. She'd have foxglove in her basket of herbs for my aches and others to mix with healing oils she'd lather on the cuts once they were cleaned. I sighed and rubbed my arms, trying to get my mind off my pains and this desperate turn of events.

For as high as I had felt a couple days ago—in the midst of the Aravanders, seeing the Maker's power flow through me and the other Ailith and into Kapriel—I felt just as low today.

From found … to lost. From invincible … to weak.

I knew he approached before I heard a sound. The chill in my cuff grew until it hurt almost as much as any other pain in my body. Then I heard the metallic scrape and click of a key in a lock, the creak of a massive, thick wooden door opening and closing. I refused to look at him. The warm light of a lamp held by the man filled the room, and I could see I was in a luxurious chamber indeed: the walls covered in elaborate paper and crowned with thick moldings, the marble floors covered by thick, finely woven rugs.

"Go away, Sethos," I muttered wearily, not looking at him. Even his presence seemed to make me hurt more.

He turned and placed the lamp on a table beside him. "Do you not wish to have some food? Some tea? A healer to tend your wounds?"

"I want nothing from you."

"Come now. This can be so simple. All I ask is a bit of information."

My eyes slipped down to his hand and I didn't bother to hide my smile. The bandage that covered his palm felt like a medal on my chest for at least trying to fight my capture.

His dark eyes followed mine and then narrowed. "Take pride where you can, Remnant. It will be the last time you harm me."

"Oh, I hope not," I said sweetly.

He sat down on the edge of the sprawling bed and leaned closer. I had to fight the urge to push away. "Perhaps you need another day here, alone, before we have this conversation."

"Perhaps," I returned.

We stared at each other for a long moment. "Very well," he said, rising. "I'll return tomorrow." He moved toward the door, taking his lamp with him.

"Wait," I said, before I could stop myself.

He turned partially back toward me and lifted a brow.

"When does Keallach return?"

"I fear his business will keep him away longer than he first thought," he said, a tiny smile lifting the corners of his lips.

I refused to react or say more. Doing so only made me more vulnerable.

Sethos still stared at me. "I can allow you out of here. Give you time to walk the emperor's gardens. See his library. Bathe in his amazing baths. Just tell me where the rest of the Ailith and Aravanders went."

I ignored his request. "I'm here for Keallach. Not you."

His gaze hardened. "There is some preparation that needs to be done before you and the emperor are ... reunited."

I frowned but clamped my lips shut. I didn't like the unspoken menace in those words, in particular, *preparation* and *reunited*. What did they plan to do to me? And surely they didn't think I had any romantic intent ...

"You must be in far better order before you see the emperor," he said. He sniffed and wrinkled his nose, as if he found the odors in the room offensive. "Bathe. Dress in proper Pacifican dress. Eat. Allow a healer to attend you. And then we'll talk about you seeing his highness."

"I'd rather be thrown into the dungeon," I ground out.

"That can be arranged," he said, then turned in a swirl of crimson fabric to leave, his boots making a distinct clipped step as he turned to go.

"Wait," I said, hating the pathetic edge to my tone as I pushed back the covers and eased off the bed. He was ten paces away and paused, but did not turn. Ignoring the ache in my head, I concentrated on casting emotion toward him. Mercy. Care. Love.

He turned partially back to me, so that I could see the straight line of his nose, the curve of his chin in profile. And then I heard his soft, mocking laugh. "Your gift is of no use in this palace, against me, Remnant." He lifted his hands. "It is a Sheolite outpost. So try all you might, little girl. But it will be for naught."

With that, he left the room, closing the heavy door firmly behind him. I rushed toward it, my hand on the knob, when I heard the thick bolt slide shut outside. I tried to ignore the idea, but the door felt like a lid of a coffin, slamming closed.

Then I leaned my forehead against the wood and closed my eyes, feeling every beat of my racing heart in my temples, injured eye, and base of my head. "I'm a fool," I muttered. Pride and anger had kept me from what Sethos would have likely offered — water and food, at the very least. Even if I hadn't told him what he wanted to know.

I turned and moved to where I'd glimpsed what I thought might be a window, behind long, thick drapes. My groping hands found the far wall, and moving left, then the fabric. I pulled it aside, my heart thudding heavily with hope.

But my hope was short-lived. Thick glass covered the window — which appeared to not open — and outside, heavy wooden shutters and metal bars eradicated any dream I had of escape. I leaned my cheek against the glass and watched the dancing flame of the single candle in my cavernous room dance in its reflection. I wondered how this — me being here, injured and in the court of the enemy — could at all be a part of the Maker's plan.

RONAN

Niero and I joined Tressa and Killian and made our way to the rendezvous point in what I came to find out was northeast

Pacifica, halfway between Chaza'el's village and Wadi Qelt. Five Aravander men and one woman joined us, pledging their lives — and their bows and arrows — to protect us and help us see through our mission. "I don't know if I feel relieved or more vulnerable with them with us," I muttered to Niero.

"Dri would be able to tell you," he said, casting me a mournful look.

I frowned. I didn't need any additional reminders of Andriana. She was on my mind all day. I even dreamed of her at night.

Niero moved back to the Aravanders. "Get used to extra company. It's just the beginning. These people will be an aid to us."

We moved at a fairly slow pace the first day to accommodate Killian — remarkably healed and yet not feeling completely whole — which was fine by me. Every one of my injuries, bruises, and strained muscles seemed to be shouting at me to slow down. It was as if my entire body echoed a complaint my heart cried first. But we fought our way forward, climbing a shorter mountain pass. The second day we moved much faster and sensed we were drawing closer to our fellow Ailith. "We'll find them by nightfall," Niero said, clasping my shoulder.

The Aravanders had gladly positioned themselves as our scouts — three in front, three in back. And twice they'd sounded an alarm just in time for us to take cover and avoid Pacifican drones. After the second one circled and moved off, we watched it. The bird-like contraption circled in what seemed like a mile-long pattern, edging forward slowly. "We think they record what they see," one of the Aravander men noted, shifting his bow strap higher on his shoulder. "We shot one down once. They are mechanical, filled with glass and metal and cameras like some of old."

I didn't like it, this advantage the Pacificans had over the Trading Union. What else did our enemies have access to? What would happen if it came down to battling them outright?

When we reached the next valley floor, surrounded by rocky soil and towering trees but no ground cover, Niero led us to a small game trail and we followed it toward the next mountain pass. We curved in and out of rock fields and gradually among boulders, which gave me comfort in case the drones showed up again. Onward we climbed. Soon our water bags and canteens were dry, but we'd yet to encounter a stream or spring. We kept moving, hoping that the higher we rose, the greater the chance we'd find water. But for hours, we found none.

We'd paused, panting, letting the last drips of our containers drop into our open mouths, when Niero sent all six Aravanders out farther ahead to see if they could locate water, half a bit to the west and half a bit to the east. As they set off, we sank gratefully into the recesses of the boulders about us, squeezing down and under the curves of the great rocks, eager to soak up the break from the relentless sun. How many times in the Valley had I prayed for a full day of sun? Now it seemed like a curse.

The Aravanders eased away, and I was again impressed with their stealth. Our trainer would've been proud. I didn't even hear the swish of leather sole on rock or the movement of pebbles as they padded away.

"Try and grab a bit of sleep," Niero said to me and Killian. "We might have to hike into the evening, depending on what they find—and you two are still on the mend. Tressa, you look weary enough to fall asleep on your feet."

He didn't have to encourage us twice. I closed my eyes and immediately gave in to the pull of slumber, hoping I'd encounter Dri in my dreamscape again, the closest I could get to her.

■ ■ ■

I awakened to a tiny pebble hitting my forehead. I frowned, rubbed where it had hit and squinted out into the fading light to see where it had come from. My hand moved to the hilt of my dagger. Did we have company?

I eased out from beneath my rock and slowly rose, just high enough to peer over and around my sheltering boulder. I turned slowly, not wanting to draw attention to my movements, and saw Niero rising and doing the same. He put two fingers to his eyes and then made a circular movement, silently asking me to help him spot whoever was with us. Friend or foe?

Niero edged toward where Tressa and Killian laid, obviously angling to awaken them, in case we were about to —

I saw the pebble this time. It sprang from a rock above us and struck the back of Niero's head. He whipped around, knife in hand — and narrowly kept himself from releasing it.

I heard her laughter, then, along with the low laughter of a man. Saw Niero's face break into a rare grin as he shook his head and sheathed his dagger.

They emerged: Azarel and Asher.

Azarel raced down the trail and sprang into Niero's arms for a hug, then reached for Killian and Tressa. I joined them, clasping Asher's arm and accepting Azarel's embrace. I waited, my smile fading as I saw her look for Dri and then search my eyes. "Your Remnant ... Andriana is gone?"

"*Away.* Not gone," I said.

"Keallach has her," Niero said, accepting a canteen from Asher, drinking deeply, and then passing it to me.

"Or Dri has *him,*" Tressa put in, taking a water skin from Azarel. "She thinks she can turn Keallach. Bring him back to us," Tressa said.

Azarel and Asher shared a long, sober look, all trace of humor leaving their faces. "I fear that is a long shot," Azarel said to Niero.

"I fear it is a long *shot in the dark,*" Niero returned. "But we had no choice. They captured her. To try and rescue her would have meant that we four would all have been lost." His black eyes remained on me; I knew he hoped his words would reinforce my constantly crumbling wall of resolve.

"I can't tell you how happy we are to see you again," Tressa said to them both.

"And we, you," Asher said, eyes gleaming again. "Come. We have your Aravander friends back at our campsite. We told them we wanted to be the ones to come and fetch you."

He turned and led the way up the trail. With a bit of rest and water in my belly, I could force my way forward. But I prayed that we weren't far from their camp. Stopping had almost made my weariness worse. Or was it the talk of Andriana?

We climbed up the trail, pausing when we thought we heard a drone, then moving onward. "What brought you into Pacifica?" Niero asked. "I thought you didn't dare any farther than Castle Vega."

"Castle Vega is the worst place for us," Azarel said. "But we found friends to the north of the castle and gradually heard rumors of what might be happening to our Ailith friends in Pacifica. Eventually, we felt the Maker's pull to head toward you, in case you needed help. But here you are! Safe and sound."

"Well, most of us," Killian said.

I closed my eyes, hearing his words as condemnation.

It took me a while to realize my armband was growing warmer, since I was sweating so much with our climb. The heat wasn't fading when night came on as I'd expect it to. Was that because we were so close to the Great Expanse? But then I felt them, their presence, and noted the other Ailith grinning from ear to ear. They'd recognized what I hadn't because I was so preoccupied with thoughts of Dri. But they were here.

We turned the corner, entering a cave crevasse that forced us to suspend ourselves between the two walls, shimmying down twenty feet to a dirt path that led deeper into a cave. We could hear the chatter and laughter ahead, then the gasps and shouts of hope as they sensed our arrival too. It wasn't long before we were surrounded by Bellona and Vidar, Chaza'el and Kapriel, as well as our Aravander scouts and about twenty more of their tribe, including Latonia and Jezre and their baby.

And for the first time in days, I experienced joy and hope again. The Maker had seen to our reunion.

Surely somehow, some way, he could bring Dri back to us too.

CHAPTER 18

ANDRIANA

I had no sense of time. Had it been days since Sethos had come to visit me or mere hours? I drifted in and out of sleep, curled up on my side, teeth chattering as fiercely as the night Ronan and I spent in the cave. No maid had come with food, no healer with balms. The fireplace in the corner remained cold, and the room was so frigid that even the thick blanket could not ward off the chill. Or perhaps I ran a fever ...

By the time that Lord Maximillian Jala came to see me, I knew I had no choice but to capitulate — if only for show — in order to survive. I would not do the Remnants any good if I died of thirst. The least I could do was die with a sword in my hand.

I awakened as I heard the heavy wooden door scrape open — wide open, I realized — and I wished I had the strength to rise and fight my way out, to escape this cursed palace. But I felt as weak as an old woman on her deathbed.

His boots scuffed to a stop a foot from my bed and I forced myself to look up with my good eye. Lord Jala was one of the Council of Six, the head of Keallach's advisors. The one we'd almost killed in Castle Vega.

"Hello, Andriana. Welcome to Pacifica Palace," he said sardonically.

I tried to think of a witty comeback but nothing came to me. I was tired, so very, very tired.

He crouched and let out a sound of disgust. "The emperor would not be pleased that she was left in such a state," he said over his shoulder.

"Lord Sethos demanded—"

"It doesn't matter what Lord Sethos demanded. The emperor's demands surpass them. She's had no food? No water?"

"No, m'lord."

Maximillian ran a hand briefly across my forehead and then muttered, "She burns with fever. And that cut! She's as filthy as an alley dog. See to it that the maids bathe her and put her into something decent, and summon the healers."

"Yes, m'lord," said the other man behind him.

Maximillian moved away and two others came and lifted me between them like an awkward sack of potatoes. But again, I felt too dizzy and weak to complain. They were moving me, hopefully to warmer quarters. Somewhere they'd give me water to drink. Lots and lots of water.

The guards partly dragged, partly carried me down a hall two stories high. Sconces burned at regular intervals, and the corridor stretched out before me. I remembered how we had tried to drug Maximillian and escaped that terrible night at Castle Vega—all of us—and longed for my fellow Ailith. Only my captors' attempts to ask me where my friends might be gave me comfort. If our enemies didn't know, there was a good chance the Ailith lived and were on the move. And headed toward … where? I racked my mind but could not remember where we were to meet. It was like a bad dream with a hall full of doors, where you once knew the right door, but now the hall stretched and stretched, so long and with so many options you thought it might take days to open them all.

Finally, the men turned into a room full of white pillars and steaming water. The walls were covered in tiny tiles, mosaics depicting fish of every size and shape beneath the waves. And down below were pools, vast baths that sent steam up in tendrils as offerings to the domed ceiling covered in gold.

A matronly woman in Pacifican dress came into focus before me. "Here, my dear. Drink. Drink. This will be the first step toward healing."

I sucked eagerly from the narrow lip of the bottle, relishing the lemon-laced water as if it were from the afterworld itself. When I'd drained one, she motioned for another. When I'd finished that, two women came and helped me to the edge of the nearest tub, sunken into the floor. It was as big as a small cottage in width, and sprawled across the corner of this bathing room like a private, steaming pool. In quick order, they'd undressed me, pausing to gawk at the crescent-moon-shaped birthmark on my hip, whispering behind their hands and then hurriedly moving on as if I'd missed their attention. But it didn't matter. I witnessed it all as if in a dream half a world away.

They lowered me into the water and I cried, unable to tell if the water was so hot that it was truly burning me or if the heat was caused by my fever. But the women clucked and soothed and two of them actually got in with me, setting me upon a ledge, and set to washing my hair and scrubbing my body—pausing in wordless wonder when they realized that my arm cuff was fused to my skin—and eventually carefully, tenderly washing away the blood on my face.

I cried harder then, despite my shame. But the thought of my battered face, combined with their careful ministrations, felt a bit like a touch from my mother herself, and I was overcome. *Mom.* My beautiful mom. So worried for me when it was I that should've been far more worried for her …

They looked at each other in concern, then quickly completed their task.

"Come, mistress," murmured one. "Gain your feet beneath you and we'll help you out."

I did as she bid and was up and fairly lifted out in moments, thankful that I had ceased shivering for the first time in what seemed like days. Had a mere bath helped drive away the chill or had my fever finally broken? On shaking legs I made my way out of the bath and along the floor, an intricate mosaic of all sorts of fist-sized marble pieces: twilight purple, olive green, and fools-gold yellow. I stared at it as the women patted me dry, rubbed oils across my skin and ointment into my cuts, then slipped the sheath of the Pacifican gown over my shoulders and pulled it down, long and clinging, across my body, and then over it the gossamer-thin, billowing second layer opening in slits all along my arms.

I could feel sweat beading on my forehead as they tied a soft rope around my waist, and saw the concerned looks shared between them. "Not out of the woods yet," I said, laughing to myself, remembering something my dad had always said, amused by the understatement even in my foggy state.

The motherly servant appeared before me. "This way, please."

I allowed her to take one arm and felt another take my second, leading me to a new room with a sprawling bed. I'd never seen such a thing. It was huge, big enough for a family of five, with posts at each corner and luxurious draped linens atop it that reminded me of a tent. The women helped me into it and under the covers on one side while I trembled, well aware that the fever still plagued me, spiking again now. The bath had only been a temporary reprieve.

One servant girl set to feeding me broth from the edge of a crystal cup until a man entered the room and all conversation hushed. The man strode over to me just as I was nodding off and roughly pulled aside the blankets. Instinctively, I moved to defend myself but I was far too slow and weak; even the maids were able to hold me down. One whispered, "It's all right, miss. He's a healer."

I didn't care who he was. I didn't trust anyone in this place. But I had little choice but to succumb.

Swiftly, he ran his hands across my arms and legs — presumably to check for breaks — then moved his attentions to my ribs. I sucked in my breath as he ran light fingers across my right side. He paused, studied my face, and then probed again. I gasped.

"Bruised or broken ribs on her right side," he muttered. Then he moved up to my face, leaning close enough to check out the cuts at my eye and lip that I could smell garlic on his breath. "Too long since injury for stitches," he said again, almost to himself. "They will heal as they wish."

"Surely there's something you can do for those cuts," said the matronly servant. "They will scar if — "

"I will leave herbs for a poultice," he said abruptly. "It's all I can do. Give her a cup of foxglove tea and evening wine. That will see her through most of the night. If she wakes, give her another cup of both. The girl needs warmth and rest. Food and water. She's strong. With care, she'll heal." His gaze moved to the silver and gold cuff on my arm and studied the intricate knots, one weaving into the next. He ran his finger along the edge, where the band had fused to my skin, and then looked at me, a hundred questions in his eyes, but remained silent. Then he turned to go. I think I started to fall asleep because I let my eyes droop, opened them with a start, and he was gone.

The maid poured a cup of evening wine as another set off to fetch the tea. I well remembered how the wine had affected me last time and took a few sips — just enough to help me sleep and shake this fever, but not enough that I would sleep through anything I didn't want to. "Do you know where Keallach is? I need to speak to him."

The maids shared a look of surprise. "No, miss. I haven't heard anything about his highness and where he is. Only that he is away."

I grabbed her hand and tried to will my urgency and anxiety into her, but she just looked at me with irritation. Confused at my inability to use my gift, I held on, still trying. "What about other prisoners? Was anyone else brought to the palace besides me?"

"I know naught, miss," she said, gently prying off my hand and tucking my arm beneath the covers. "But you need to rest through the night before you go asking. You're too weak to do anything but concentrate on healing. Agreed?"

I said nothing, but turned over. I wished I had the strength to go and search the palace to make certain that none of the other Ailith had been taken captive, but I assumed this palace was no smaller than Castle Vega with its acres of halls and rooms. I'd gotten lost in that one before. Chances were greater that I'd be caught, and if they sent me to the dungeon ... My trembling doubled in response to the thought.

No, I had to sleep. Sleep so I could rise tomorrow and have the strength to fight.

■ ■ ■

I awakened in the early dawn hours, a light breeze and pale sunlight streaming through my open window. It took me a moment to realize where I was. But then it all came to me at once. My fever had broken during the night. I was in Palace Pacifica — upstairs in the guest quarters — a prisoner of the empire. But I was hardly being treated as a prisoner any longer. In a rush of guilt, I sat up quickly, and then gasped in pain. My ribs ...

But that's when I saw I had company: Lord Maximillian Jala.

He sat in a chair in the corner of my cavernous room, calmly sipping something hot from a china cup with his legs crossed, as if he'd been prepared to wait for me to wake all morning.

Hurriedly, I pulled the sheet and blanket to my chest, as if they might lend some sort of protection, which he seemed to find charming.

"Ah, do not fear me, Andriana. If I was bent on retribution for the harm you and yours did me, I would've slit your throat in the night, or during any of the previous nights." He set down his cup and waved in the air. "But my emperor has commanded me to forgive you, and forgive you I have." He lifted one brow. "No, you are to be kept in good health, unmolested by me or anyone else."

"Why?" I said, my tone dull, my eyes narrowing. "You didn't hold back before."

"Right," he said, striding over to stand beside me. "But circumstances have … changed. You are now the emperor's … *guest*. Not an enemy masquerading as my servant."

I stared up at him. "That is not how Sethos treated me."

"Indeed. Had I been here, I'd have put a stop to it. I did so, as soon as I arrived. Sethos has been reprimanded and is to come to you to apologize at some point. He is finding it … *challenging* to treat you as the emperor has dictated." A small smile pulled at the corners of his lips as his eyes searched my face and exposed arms. "I'm afraid his highness has taken quite a liking to you. And his Council of Six, including me, shall follow his lead." He paused to put his hand to his heart and bow slightly.

I sighed and sat up, wincing over the breath-stealing pain in my torso, but all the while keeping him in my sight. I tried to read him, and clenched my teeth in frustration when I failed. What sort of spell had Sethos woven here? And how might I break it?

Maximillian smiled gently. "Are you doing it now?" he asked with delight, sitting on the edge of my bed, beside me. "Attempting to use your empathic skills?"

I said nothing, resorting to trying to interpret his expression, body language, tone. From what I could tell, he seemed honest in his new pledge to protect me. Hadn't it been his doing, seeing to my care? Bringing me here?

He reached out a hand. "Now try and cast emotion into me, as you did with Keallach. As you tried to do with Sethos." He lifted it closer. "Go on."

I knew he was baiting me, curious about the strength of my

gifting. And I knew that it would likely be difficult given the spell that Sethos had wound around these halls, but I couldn't resist the opportunity to try. How else would I find out how strong the sorcerer's spell was? Tentatively, I reached out and held his wrist, the most I was willing to touch him. Then I tried to summon within me a sense of mercy. Care. Grace. But all I seemed to reach was my own anger, hatred, frustration, and no conduit at all opened between us.

His smile grew and he pulled away. "No? It is as Sethos says then—"

"Clearly I am of no use to you," I said, pulling down the edge of my gown when I saw his eyes lingering on my bare calves. "Let me go. My gifting has left me."

"Oh, no, no, no, my dear Andriana." He leaned close, one lock of his dyed-blond hair falling over a brow. "It is not gone. We are simply in the process of putting it under proper restraints," he said lightly. He straightened and smiled, hands out as if announcing something glorious. "We cannot have a Remnant in full command of her gifting out and about the empire, wreaking havoc, sowing seeds of discontent. We are all about peace here in Pacifica. Prosperity! You'll soon see."

He strode toward the door and opened it. "Sethos doesn't wish for you to read him. But me?" He grinned, showing off his straight, white teeth. "I'm an open book. I'll tell Sethos that I've granted you permission. I, for one, find it fascinating. Until tomorrow?"

I grimaced, visualizing Maximillian at one of his Castle Vega dinner parties, forcing me to use my gifting as some sort of odd parlor trick for his guests' entertainment. "Don't rush back, Lord Jala."

He laughed at that, so hard he looked up at the ceiling, then back to me. "Oh, this will be fun. We haven't had a woman with a backbone in the court in ages. Rest and heal, Andriana of the Valley. There is much ahead."

With that, he exited and carefully closed the door, locking it behind him.

CHAPTER
19

RONAN

We all stared at Niero, wishing we'd misheard him. That he'd forgotten his mad plan.

"You want us to go back," Vidar said flatly. "To places and to people who tried to kill us."

"Yes. That is where the Maker calls us — to the people in most desperate need of hope," Niero replied. "We are to go to the Drifters. To Georgii Post. To Zanzibar."

We were all silent again.

"People that desperate," said Killian, "will make martyrs out of the faithful. We cannot change the world if we are dead."

Niero turned kind eyes on him. "The Maker will make use of our lives, whether our days stretch far or short, right?" He waited Killian out, not releasing him from his gaze.

"Right," Killian said at last.

"But I'd really, really rather go for that long stretch," Vidar said. "Who's with me?"

We all smiled and laughed under our breath. But I was certain every one of our mouths were dry.

"Why?" I asked. "Why go back to those places? Where they know us? Where they might be on the lookout for us from the beginning?"

"Because it is there," Asher said, eyes alight, as if in silent communion with Niero, "that the story of the Way is already whispered and shared. If you return now, with our Remnants in full command of their gifting" — he paused to gesture toward Tressa, Chaza'el, and Kapriel — "our healer, our seer, our miracle worker ... our Prince," he amended, "the whisper shall become a shout!"

Asher clasped his hands, eyes shining, and then lifted his face and hands to the top of the cave. "Glory to the Maker!"

"Glory to the Maker!" we repeated, caught up in his joy.

"Is it possible?" I asked Niero. "Do you really think it is possible for us to enter and exit these cities and not be imprisoned?"

Niero's smile, which had spread with Asher's words, melted into a sober, somber line. "I think it is possible we will be imprisoned and tortured, even unto death."

"You do know how to rally a crowd, don't you?" Vidar said with sigh.

"But I am certain that the Maker has asked us to go," Niero pressed on, ignoring him. "We must trust him to sustain us regardless of what is to come. He did not bring the Ailith into this world for you to cower in caves, hiding from the enemy. He brought you into the world to bring together the people, to lead them back to the Way. To bring hope and direction and light for people long lost to the darkness. It is time for the awakening. And that shall not come easily. Are you ready?"

His dark eyes shifted around at each of us, even the Aravanders behind us, and he then reached out his fist.

"I've never been fond of caves," Vidar said, putting his hand on Niero's.

Silently, the rest of us placed a hand atop the others. The Aravanders clasped our shoulders.

"Are you ready to go where you are called?" Niero asked again.

"We are ready," we said as one.

ANDRIANA

With each day that passed, my pain eased. Sethos and Lord Jala appeared to have left the palace, which both aggravated and pleased me. It pleased me in that time with them would only mean taunting and trouble; it aggravated me because they were the only people I knew of in the entire palace who might be able to tell me when Keallach would return.

By day five I was pacing the room for hours, eating only what was necessary from lavish food trays that could have fed twenty. By day seven, I was pacing the room and continually trying the door, as if it might magically open. The guards became more and more wary as they entered, and I noticed they added two more to their retinue when delivering food and taking away the picked-over trays.

I awoke on day eight knowing that something had to change. I got out of bed, stripped to my underclothes and stretched, noting that for the first time my ribs weren't killing me. I ran my fingers over each one and felt the odd bulge that

I figured was a broken bone healing oddly. It was still more bruised than the others — a dark purple where the rest were turning green — and there was a cut that had scabbed over. Perhaps the rib had actually punctured the skin. I was just lucky that infection hadn't set in over those days where they'd left me alone in my fever. Or maybe it had.

I shook my head and fell to my toes and hands, doing five sets of ten push-ups, then turning to make my way through some sit-ups too. That still made my torso cry out, but I knew I had to work my muscles if I was to regain my strength. And I'd need my strength in the days ahead. Without Ronan to take the lead in my battles ... I rose and jogged around and around the room after throwing open the curtains on all three tall windows, each covered with bars on the outside. When I'd worked up a sweat, which didn't take long in my weakened state, I went to the bathroom that attached to my room. As much as I loathed being imprisoned here, I knew that as long as I lived, I'd dream about the comforts of this small room.

A toilet that flushed and paper beside it. A sink and shower with hot running water that never seemed to come to an end. Soft, scented soaps. Thick, luxurious towels. Lotions and oils. Combs and brushes. And a full-length mirror. I was embarrassed by how long I stood in front of it, probing and examining my body — both the wounds that were healing and my skin and curves. Never had I seen my whole body from my hair to my toes. And in such clarity.

Even with the cuts at my eye and lip that were still an angry red, I figured I was pleasing to look at. At least Ronan would think so ...

A knock sounded at my bedroom door, and I turned away from the mirror in confusion. No one had come to see me in days. Hurriedly, I slipped on my undergarments, then the satiny sheath of the gown, and finally the outer gown. I went out to the main room and to the door, pausing when someone knocked again.

"Andriana? May I come in?"

It was Keallach.

Taking a deep breath, I turned the knob, and with some surprise, felt no resistance of a lock.

He smiled, but it quickly disappeared as he stepped across the threshold and waved back two guards who seemed intent on coming with him. His hand lifted to my face and his eyes darkened. "What ... *Who* did this to you?"

"Sethos," I spat out, silently cursing myself for being glad — *glad* — to see him. He wasn't my friend. We were connected, bonded in a way, but I had to remember —

His frown deepened. "Sethos? No. He wouldn't ... He knows ..." His lips clamped shut and he seemed to gather himself. "How? When?"

"More than a week ago," I said. "When I was brought here. Where have you been, Keallach?"

"I'm sorry for that," he said, giving me a rueful look. "I had to see to an urgent matter in the southern region of —"

Another knock sounded at the door.

"Come," Keallach called. He was dressed in Pacifican ivory, in a billowing shirt that hung loose at his collar, revealing toned muscle and smooth skin, golden from time beneath the seaside sun. I looked away as servants carried in two chairs and set them beside the gold table. Another brought a tray of tea, and another tiny sandwiches stacked on a triple-layered china plate, each one smaller than the next.

When they left, Keallach stood beside one chair and

gestured to the other. "Andriana. Let us sit and discuss what has happened and what shall happen next."

I searched him, trying to read his emotions. All I got was hope. How could I argue with that? Didn't I myself hope that by some miracle he'd allow me to leave? And maybe even come with me?

Tentatively, I went to the other chair and perched on its edge. I made myself put my hands down, feigning relaxation when every nerve in my body was on alert. He sat down and leaned in the corner of the huge high-backed chair, lazily crossing one boot over his other knee. His breeches were soft, brushed leather, tawny gold. I resisted the ridiculous urge to reach out and touch them.

His eyes followed mine. "Aren't they marvelous? The fabric comes from a leather factory on the eastern edge of Pacifica. They're experimenting with various colors. I'm so weary of the whites of Pacifica," he added, fluffing his shirt. "I think I'll decree a change of royal dress. Soon the empire will be full of clothes in all sorts of colors. We've just re-established trade with those across the Great Sea who can bring us amazing indigo and purple and green."

I tried to summon polite pleasure to mirror his, but my mind and heart were screaming about a hundred other more important things ... one, in particular.

"Keallach, why have you brought me here?" I asked. "Am I your guest or your prisoner?"

His smile faded and he looked into my eyes. Then he leaned forward and took my hand. Although everything within me wanted to resist his touch, I allowed it. If I was to find out anything, he had to think I was open to him, that I was willing to give him a chance. And if we were touching, I might find it easier to read him. His skin was warm, and he put his other hand over mine.

"Go ahead," he said, nodding a little. "Use your gift. I shall be open to you for a moment."

"I can't. Sethos —"

"Sethos has not created any barrier that I can't supersede," he said. "By choice, I can take down the wall between us. And Andriana, I don't want any wall to remain between us. I brought you here so that you could know the truth about me and my country. No secrets."

I hesitated, feeling a blush rise at my jaw at this sense of intimacy, this understanding, then gave in to it. Again, I felt nothing but hope in him. Intense hope. And joy.

"Do you sense anything in me that makes you fearful?"

I shook my head.

"Having you here," he said tenderly, reaching up as if to touch my face and then thinking twice, "has given me the first measure of hope I've felt in some time. I mean, it's the first I've felt of the Maker's presence since ..." The grief rose up in him then, in memory. He shook his head. "Well, for a good while." He concentrated again on my face. "Those responsible for your wounds ... shall face consequences." I felt a flicker of rage in him, darkness yawning, but then it was gone so quickly it stole my breath. Alarmed, I pulled my hand away.

I leaned forward to pour myself tea and then another cup for him. He took it from me with a small smile, as if he were thinking he could get used to such niceties. Suddenly I wanted to slam the cup into his face, my own anger rising now. He was ultimately responsible. For my capture. For leaving me here alone, with Sethos. For my injuries. But I had to find my way, my time. I had to think, not give in to feeling.

"I'm glad you're here, Andriana."

He said it as if I'd finally answered an invitation.

"There is so much I want to show you in Pacifica. So many things you and the Ailith have ... misunderstood. While we've been apart, I've been doing some research. And I've figured out how things have gotten skewed out there, in the Trading Union. Lies passed on from one to the other."

"Skewed," I repeated flatly. "Or lies. Which one?"

"Well," he said, popping a bite of sandwich in his mouth. "I do not know if it began as malicious intent to slander my reign, or if it was an innocent misunderstanding, but you can help me make it right."

I studied him. "Do you have an example?"

He nodded, clamping his lips together solemnly. "Take, for instance, your accusations about children being kidnapped at Georgii Post."

"Something," I said slowly, "I saw with my own eyes."

"Right," he returned carefully, one hand outstretched, palm up. "Eat a bit and then I'd like to take you to see a couple of places that will give you ... context."

I paused. He was offering to take me out? Out of the palace? If nothing else, it would be good for me to know a route of escape, if I ever got past the cursed locked door ...

"Yes," I said with a nod. I hurriedly stuffed a sandwich in my mouth and grabbed three more. "Shall we?" I asked, still chewing as I moved to my feet.

His dark, sculpted brows rose in wry entertainment over my haste, but seeing my lack of humor, he quickly stood behind me. "We shall," he said.

CHAPTER
20

ANDRIANA

We walked out of my room as if it were never locked, as if I'd dreamed the whole thing. The guards outside stood relaxed, their swords sheathed and sidearms holstered. Keallach offered me his arm again. I tentatively took it, feeling at odds but wanting any anchor I could find. He smiled a little, and I felt the pleasure of the small victory surge through him, but I still couldn't summon the courage to release him. I even gripped tighter as my arm cuff began to turn cool when we neared what appeared to be the main hall of the palace.

The Six lounged about on luxurious chairs before a crackling fireplace that was taller than I. They looked up as we entered the room and appeared only pleasantly surprised at my presence. Keallach placed his warm hand over mine, but kept his eyes on the group. "Gentlemen, I think I'll take Andriana for a little drive. Show her a bit of Pacifica. True Pacifica, not the dark legends that have permeated the greater Union."

The men, as one, returned their gazes to me, looking intrigued and entertained. I reached out, searching for warning signs of anger and malice, but for each of the Six, Sethos's wall remained firmly up. No doubt I'd made no friends the night we'd attacked Lord Maximillian Jala and escaped Castle Vega, making them all look like fools. And Lord Fenris ... well, the word *hate* probably didn't begin to cover what he was feeling toward me. I'd taken him down in front of all the rest of the Council. But it was Lord Fenris who rose first and came to us, extending a hand until I allowed him to take mine. He promptly bowed and kissed it, his lips soft and featherlight on my bruised and scabbed knuckles. He didn't release it as he rose, holding it instead, between both of his. "May you find the truth, Andriana. As the emperor will show you, I believe we started out on the wrong foot, but we'll soon find our way in the dance of friendship."

"I have reason to doubt that," I said.

His own smile grew, then he threw his head back and laughed, the others with him. As if I'd just said the funniest thing. He dropped my hand and put his fists on his hips, staring at Keallach. "You're quite sure, Highness? That you can convince her of our merits?"

"Quite," Keallach said, with a nod, already leading me away. "Give me some time."

The massive doors in the front of the palace were opened by doormen, and it was with some relief that I felt them close behind us. Keallach was enough for me to handle and sort through, without the rest of the Council or Sethos about. I blinked against the bright afternoon light and rubbed my arms against the chill. Even here in Pacifica, where the sun shone far longer and more often, the change of seasons clearly approached.

"Forgive me," Keallach said, grimacing. He snapped his

fingers and sent a servant off to fetch a "wrap" while another opened a car door.

I paused beside the car and then looked guiltily back to the palace. I was out here enjoying such luxuries while the Ailith were somewhere in the wilderness, likely trying to find food, shelter. And yet if I didn't find out all I could, discover a possible escape route, as well as try to establish a true bond with Keallach, was I not wasting time?

"We'll return here?" I asked Keallach. "By nightfall?"

He nodded, once, his eyes sparkling with curiosity and a bit of gratification in his heart, as if he hoped I liked the palace so much that I wanted to return to it at my earliest opportunity.

I sighed and slipped inside the vehicle, my nostrils filling with the scent of new leather. I pushed to the far side of the wide seat, making room for Keallach. He followed me in, and after a moment the servant returned and pressed a soft white bundle inside the car. It was a fur — or rather countless white furs — stitched into a blanket. Keallach absently handed it to me as he leaned forward to respond to the driver's question.

I rubbed the impossibly soft blanket, hugging it to my chest while I watched Keallach interact with the driver. He was kind, polite, not at all the lordly tyrant I imagined he might be. Or was it all an act? All I could detect was respect, joy, and anticipation.

The car pulled out and I stared outside, amazed at the sprawling green lawns, the leafy trees laden with fruit, and the bushes covered in flowers, even this close to Hoarfrost. My eyes could not seem to get enough of the color, the vivid color all around me. "Is all of Pacifica this beautiful?" I asked.

"Most of it," he said, taking the blanket and shaking it out, then gently spreading it across my lap. "There are parts of it that are quite dull, nothing but vast acreage of sand and cacti." He sat back and looked out his own window, a finger across his lips. "But yes, most of it is like this. Why? Is it so different from your Valley?"

"I suspect you know what my Valley looks like."

He stared back into my eyes and lifted his brows. "Honestly, I've seen pictures, but I've never been there myself. It's never quite the same ... Don't you agree?"

"Pictures?" I said. "You mean drawings?"

He quirked a small smile and then shook his head. "No. Pictures." He pulled a device from his pocket and pressed a button, then two more, then handed the device to me. I gasped. Because what he showed me was a picture — in full color — of my own beloved woods. He ran a finger across and the first image went away, leaving a new one of a mountain peak I knew well. After another swipe, there was a thick fog over a pond where my father had loved to fish.

"*Pictures*," Keallach said with a nod. He flicked off the device and tucked it back into his coat pocket. "I take it you don't have a device like it back in the Valley?"

"No, we don't," I said in a low tone, thinking of the drone birds and how the Aravanders thought they took pictures. Of how much Tonna might pay for such a thing back at Nem Post. "It's marvelous. Does everyone in Pacifica have one?"

"No, but I see a day when everyone will," he said, with confidence. "Pacifica is on the rise, Andriana. Wealthier by the day."

"As the Trading Union becomes poorer," I said. I shifted uneasily beneath my fur blanket, which was probably worth more than I could ever pay.

"We are not using the Trading Union, Andriana," he said,

frowning a little. "We are gradually equipping her to become a part of us. After the War …" He paused and glanced out his car window. "There is no way to change things quickly. It has to be a gradual transition. But this road we're on, toward unification, is good."

I stared at him, searching him, and he allowed it, lifting his hands.

"Go ahead. As I said — I am an open book to you." He was guileless, hopeful, excited. "Don't you see?" he said, leaning toward me, green-blue eyes intent on mine. "Don't you see how this could all be the Maker's way? For us both?"

"The Maker's way is one of freedom." I stared back at him for several seconds. "So may I leave Pacifica any time I wish?"

His enthusiasm faded and I sensed guilt in him before a wall went up between us.

"I thought you were an open book."

"For certain chapters. One day at a time, Andriana."

"When will you release me?"

"Not until you give me the chance to show my side of this story. 'A fair shake,' as they used to say. I want you to know for certain that I am your true Remnant brother, not your forsaken enemy. Then I might allow you to leave me."

I considered him, wondering if that was all he truly sought. Troublesome words from the Six came back to me. "*Brother* I can tolerate," I said, deciding to test him. "*Husband* is not something I'm ready to say."

He quirked a smile, and the chill disappeared. "Frankly, as lovely as you are, Andriana, I'm not quite ready to call anyone *wife*."

I sat back, breathing a little easier after hearing him say it. And yet he'd not specifically said it *wasn't* a possibility. I returned to staring outside, glimpsing the wide blue arc of the sea from time to time. "Have you been swimming in it?"

He followed my gaze. "In the ocean? Sure. Every day as a child. Less now. Imperial business doesn't allow for a lot of swimming." I struggled to not smile with him.

"Remnant business *kept* us swimming at home."

"Lots of training, I assume," he said lightly. "I could see it in your dive in that river and how long you stayed under."

"Lots. For you too?"

"Every day, classes in the morning and warfare in the afternoon."

"What's your weapon?" I asked carefully, after a moment. I couldn't remember him drawing a sword in Wadi Qelt, only watching us.

"I'm most adept with an iron-tipped staff, but I do well with swords too."

I nodded and then resumed my watch out the window. I remembered Sethos, with his double-tipped sword. Had he trained Keallach to use his?

After a few minutes, we pulled up to a massive building that looked hundreds of years old. "Pre-War?" I asked in surprise. As I'd understood it, almost everything in this region had been leveled by the bombs.

He got out of the car and stared up at the façade proudly. "It was nothing but rubble in a ravaged town. I had my people put it back together, brick by brick." He came around the car and put a light hand at my lower back, leading me forward. "I partially favor old things, old ways. In a new country, it helps to remember the things that were good once, the things we want to recreate now. It's definitely not in fashion here, but I try to incorporate some of the old, now and again. It brings me ... comfort."

I nodded. A glance left or right down the street affirmed his words. Most of the buildings showcased flat, barely angled roofs and wide windows, clean and simple. But this building flaunted concrete ornaments in fanciful curves. Everything about it led the eye upward, and there was a sense of lightness that counterbalanced the heavy building materials.

We walked up the stairs and he opened a glass door with a long, brass handle, gesturing for me to go before him. He wasn't even through the door before a man and woman were coming around a desk to greet him.

"Highness, welcome, welcome! We didn't expect you here today," said the woman, lifting a hand to her cheek as if she might faint from the surprise.

"Yes, well," he said, "I like to see how the facilities are doing when my people don't have time to prepare. I'm sure my guest here, Miss Andriana, would like to see the same," he said pointedly.

"Right, good," said the man. I found it oddly reassuring when Keallach offered his hand in greeting—familiar and welcoming—rather than accepting a bow as some aloof monarch might. "You're welcome any day, any hour, Highness. We're honored to have you visit us at all."

"I'd like you to give Miss Andriana a tour. Show her how our operation with the children works here. Tell her everything. Hold nothing back. Answer any question."

"Certainly," the man said slowly, obviously feeling anything but certain inside. Perhaps it was only because no one had ever asked before, or expressed interest. He undoubtedly wondered who I was and why I had a right. But he wasn't going to question the emperor.

"Please, follow me," he said. He turned and went through

211

double doors to the right, leaving the woman behind at the desk, presumably to intercept any other visitors who entered the building. The doors shut with a locking sound behind us.

We followed the slight man down a long hall. "We house over two hundred children, none of whom have reached their first decade, but all rescued from the greater Union."

"Rescued?" I asked carefully, remembering the reaping in Georgii Post.

"Yes. They are orphans, found among the streets of the various cities and brought here to begin a new life."

"I thought they were brought here to be adopted into Pacifican homes."

"Most shall be, in time. Nearly every home in Pacifica houses at least one or two. But the children must first learn to live as civilized humans rather than the street urchins they arrive as. And the older they are, the longer that takes. Here," he said, gesturing about as we passed a wide bank of windows that looked out to the sea, "they learn how to bathe, sleep regularly, eat as if it might not be their last meal. They are given a bit of an education and learn the value of hard work."

We moved through another set of double doors, and I heard the *click* of another lock behind us.

This hall was full of what appeared to be classrooms, and the children sat in neat rows, all in gray uniforms, their hair tidy and their hands folded on their desks as the teachers lectured. It was like something out of a scene from the Pre-War days, something I'd longed for, wished for. Even in the Valley, only a few chosen children received such instruction. What would happen if all had access as these did?

"They go to school all day?" I asked, moving from one window to the next.

"Perhaps someday," said the headmaster, looking a bit sorry for his answer. "For now, all we can do is provide them a few hours of reading and writing and mathematics. The brightest receive instruction in science and history. But the other part of their day is to learn the value of hard work."

I was torn as to what to pursue first, and yet did not want to appear too accusatory in front of Keallach. He wanted to impress me, win me. So I chose the positive first. "You teach these children to read? I thought it was expressly forbidden."

"In the Union," Keallach said gently. "Out there, it tends to breed rebellion. But as I told you in Wadi Qelt, I am in pursuit of enlightenment, for my people as well as myself. If we can all come together, I do not fear the power of intelligence. It can only benefit our people at large, help us move forward as a true empire. So we are experimenting with it here."

My mind raced. He was educating children that had once belonged to the Trading Union. How long until the practice spread beyond the Wall? I thought of Asher, and him teaching the children the sacred words. Did any of these children in these classrooms whisper of them? Dare to write them down? My pulse quickened, partially in fear, partially in excitement. And as much as Keallach or the headmaster might wish to control or shape these children, they were undoubtedly beginning to develop their own thought processes.

We heard the hum of machinery before we opened the next set of double doors. The sound became louder as the doors slid open, but at the sight of Keallach, it faded to a stop. I saw that each boy or girl sat before a sewing machine, stitching together fabric, their eyes dull, mouths slack. But when they saw Keallach, joy lifted each one's lips in a smile and they came to him, surrounding us, hands lifted for him to touch, crying out greetings. Their combined joy and hope flooded through me in such a sudden wave that it took me aback and tears streamed from my eyes.

Keallach lifted a boy in one arm and a girl in the other and turned around, shouting out a jaunty tune, wading forward through the fifty or so children, as if to allow them all to reach out and touch him. He looked at each of them — really looked them in the eye — and my mouth dropped open when I realized that he was greeting them all by name with a word for each one. Finally, he looked back at me, and seeing my tears, gave me a puzzled smile. I hurriedly wiped them away as the children quieted.

"I see you all are doing a most fine job here today," Keallach said, his attention on the children again. "If you hit the headmaster's quota this week, I shall invite you all to the palace for a party. Would you like that?"

The children laughed, clapped, and cheered.

"Well, don't just stand here," he said, eyebrows lifting. "Get working!"

The children all ran back to their machines and the hum again filled the air. We moved out of the room and to the next, a large, empty hall filled with long tables and benches.

"Our dining hall," said the headmaster. "The children are fed three times a day. Most of them used to get only one meal, if they were so fortunate. It takes them a while to relax, to eat slowly and not so much that they vomit. They are unused to the idea that there will not only be a next meal, but countless after that."

I nodded, my hands behind my back as we walked down yet another hall. Outside this bank of windows was a large sandbox and what looked like brightly colored bars and slides on which to climb, though no little ones were out there. "What happens to the children after they reach their first decade?"

"Most are adopted by then," he said. "Though our families seem to prefer younger children, despite our good work with them here in the home."

"And if they're not?"

"Then they are placed where they can earn their keep," he said easily.

"You put them to work," I said slowly.

He nodded earnestly. "In homes, in factories, some in mines. All become model Pacifican citizens."

"You make them slaves," I said, at last landing on a place to focus my anger.

Keallach stopped abruptly and faced me. "No. They are paid."

"Paid, but somebody else makes a great deal of money off of their hard work."

"Is that not enterprise? Progress? Life as this land once knew it?"

"But is it life as we want to know it again? What are their hours? Their conditions? Where do they live? A child of one-and-one is hardly ready to take care of himself!"

"And yet they were taking care of themselves on the street at a far younger age." Keallach stepped closer to me. "Were they not? And were they not working twice as hard, merely to survive?" He rubbed his forehead as if trying to find the right words to reach me. "What we're creating here is opportunity for everyone, Andriana. Opportunity to become a part of a Pacifica family — which undoubtedly is the chief goal — but for those who are not chosen, opportunity in the empire. We are forming these street urchins into contributing members of society."

I wanted to take issue with it, but was it so different than at home? Every child had to work from morning until night to help keep themselves and their families alive. Only a few were educated; the rest worked. But something about this place around me made me feel uneasy. Something was off.

"Keallach, not all of these children were orphans. I saw, with my own eyes, Pacifican soldiers wrench younger children from their parents' arms."

He frowned. "That is not sanctioned action. I've told you I shall inquire about it. Perhaps you saw a few rogue soldiers, out to make some extra coin." His look soured. "Younger children are sometimes purchased by desperate women unable to wait for their allotted adoption chips. It is something we're trying to stop at every opportunity."

"Why is it that your women do not bear their own children?" I asked, looking toward Keallach. I thought I knew the truth. I wanted to hear his version.

He began walking again and I turned to catch up. "After the War, the toxins left us with generations of infertility. It was in our water, in our soil. And while our land and water is now clean, our women still struggle. In fact, it seems worse than ever before."

"But the men are not infertile."

He shook his head. "By and large, no." He studied me then. I shook off memories of the Six jeering over my supposed fertility and how I might make the perfect bride.

"What of ..." I began. "I've heard mention that your women prefer to not put their bodies through pregnancy, even if they can get pregnant."

He frowned and looked to the headmaster, gesturing for him to go, then back to me, once we were alone. "There is some truth to it. In the last three decades, only about a hundred children have been born in our land, Kapriel and I being two of them. If you do not grow up seeing older women bearing children does it not become ... foreign? Vaguely frightening or even ... repugnant?"

I considered that. He'd risked much, telling me of their plight. His vulnerability and understanding of his people moved me. We stared at each other and I felt his need — for his people. For himself.

"How long has it gone on then?" I said, forcing words out to break our awkward moment, ignoring the heat of my blush. "This ... incorporation of Union children into your populace?" My mind was racing back to Zanzibar. How long until the Pacificans realized they could take a wife from the Union and break this endless cycle of infertility?

"Only a decade or so," he said. "My father began the campaign, well aware of the plight of the children beyond our Wall and the need among our own populace. It seemed the perfect solution. At first, every child was placed in a home. Now, there are so many in need ... Well, you've seen our solution."

A cold thought came to me, again born in what I'd seen in Zanzibar. Many of the children back there had been girls ...

"You suspect wrongdoing," Keallach said, sounding shocked. The warm feelings between us quickly chilled. "You suspect me, even after seeing this?" he said, lifting a hand about the clean walls and sparkling windows.

"I have seen hard things, Keallach. Dark things. Are you aware of what goes on in Zanzibar?"

His brow lowered and he rested his chin in his hand. "I am."

"Then you are aware that the men there are short of women. That girls, far short of their second decade, are sold into 'marriage.'"

He nodded once.

"How long?" I asked, lifting a hand to the windows. "How long until your men demand a wife of the Union too? From among these children?" I waved in the direction of the sewing hall, the image of all those little girls among the boys sending a shiver down my back. "And how are those girls, now Pacifican brides, to be treated among your people? As equals? Or something less than?" I paced, my thoughts coming together now. "And how long until the men of the Union realize that what you're doing is basically importing breeders for you, stealing away the women, putting their children — even orphans — to work in your factories or mines? Will that produce unity? Peace?"

"It is not like that."

"Isn't it?"

"No."

"But you have to admit, it's a likely outcome. You said it yourself, in so many words — without changing things, you will gradually die out. Women who can produce a babe will become a prize. You will become like the Zanzibians."

"No. I won't allow it. We will never become like that scum. We will not take to their ways! I intend to force *them* to civility."

"Truly?"

"Truly!"

I stared at him a long moment. "Then tell me why Sethos was sent to capture me. Tell me — "

"Because I wanted you to know me," Keallach said, lifting

218

a hand to his chest. He stared at me with earnest eyes. "Even after what happened on Catal ... I still wanted you to know me. I want you to decide for yourself if I am the monster that others made me out to be or your missing brother."

"Not to become your bride," I said, not dropping my eyes.

"No," he said with a grimace, but he looked away and I felt his flash of guilt.

"Not to bear you a child," I pressed.

He dropped his head, turning it this way and that as if my words hurt him.

"Not to use my gifting for your own purposes and—"

"Enough! Enough questioning!" He strode to the window and stared out at the sea, arms crossed. I licked my lips, tried to gather myself, and then forced myself to follow him. I leaned against the windowsill, staring out at the clouds gathering on the horizon.

"I know you are not all bad," I said.

He huffed a laugh. "There's a start."

I didn't smile with him. "I think the Maker continues to urge you toward us because you know it's where you belong. Your path diverged from ours, but there is a way back. There is *always* a way back."

He shook his head and rubbed the back of his neck. "I have to make my own way. But I don't want to do it alone. I need you, Andriana. Here. By my side."

I battled between objection and compassion, staring at our ghostly reflections in the window, not daring to look him full in the face. On one hand, he was still my Ailith kin. He was meant to be with us, one of us. But he'd all but killed his parents. Allowed his knight to die fighting Kapriel's. I tried to imagine watching Ronan battle Killian or Bellona, and them both dying. Thoughts of death led me to my parents. He was responsible too, in a way, for their deaths. Did the Sheolites not report to Sethos, and Sethos to Keallach?

And what was I attempting here? I remembered the alarm in Chaza'el, Vidar, Raniero, even the knights, whenever we spoke of Keallach's potential redemption. They clearly all thought it impossible. I reached up and rubbed my throbbing temples. Was I going mad? Doing what the Sheolite wanted of me instead of the Maker? I needed my fellow Ailith. I needed their strength. Most of all, I needed Ronan.

"I've taxed you," Keallach said, glancing over at me in a tender way. "We both have said much and have much to think about. Come, we'll get you home to the palace where you can rest."

I walked beside him out of the facility and out into the cool air of evening. I was eager to get to the car and back to that marvelous fur blanket. But once I was settled beneath it, the car door shut and the engine purring beneath our feet, the ocean sprawling outside my window, Keallach's words came back to me.

Home to the palace.

I smiled, thinking of what Vidar would say about that.

"Is something amusing?"

I glanced over at him, embarrassed to be caught in my reverie, and shook my head.

"You are very beautiful, Andriana," he said softly. "Especially when you smile."

He wasn't flattering me idly. He meant it.

I quickly looked out the window, feeling the blush burning up my cheek. "It is not our way to speak of outward beauty," I said lowly.

"Bah," he said dismissively. "It's a foolish Valley tradition."

"It's the tradition of our elders. Presumably of yours too."

He shook his head a little, irritated. "You are as beautiful inside as you are out," he said. "I see no harm in recognizing that fact."

We pulled up along the sweeping drive before the palace, then past armed guards and gates. He got out and offered his hand to help me, but I ignored it, leaving the fur behind and feeling guilty for accepting it at all.

"You will join me for supper," he said, a few steps behind me.

"No," I said. "I think I shall take it alone, in my room tonight. As you noted, I am suddenly weary."

"Please, Andriana. Rest. Then join us in the dining hall."

I thought of the Council of Six, and all I could visualize was that horrific dinner table at Castle Vega. "No thank you."

He let out a sigh of exasperation as we strode down the long hall to my third-floor quarters. At least I hoped I was heading to my quarters. "You do realize that there is not another woman in the empire who has been allowed to refuse me outright."

I rolled my eyes, and turned to face him. "Are you an emperor? Or a spoiled child?" I said the words without thinking, and instantly regretted them.

Fury, black and roiling, burst forth in him and the muscles in his jaw tightened. For a moment, I thought he might hit me. But then it was gone, and he resumed his composure. The flash of all we'd both just felt left me stunned. Reeling. He ran his hands slowly down his sleeves, as if they were out of order, and then looked down at me. "You ... seem to bring out the best and worst in me."

I considered him for a long moment. "As you might, with me," I allowed.

"The Council," he tried again, "will wonder why you are not at our table this night."

"Let them wonder. I don't care." His anger had ignited my own.

His lips clamped together. Then he took a firm grip of my elbow, hustled me to my quarters, and let go of me inside. "You are not a prisoner in this palace," he said curtly. "But you are not behaving like a proper guest. Keep in mind I do have limits, regardless of my fondness for you. I shall send a servant with a tray. You may explore this third floor or the second. But no further."

I huffed a laugh and crossed my arms, feeling like a bundle of agitation and confusion. Why had my refusal so totally sent him into such a state? Were we now enemies? Doubt ripped away any fresh, light cords that had been woven between us in the last hours.

Whatever had transpired, I knew this: If he was ever to join the Ailith, he had to get over his pride. Pride was forbidden among my brothers and sisters and quickly weeded out — it inevitably led to other sicknesses.

Keallach stood just outside the threshold of my door, and I was only a few steps away inside my room. And while I was as angry with him as he was with me, I couldn't help feeling sick over the fact that we were so close, and yet it was like miles now stretched between us.

"Good night, Keallach," I said.

Then I reached forward and slowly, but firmly, shut the door in the emperor's face.

RONAN

There was no long, horrible journey back across the Great Expanse. This time Asher and Azarel had secured rides with Drifters that had a camp to the northwest of the Hoodites. We rode in the backs of trucks and Jeeps, meeting every furtive glance of the Drifters who were our hosts, wary that we were entering tenuous territory. But our armbands remained warm, and while the Drifters seemed cautious and suspicious, they had taken significant risks in order to aid us. If Asher and Azarel — and most of all Vidar, with his gifting to discern light from dark — thought they were trustworthy enough, then I had to believe my friends were right.

But it did not escape me that every one of these Drifters was armed for war, many of them with guns I wished that Vidar could carry on this quest. Granted, the way the Drifters made a life demanded such armor. Yet if we ended up combatting them, it wouldn't be long before we were disarmed, wounded, or dead, no matter how good we and the Aravanders were with our ancient weapons.

My eyes moved to Asher, who was grinning and shouting back and forth in conversation with one of the Drifters riding beside him. He still seemed at ease, confident. But then that was his way, wherever he was. My eyes went to Vidar again. If he wasn't sensing darkness ahead … well, I'd rest in that.

We left the main road that cut through this part of the desert and rambled over a rocky plain, then entered the end of what appeared to be a dry arroyo. Trees and shade instantly cooled us the deeper down we went. It felt good to be away from the exposed plain of the desert, constantly fearful that a Pacifican drone or scouting party might spot us when we had nowhere to hide. And yet I kept reverting to fear, remembering how Dri was treated the last time we encountered Drifters. How Niero had been shot … How they'd hated our friends among the Hoodites.

The Jeep that Killian, Tressa, Chaza'el, and I were riding in came to an abrupt stop, sending a big cloud of dust up and around us. The five other vehicles did the same. I coughed and squinted in the golden, dusty evening light, trying to see who all approached. There were more than fifty or sixty Drifters here in this camp. I could smell roasting meat on a spit and my mouth watered.

Chaza'el edged past me and stood in front of us as we gathered together. "We are grateful that you provided us passage across the Expanse and a place to rest for the night. But we must see your blind leader now. It is most urgent."

Niero stepped up beside him, gave him a long look, and then folded his arms, waiting.

The Drifters frowned and looked alarmed. Eventually, a burly, scarred, bald man was led through the crowd, stopping ten feet from Chaza'el. "Who told you I was blind?" he asked, letting go of the shoulder of the boy who led him.

"The Maker told me," Chaza'el said quietly.

The leader narrowed in on his voice and stepped toward him. Niero blocked him by placing a hand to his chest. "We mean you no harm, brother," he said quietly.

The man shoved away his hand. "You are no brother to me," he snarled. "And I will have the name of the one who identified me as blind to you. It is forbidden among us."

I frowned. What sort of mad control was this? Who could not refer to this chief without mentioning his weakness? And yet, maybe that was it. He didn't want to appear so at all among a people famous for preying upon the weak …

Chaza'el didn't wince in the face of his brawn or fury.

Instead he stepped forward, and I saw Tressa move to stand behind him, and Killian behind her.

"I'll tell you again, brother," Chaza'el said. "We were sent here by the Maker, to a blind chief among the Drifters."

"A leader who shall see again this day," Tressa added in a clear, high voice.

Understanding flooded through me. This was why we'd been brought here. The work was beginning—

"What is this?" cried the blind man. "Who has brought these people into my camp only to poke fun at me?"

"We have not been brought," Tressa said soothingly, reaching out to touch his arm. "We have been sent." He started to shake off her fingers and then suddenly stopped, mouth dropping slightly open. It was as if he knew, then, just as surely as we all knew.

"You ... You are a healer?" he asked her. His voice seemed small though he was twice her size.

"I am," she said. "And I'll say it again. Today, the Maker has sent us to heal you."

"The Maker is dead," said the man. His words held not venom, but doubt.

"The Maker is very much alive," Niero said. He looked around at the others. "We are his people."

Some gasped, some scowled.

"No one in their right mind admits to following the Maker," the chief insisted. "If one of the warlords heard of it, they'd string you up!" He swore and spit, and then folded his arms. "That said, we might just do it ourselves and be done with you." This brought a laugh from those around him.

"The time for denial is past," Vidar said. "We are for him or against him. And this day, friend, I suggest you slide toward the for-him side. You know, since he seems to want to heal you."

"I am as healed as I need be," the chief said with a scowl, patting his broad chest encased in an old leather tunic.

"You are fine leader," Niero said. "A proud man. I understand that. What is your name?"

"Sesille," said the man, grudgingly.

"Sesille," Niero repeated. "The Maker forces no gifts upon his people. He only offers them freely. It is our choice whether we accept them or not. If someone came to you, freely offering a new truck to you, would you turn it down?"

The chief folded his arms again. "It depends on what that man wanted in exchange for the truck."

"What if all that man giving you the truck wanted was understanding? Kinship? As well as thanks?"

"Then I'd say that man has too many silver coins in his coffers."

The other Drifters laughed at this along with their chief.

Niero, Tressa, and Chaza'el stood their ground, waiting him out. Kapriel edged forward then, too, joining us.

Sesille's broad smile faded and his opaque, unseeing eyes swept over us. I could almost feel him trying to sort out the way to go — whether to trust this impossible promise of sight or to send us away. Finally, he gave us a shrug. "Bah!" he cried, smiling around at his people. "What will it hurt to let them try healing this old man, other than my pride when they fail?"

Tressa let everyone laugh at this, then she reached out to touch him. "Sesille, I will say my healing prayer whether you believe in it or not. But the Maker shall not heal you unless you believe in his power."

His face was utterly still for a moment. "It has been a very long time since I considered the Maker capable of anything."

"Is he not the creator of all that lives and breathes?" Kapriel asked.

"I don't know." Sesille lifted his chin. "There are a few brats around this camp that were probably my doing," he added, giving Kapriel a gap-toothed grin.

"But it was the Maker who gave you the capability to beget those children," Kapriel returned, without missing a beat. "It is the Maker who commands the wind." He raised a hand, and a breeze swept through the trees around us, sending capes swinging and hats off heads. "It is the Maker who brings the rain." He lifted both hands now. Above us, the scant clouds began to gather and darken. A woman cried out, fully weeping in terror. Everyone else stood stock still, staring upward. The cloud bank billowed, swirled, grew darker, and then with a wave from Kapriel, rain fell gently down upon us.

People gasped and cried out. Some fell to their knees.

Sesille lifted a hand to his cheek, wiped the rain from it, and then rubbed his fingers back and forth, mouth agape in wonder. "Who are you?" he asked, his brows now crooked with a combination of fear and hope.

"We are people of the Way," Kapriel said. "The prophesied Remnants and our knights, as well as others who know the truth," he looked around at the Aravanders, at Azarel, Asher, and Niero. "We were hoping that you and yours will be the next to know it."

Sesille nodded slowly and sank to his knees, his face lighter and softer with the wonder that settled in. "The prophesy. I didn't believe it," he said, his nod turning to a shake of his head. "I thought it a word for the old ones. Not for us."

"It is for all," Tressa said. "Old and new. The Maker invites us all. But right now, he wishes for you to be healed. Do you believe?"

It was raining hard now, the water carving rivulets through the sandy soil.

Sesille turned his face up to her. "I believe," he said solemnly.

She knelt before him, bending to pick up two handfuls of the mud beside them. "Sesille of the Desert," she said, "long have you wandered. But today, you take your first steps along the Way. The Maker has seen you and chosen you. Today, he gives you eyes to see too."

The rest of us fell into silent or whispered utterances of prayer as she wiped mud across Sesille's closed eyes. I'd seen her heal a room full of patients stricken with the Cancer. I'd seen her straighten the goatherd's crippled foot. I'd seen her seal Killian's would. But it was as if I'd forgotten it all as I felt the Maker draw closer, the hairs on the back of my neck and arms lifting in anticipation.

Gently, Tressa lifted Sesille's face to the pounding rain, praying as it washed away the mud bit by bit. We all stood there, spellbound, ignoring the fact that our clothes were becoming drenched. When the last of the mud disappeared from Sesille's face, Kapriel lifted his palms and the torrent of rain slowed to a drizzle, then completely stopped. Still, Tressa prayed. Kapriel made a gesture and the clouds above us divided.

We all held our breath as Tressa released the Drifter's leader.

His head bowed and he blinked several times.

Then Sesille laughed, coughed, sputtered … his hands turning slowly before his face.

"I can see," he said slowly. "I can see!" he shouted. He reached for Tressa as he rose, lifting her in his arms. Killian had moved to intercede, but Niero stopped him, gesturing toward the Drifter chieftain as he turned her in a joyous circle, celebrating, not intending her any sort of harm. "Praise the Maker!" Sesille shouted. "I can see! I can see!"

"Praise the Maker!" cried the others around us. "Praise the Maker! The Remnants have come!"

CHAPTER 21

ANDRIANA

When I'd calmed down later and tried the door, I found it unlocked, and the guards that had been there were gone. Keallach was trusting me, at least to stay within the confines he'd dictated in the palace. But if I could get to other rooms, other doors, other stairwells, might I not find a way out of the palace itself? It would be wise to seize the opportunity, in case things with Keallach took a bad turn. Today — well, today had scared me. Somehow, he was drawing me in as much as I sought to draw him away. And he wasn't consistent. One moment my brother, yearning to connect, the next moment entirely the emperor, irritated that I might not do everything he demanded.

I exited my room and quietly shut the door. No guards hovered in doorways nearby and no one appeared. I peered down the hall and gaped upward. Three crystal chandeliers had glowing bulbs on their many stems, and distantly I recalled the word — electricity. The light reflected on the shiny, dark marble floor and papered walls, and I marveled at it. What would it be like to have light anytime you wished to have it? In the bedrooms — at least mine — there were only gas lamps and candles, but in the public spaces, the palace appeared to be fully wired.

To my left, at the end of the hall, was a doorway that I supposed would lead to a servants' staircase. To my right, in the distance, I could hear voices rising and falling. An argument? I was torn between my desire to find out who was there and what they were talking about and my need to figure out an escape route. I chose the stairwell. There'd be time enough for intrigue; there might not be ample time to figure a way out.

Sucking in my breath, I entered the stairwell and curved down it, rushing past the second floor and down to the first, assuming that'd be the best place to find an exit. My heart leaped with hope until I rounded the final curve and saw two guards in gray uniforms, who each quickly rose when they saw me.

"Good evening, miss," said one, bending his head in a slight bow. "Is there something you need help with?"

"No, no, I, uh … I seem to have become lost." I noted the barricaded door behind them. *My way out …*

The two shared a knowing look and then glanced to me. "The captain said you're not to go past the second floor. Anywhere on the second or third is all right, but not down here. So if you want, you can go up one floor. That's where you'll find a library and sitting room. Or go back up to the third, and you'll be on your floor again."

"Oh, right, right," I said, feigning relief, knowing they

knew I lied. I turned and scurried up the stairs with the irrational fear that they might decide to chase me back up to my quarters.

I made myself pause at the second floor door. If I couldn't flee, might I discover something else that would prove useful in time? Carefully, I opened the door. It was with some relief that I saw that this hall too was empty, but I also could hear ghostly voices, ringing in echoes and then fading. Whoever they were, they were closer on this floor. With a glance downstairs to make sure the guards did not follow me up to see where I went, I slipped through the door and padded down the hall, the marble beneath my feet cold and smooth, the voices growing steadily louder. Two guards stood at the far end of the hall, near the main staircase, but their backs were to me. They nudged each other and laughed, chatting, clearly absorbed in their own conversation.

As I stole closer to the room with the arguing men, I knew that Sethos had to be one of them.

So he was back. I swallowed hard, forcing myself to take another step forward, hovering near the shut door, and not flee.

"You hurt her, Sethos," Keallach was saying, his voice carrying easily across the marble floor and beneath the crack at the bottom of the door. I crouched, in order to hear better. "Left her for days in that room, her wounds unattended! Had not Max discovered her —"

"She would have been fine. I merely meant to show her that she could not behave like a rebel in your court. If you insist on her presence, I must insist on respectful behavior."

"And what could she have possibly done that would warrant such a response?"

Sethos paused. "She *bit* me, your highness. And the girl has been as thoroughly trained as you yourself were. She's hardly a Pacifican flower, incapable of self-defense."

"And you are more than capable of taking her into custody if she proves to be ... unwieldy. I do not want you to harm her again. Do you understand me?"

Sethos said nothing for a long moment, then begrudgingly, "Agreed, Highness, unless she gives me no other choice. That is all I can promise."

Keallach paused, and I could feel the tension between them from where I stood. *Good*, I thought. *Perhaps I can divide them*. It had to be done if I was to have any true chance to turn Keallach back toward the Way.

Their voices dropped to an undertone and I leaned against the door, in order to hear better. "Does your agitation not stem from a deeper draw toward Andriana, perhaps?" Sethos asked.

I froze, my back to the wall, my pulse thundering in my ears.

"You have become far too familiar, Sethos," Keallach said icily.

The other man was silent a moment. "I do not understand why you cannot find another way to resolve your past ... issues. The Ailith bond has been broken. You cannot reestablish it."

"I don't believe that. I feel it still. So does Andriana. I know she does! The Six concur with me — if there is a way for me to reunite with my kin, it will be all the easier to build the empire. Together, we would embody the foretold. Who would come against us?"

My mind raced. So he was thinking of joining us? Or using us?

"And yet the Ailith think of me as a mortal enemy," Sethos said carefully. "How do you see that resolved?"

Keallach paused. "I'll help them understand in time. We

did what we had to. The most important thing is moving forward from here."

"And you believe," Sethos said slowly, "that Kapriel will come to understand that too?"

Keallach's voice was tight. "I don't care for your mocking."

"I don't intend to mock, Highness, only to be ... pragmatic. This is not something we can simply hope for. Every step must be strategic. Planned."

"Yes, well, not everything in life can be planned, Sethos. Listen, it is enough for tonight. We can resume this conversation in the morning."

My heart stopped as I realized they were ending their conversation, and I turned to tiptoe away, freezing when I heard Keallach's boot heels clicking across the marble, coming closer, and the door swinging open with a complaining creak. When he didn't pause or come after me, I dared to look over my shoulder and took a breath. Keallach was walking away, apparently having missed me there, in the opposite direction, toward the central staircase. How could he not have sensed me? His head was bent, as if in deep thought. Maybe he was too distracted—

But what came next was worse. Sethos stepped forward, looking after his master. Then his nostrils flared and he slowly turned toward me. He glanced back, obviously waiting for Keallach to clear the hallway, the guards following their monarch, then strode toward me. I tried to flee but he wrapped an arm around me and roughly pulled me back against him, covering my mouth with one hand. "Did you hear quite enough?" he whispered in my ear. He practically picked me up and rushed me to the servants' stairwell at the far end of the hall, the one I'd used. I struggled against him, but he was too strong, his arms like a vise. Once we were through the door, he released me and allowed me to face him.

"Listen to me well, now, Remnant. If you wish to survive, you will not plant any more seeds of discontent in Keallach's mind. And if you won't do it for your own survival, do it for those you love."

I stilled, immediately thinking of Ronan. Had they … captured him? It wasn't possible. He would've died fighting them.

But then my breath caught. He would've done anything to try and free me, if he'd seen me taken …

Sethos laughed under his breath. "Ahh, yes. I know the ways of your heart, Andriana. Your strengths as well as your weaknesses. And if you don't think I'll lean hard on those weaknesses, if necessary, then you know nothing. Act against me, and your loved ones shall suffer, and in turn, you shall know the most exquisite suffering of your life."

Loved ones. Who else was he talking about, besides Ronan? Had they captured others?

"You lie," I said desperately. "You hold no one that I love."

"Are you certain?" he asked drily, lifting one brow. He grabbed hold of my arm again and dragged me up the stairs down the next hall to my room, opening the door with such force that it slammed against the wall. He tossed me inside and I went to my knees. I lifted my face, furious, longing to lash out at him again.

"Stay here, in your room," he said, pointing at me and then around the room. "No matter what the emperor has told you, these walls are the full extent of your freedom in the palace. If I find you outside this room again, those you love will suffer the consequences."

"You lie! I don't believe you captured anyone but me."

"Is that a risk you care to take?" he asked. "Cross me, and I'll take out my wrath on those within the dungeon's keep."

I switched tactics. "Keallach will wonder what is wrong with me, if I stay here. And I'll have to tell him you have limited my freedom."

That seemed to make Sethos take pause.

"You like to read, yes?" He didn't wait for my answer. "There is a vast library at the very start of the second floor, directly beside the staircase we just came up. You may spend your days there, reading novels or whatnot. Or here, in your room. Nowhere else unless you are in my company or the emperor's." His eyes narrowed. "Have I been clear?"

But he didn't wait for a response. He took a deep breath, straightened his tunic, and then calmly walked to the door. He gave me a tiny smile, as if nothing had happened at all, and bowed his head slightly. "Good night, Andriana. Sleep well."

With that, he left me to close the door. I waited until I could not hear his boots across the marble floors of the hallway, then I raced to the door, slammed it, and leaned my back against it, as if I could bodily keep him from ever entering again. Then I lifted my eyes to the high ceiling and muttered, "What now, Maker? What would you have me do?"

CHAPTER 22

ANDRIANA

I battled sleep for hours as I sat huddled on my bed, staring with burning eyes and heavy lids at the door, frightened that Sethos would return. Again and again I tried to sort out all I had heard that night, until in weary defeat, I slept.

I awakened with a start, my eyes on a fold of fabric inches from my face. I blinked slowly, then opened my eyes again. Remembering, as I stared at the elaborate stitches and ran my hand across the shiny, soft fabric that I was a prisoner in the palace of our enemy. I blinked slowly and rolled, looking up at the canopy above me, and rubbed my armband, like it was a talisman that might whisk me home, back to the Valley. Or to —

I frowned in confusion. My cuff was warm. *Warm.* My heart surged with hope. An Ailith. Ronan?

Sitting up quickly, my eyes darted to the far corners, deep in morning shadow, to the two chairs.

My heart pounded hard, stopped for a second, then pounded again.

"Oh, Keallach," I said, pulling the blanket to me as if it were a shield. "What are you doing here?"

He had been rubbing his temple as if it ached. But when I sat up, he smiled. "Good morning," he said softly, almost wistful. "Forgive me for intruding. I just ... missed you. I didn't like how we left things yesterday. That wasn't how I want it to be between us."

I stared at him, trying to sort out what was going on. He was feeling the Ailith pull for certain. "There is a lot between us, Keallach. Good and bad."

"Yes. Right," he said quickly, clearly not wanting to go into it again. "You didn't undress last night for bed," he said, rising and going to the wall to pull a long, fabric band that I had learned summoned a servant from somewhere below. "You're still in your gown."

I glanced downward, thinking the gown was hardly more than nightclothes, anyway. But I had more important matters to address before anyone else entered the room. "Listen, Keallach. I had an ... encounter with Sethos last night. And with him having access to —"

"Sethos?" he frowned. "He was here? In your room?"

"Yes."

He shook his head in anger. "I'm sorry. I thought I made it clear to him that he wasn't to ... cause you distress."

"Thank you. But, Sethos said ... He said that he holds people I love in his dungeons. Who was he talking about?"

"I don't know," he said, shaking his head. I searched him,

but while he wore an honest expression, he was blocking me to some extent. All I could feel was anger. Toward Sethos still?

"Who is in your dungeon then?"

"No one but enemies or traitors to Pacifica," he said, irritation now wafting off of him. "But this might surprise you, Andriana — I don't walk the dungeon halls every day like some evil lord. I have plenty of important things, *good things*, to do in order to see to the affairs of my people. The business of the empire keeps me busy from morning until night."

"So, you do not hold Ronan — or any of the Ailith — in your dungeon?"

"No! Search me! See if I lie!"

I did again, then. I thought he was telling me the truth. Sethos must have just been lying to me, trying to get under my skin. I summoned my courage, threw aside the covers, and strode over to the dressing table as if it was completely normal to have him in my room. He turned toward the window, as if giving me privacy, even though I was fully clothed.

"I'd like my clothes back," I said, rubbing my arms against the morning chill. "My Aravander tunic? A long-sleeved shirt?"

He went over to a trunk and opened it, peered inward and then reached for a soft, silky cape. He shook it out and brought it over to me, silently waiting for me to stand, then gently wrapped it around my shoulders, tying it at my throat. I stilled, allowing this intimacy, trying to reach out to him. Today was a new day. Perhaps this was the day I'd really reach him. But he turned back to the window, as if sensing my pull.

I sat back down, picked up a brush and yanked it through my hair with rough strokes. "You dress your women as if they were dolls. As if they had nothing to do but lounge about, eating and drinking and gossiping the day away."

When he said nothing, I dared to catch his reflection in my side mirror. He was edging the curtain aside, looking out. "It's a sign of stature, to have one's wife look as if she has no further demands on her life."

"How utterly depressing is that? No wonder they all look half dead."

He turned toward me, and I felt his agitation.

"I'm sorry," I said quickly, forcing myself to swivel on the chair and face him. "That was unkind."

But his face softened. "No," he said, shaking his head slowly. "You are right. Here we are, the wealthiest and strongest in the land, and yet we are somehow dying." His voice faded and he turned back to the window. "That is why I need you, Andriana. We need you." His keen eyes returned to meet mine and he took a few steps toward me. "You are like life itself to me. I can't sleep. Every time I close my eyes, all I see is you. This pull . . ." His hand went to his chest and he rubbed it, as if feeling pain there.

He was open to me again, any trace of anger from last night gone. Full of such need and hope. And . . . love?

I tried to gather enough saliva to swallow and failed. Surely I was misreading him. "You . . . Keallach, you are sensing the Ailith pull between us and mistaking it for something more. You feel it as life because you have been separate from the body you were meant to be a part of for so long. It's like you were a severed, dead limb and now you've been reattached, in a way. At least to me. Allowing blood to flow."

"Yes," he said, nodding, and crossed the distance between us.

I froze. His words from the night before hadn't been forgotten. His plan to join the Remnants, possibly use us, for the empire's gain. And yet he was my brother too. I found it as impossible to resist our connection as I would Vidar or Tressa or Chaza'el or …

He knelt in front of my knees and then slowly, almost reverently, laid his head atop them, not touching me anywhere else. We were silent and still together for a long moment. Then he said, "I know you wish to leave here. But I beg you not to separate me from this flow of life, Andriana. I couldn't stand it. Not again."

Now my mouth was truly dry. My heart raced. Was this an opportunity or a trap? I felt the ache within him — the loneliness, the pain, the regret — and I longed to assuage it. He was so humble, in this moment. So full of need. Tentatively, I sighed and reached out and laid a hand on his head, watching the morning light dance on the dark, clean strands. "There is much for us to sort out," I began. "If we are truly to be friends."

Hope sparked within him, and he lifted his head, gently grabbing hold of my hand in both of his. "Might we?" he asked softly. "Be friends? Or even more?" He lifted my wrist to his mouth, and eyes never leaving mine, gently kissed the inside of it.

I seemed to feel the power of his lips on that bit of skin all the way to the ends of my hair. Dismayed, I pulled my hand from his and cradled it to my chest as if he had hurt me.

He smiled softly as if he understood, and that angered me, confused me. Alarmed me. He rose and moved to the table.

I turned to watch the footman who'd silently arrived, setting down a tray, moving about my room, making the bed, removing a goblet from the side table. He acted as if it was nothing to find his emperor in my private quarters, and I wondered how many times he'd found him with a woman.

I shook my head, willing myself to concentrate. What did

it matter to me how many women Keallach had bedded? I was losing my focus, losing sight of my mission. *Maker* ...

Keallach paused in his pouring from the silver pot and studied me. It was as if he had heard my silent prayer. His jaw clenched. But then he turned back to his task and lifted a cup to me. "Come."

Reluctantly, I sat next to him in the second chair. He was close enough to reach out and touch me again, but didn't.

"Why am I here, Keallach?" I asked, accepting the delicate cup and saucer. "Really?"

"I've told you. I wanted you to myself for a bit," he said, leaning back in his chair and sipping from it.

"And when I wish to leave?"

"Let's address that when the moment comes, shall we?" he said easily, as if he meant it. But I felt a flash of frustration in him. "Surely you realize what a gift this is to me. To have you here. In the midst of this crazy battle that is simmering between our people. Don't you see? We — the two of us — form the bridge." He set his cup and saucer on the narrow table between us. "Andriana, can you not help me? Together, can we not find a way to work together to broker peace?"

I took a sip, considering him. "I was born to save our people, just as you were. But Keallach, saving them cannot be done through enslaving them."

He frowned. "Are we back to this?" he asked, agitated. "I wish for no such thing."

"Regardless of what you *wish*, that is what is happening. Pacifica leaches off the Union's resources, but what does she give back? You sit here behind your wall, enjoying riches far beyond anything we could've ever imagined, growing up." I waved about the room and shook my head, then lifted my cup.

"We sipped from earthenware. Pine needle tea. And you serve me what?"

He lifted one shoulder. "Tea from across the Great Sea."

My mind went to the ships and busy port, my heart quickening. There it was again, a reference to other countries. "Have you been there? Across the Great Sea?"

"No, but my men have." He reached forward for a biscuit and, with silver tongs, placed one on the edge of my saucer, then one on his own.

"Are there many survivors there?"

"About as many as here," he said. He bit into his biscuit, chewed, then reached forward for a spoonful of an orange-colored jam. "It is part of what concerns us."

"That there are survivors?"

"That there are potential enemies. We must bind our empire together so that we are a force that compels our neighbors across the sea to never consider trying invasion again. Trading is all well and good, but we should keep to our own lands as the Maker created us to do."

I considered him. "But the Si — Sethos," I said, narrowly avoiding the tension that came up when I mentioned the Six. "Will he not want more, if he was to see you establish your empire of peace? Would he not eventually look beyond our shores to others?"

Keallach's brows knit in confusion. "No. Why would he do that?"

I thought of the combined need I'd discerned while first with the Six — no matter what they wanted me to believe of them now — of the insatiable lust the group had for everything in their path, whether people, pleasure, or possessions. But I chose to stick with Sethos, my declared enemy, to test

Keallach's thoughts. "Because Sethos is ruled by the dark one, Keallach. Because he has a hunger in his heart that will never leave him satisfied. All he'll want is more. And the longer you remain in his company, the more you will be like him."

His face became like stone, and he set down his cup and half-eaten biscuit with care that belied his tension. "I cannot allow you to continue to speak against him."

"It is simply the truth."

He didn't blink. "I know Sethos has his faults, but you speak against my oldest, most faithful friend."

"But you were knit together in your mother's womb as *my* brother. An Ailith. Our kin, not his. Does that not make me an even deeper friend?"

We stared as each other in silence.

Then he smiled, as if cajoling me. "Can we *all* not be family, of a sort, once again? Is reconciliation not the Maker's way?"

I felt the dissonance of his words deep in my heart, but struggled to find reason to argue. "The Maker does love reconciliation. It's the reason why there is a way back for you, Keallach, no matter what you have done. But he also wants us to recognize it — own up to it — when we wander from the Way. And there is not an ounce of contrition within Sethos that this empath can discern. He endeavors to lead you far from the Maker."

Keallach stood up quickly, his rage gathering. "I didn't leave the Maker. He left me." He leaned toward me as he said it, and I forced myself not to shrink from him.

"That is untrue. If we feel far from him, it is because we have not sought him out as we should."

Keallach let out a scoffing sound and strode toward the window. After a long moment he said with a quaking voice,

"I've gone as far as to build a palace in Wadi Qelt in order to seek him out."

"And have you found him there?"

He paused a long moment. Then whispered no.

"It's because you do so," I said gently, "out of your own ambition. You seek him because you long for power, for dominion, rather than to bow to his own. You want to control the One who cannot ever be controlled."

"That isn't true," he said, glancing at me over his shoulder.

"Isn't it?"

He held my gaze for a long time, then slowly turned back toward the window. My trainer's words ran through my mind, reminding me of the truth I had to share with Keallach.

I rose and went to stand at the window beside him, daring to take his hand in my own. "When we rely on our own gifting, our own abilities, it diminishes the Maker's power in our lives. We can only get so far. But if we truly bow down to him first, if we allow his power to flow through us, allow *him* to use *us* rather than the other way around ... that is what we were born for. All of us, whether Ailith or not. That is why we were born, Keallach." I turned slightly toward him. "Not to wield our gifting as gods. But to yield to the One who holds us all in the palm of his hand. To reorient this dark world on a dark path back toward —"

"Enough," he said curtly, dropping my hand and lifting his to me in warning, but he wasn't furious any longer, just confused. "No more." He took a breath, then another. "For now. You've given me much to think about."

We stood there together in silence for a long while. Then, "Andriana, will you tell me of the other Remnants and their gifting? Besides Kapriel."

I paused. To speak of them felt vaguely dangerous, treasonous. And yet he had to be so curious about our brothers and sisters too. Conflicted, I remained silent.

He ran a hand down the windowsill and looked outward again. "We've heard stories ... of a female healer. A brother who prophesies. They perform miracles, and then they move. Even now, their following grows out there in the Union."

It was happening, just as the elders said. Finally, the Remnants weren't on the run. They were claiming territory.

Keallach took a deep breath and let it out slowly. "In this, there are the seeds of anarchy. Total social unrest."

"I don't know if you've wandered farther than Castle Vega or Georgii Post, but out in the Desert, I can tell you, it's anarchy anyway."

"I want to bring the Drifters to account. I want to bring every town, every kingdom to account. I want to bring them together. But the Remnants ... Well, if they continue on this path, they may just divide everyone further."

"That isn't what you fear," I said, with a shake of my head. "You fear the Remnants will unify the Union. Make them stronger, against Pacifica."

"You believe the Remnants can bring together the Drifters? The Zanzibians? They don't have the strength."

"No. But they have the power."

We were both silent for a moment.

A buzzing sound startled us both. He reached for a small device at his belt, looked at it, and then at me. "I must leave you," he said, a touch of regret in his voice and in his eyes. "We must not always devolve to such serious matters, Andriana. There's a gathering tonight. I'd like you to come with me."

"What sort of gathering?"

He was backing away, a teasing glint in his eyes. "A dancing sort of gathering. I'll send a gown for you. I'd like you to wear it."

I shook my head. "No. That would be entirely improper. I'm hardly in a dancing mood."

"You might be surprised, once you're there. I think you'll find me a good dance partner."

I shook my head again. "I can't, Keallach."

He rested his hand on the knob of my door, his jaw clenching. "I must insist."

We were again back to Keallach as a petulant boy, demanding his own way. I longed to deny him, to show him that a man could take a refusal and move beyond it. That there were more important bonds between friends. But I understood that this would somehow destroy every rickety bridge I'd forged with him. "I don't even know your Pacifican dances," I tried. "I'll embarrass you."

"Nonsense. It will be great fun, teaching you. And you can teach my people a dance of the Valley!" A smile broke across his face. "It will be just the sort of thing we need to begin to do. A small step toward diplomacy."

My stomach clenched. It felt so wrong. To dress up, dance, when my Ailith kin were probably bedding down on dirt floors.

Keallach said simply, "Be ready at sundown," the decision clearly already made. And then he left, quietly shutting the door behind him.

I returned to staring out the window, thinking of Ronan, wishing he was here to help me sort out what was going on. He would hold me, reassure me, help me come up with a plan.

I wondered over all I had shared with Keallach earlier, and

realized then that my trainer's words hadn't been only for him. They were for me too. I'd been relying on my own gifting, my own power, for too long now. I needed to return to the Maker. To concentrate on him, especially in this palace, surrounded by so many of his enemies. As much as I felt I was making inroads with Keallach, I couldn't help worrying that he was making as much progress with me.

And with that thought, I moved to my knees and bowed in prayer.

CHAPTER 23

RONAN

Healing the Drifter leader resulted in motorized transport for the following week. We were led from camp to camp, where Chaza'el continued to share visions of the future — which came to pass, time after time — Kapriel commanded wind and rain, and Tressa healed. Some refused to follow us after that, terrified by what they saw; many more pledged their lives. The various groups of Drifters became one, in a fashion. And they were a rowdy, chaotic group, far from the kind and gentle Communities we'd come across to date. But it didn't bother Niero.

"Just as the Maker planned," he said with a grin, as we sat upon a rock watching the tenth sunset since I'd last seen Andriana. Below us was a sprawling camp, full of hundreds of men, women, and children, the Drifters' vehicles forming a wall of sorts on the outskirts.

"A beautiful sight, are they not?" Asher asked, climbing up

beside us. Behind him were Azarel and Chaza'el. I assumed Kapriel, Tressa, and Killian were all down below, moving among the people, continuing to heal.

"Beautiful?" scoffed Azarel, accepting Niero's hand to help her up onto the last boulder. "They're the ugliest, dirtiest bunch I've ever seen."

"Beautiful," Asher confirmed, eyes shining as he looked over the entire camp, then to Niero, who crossed his arms and nodded in similar satisfaction.

"The Maker begins with the humble, the outcasts," Niero said.

"I don't see humble outcasts," Azarel said, shifting her bow strap higher on her shoulder. "I see an army."

Her word startled us all. We'd sensed the growing power, felt purely from our swelling numbers. But an army? She was right. Between the remaining Aravanders — who continued to pour out into the desert after us — and the Drifters, with all their weapons and vehicles and their declaration to support and follow us wherever we led ... If we could gather twice as many as we had here, we might be able to take on a contingent from Pacifica. *Maybe ...*

A woman screamed below. Men were shoving one another. I turned to make my way down, but Niero stopped me. "Wait. Watch," he said, nodding back at the group.

Kapriel was pushing two men apart, speaking to them in sharp tones, but we couldn't make out what he was saying. Killian and Tressa edged through the crowd, into their circle, then Vidar and Bellona, and I was able to breathe a little easier. They'd protect the prince.

But it turned out the prince didn't need protecting. Each of the Ailith took a knee as Kapriel lifted his arms, and instinctively, we did too. The others did as well — at least those

Drifters and Aravanders who had already committed to following us. Kapriel was looking intently at the sky, his fingers waving in such an elegant manner that I thought it belonged in a dance.

The clouds above us began to wave, as clearly as we'd seen waves wash ashore while in Pacifica. Except this action felt far greater, covering the entire sky and growing in intensity. My cuff warmed; my breath caught. People below cried out in fear; anyone still on their feet sank to the ground. Some cowered as if they feared that Kapriel would call down lightning.

But his face was radiant, a smile lighting up his entire face. Our armbands grew hot and Vidar raised his arms, praising the Maker so loudly we could easily make out his words from high above. Kapriel was still speaking — sharing words of the hope and glory available to all, I was certain — and I felt the tears slip down my cheeks as I smiled, smiled at the blessing it was to serve with these fine people. And yet the joy was fleeting; I also ached, deep within, that Andriana was absent. Not observing, experiencing this unfolding with us. It was happening, and she was missing it.

Niero put a hand on my shoulder, and I saw that there were tears on his black cheeks as well. "Trust in the Maker, brother. And his timing. As well as your Remnant."

I nodded, but inside I thought, *How will we ever get her back?*

ANDRIANA

The maids bustled in as a veiled sun sank over the ocean. The skies were heavy with clouds, a marine layer that seemed to creep inland every afternoon, blocking any view of what I knew had to be a beautiful sunset beyond it. It was much like the Sheolites, I mused. In the last couple of days, I'd realized that I was growing accustomed to regular meals, servants at my beck and call, quiet, stillness. But it was a dulling sensation I had to fight against, a cajoling that might steal away the fight. I could not succumb to it. I had to escape as soon as I could, and hopefully instill enough connection with Keallach that he would come too, leaving our enemies behind.

I turned from the window as servants unfolded a wide blanket to show me the gown beneath. I sucked in my breath. It was the most beautiful thing I'd ever seen, far more beautiful than anything I'd ever thought to wear. It was a creamy ivory with a wide neck and narrow sleeves, a tight bodice covered in tiny pearls, and a voluminous skirt with folds of heavy silk fabric. I looked to the nearest maid. "I cannot wear that," I said.

"Why not?" she asked in confusion. "It's beyond lovely."

"Well, yes. But it looks like ... Well, it looks like a bridal gown."

Her brown eyebrows lifted and then she laughed. "But it's not," she said, waving toward it and then placing her hand on her hip, as if to dare me to protest further. "All the ladies will be in hues of white."

"If this is not a betrothal gown," I said, frowning, "what on earth do you Pacificans wear for a wedding?"

The maids laughed at that, together, as if I was a funny actor in a play. "Everyone knows we wear blue for the betrothal ceremony," scoffed one. "As everyone shall, once the empire is unified." She moved behind me, unhooking the neck of my gown, but I pulled away.

"No, I, uh ... I cannot wear that one, still," I said, staring at it and then back to them. The trio looked back at me, baffled. "Don't you have another I could borrow? Something more plain, perhaps."

The older one frowned and took charge. "No, m'lady. This is the one his highness has chosen for you, and the one you shall wear."

"I can't," I said, shaking my head, feeling this all was more wrong than ever. Even if I'd given in to attending the dance.

"I'm afraid you think you have a choice," said the older maid, sorrow hooding her eyes. "If you do not allow us to dress you, we will force you into it."

"And if I fight you off?"

A pall of silence covered us. "Then the captain and his men shall come and do so. And you don't want that."

Sethos? Sethos and his men would force me into a dress? The thought of it made me want to laugh and cry at once.

"Come," said a younger girl, taking my hand. "Why not enjoy it, m'lady? When else will you have such an opportunity? To wear a gown this fine? To dance with a man as handsome as our emperor," she added in a whisper, then turned to giggle with the other girl.

But my eyes were still on the older woman. She stared stonily back at me. I had no choice in this, just as I had no true freedom in where I went here in Pacifica. I could do this easily, or I could do this in a far more difficult manner. But one way or another, they would have their way.

I allowed them to peel the Pacifican day gown from me, leaving only the band I wore wrapped around my breasts. When a maid reached to unpin it, I grabbed her hand. "No, leave it."

"But it's unsuitable," she protested. "It will show under the gown."

"We have another undergarment," said the older maid,

lifting an elaborate contraption that looked more like an old corset I'd once seen in Tonna's trading post tent. But I assented. They wrapped the device around me and fastened it at my lower back. The ribbing in it forced me to stand straighter. But when they slipped the gown over my shoulders, I could see why the banding I routinely wore wouldn't work. The shoulders of the gown dropped into a deep V behind me. I could feel the cool wash of air across the skin between my shoulders and shivered. I shook my head. "Please," I said to the older maid, the leader, "isn't there another I could wear?"

"No," she said, turning me abruptly and tending to a row of buttons at my lower back. "This is the one the emperor chose," she said again.

I closed my eyes and bit my lip, concentrating on the one fact that assuaged my horror over all of this: attending this party just might give me the chance to win over Keallach, once and for all. It was a delicate internal dance of its own — this process of wrenching open the iron jaws of the dark and pulling my brother toward the light using every method I could think of. Even a dress . . .

Once it was on, the maids led me to a stool and lifted the skirt over the edge, so as not to rumple it, I assumed. Then the two younger women set to brushing out my hair, each on one side. When they were finished, they took to taking sections and winding it up and then pinning it to my scalp. In some sections, they wound either strands of tiny pearls or silver thread into it. I winced and complained as they pulled and rammed pins into my scalp while another woman brushed and swiped makeup on me, but at last they were done.

They stood back, and I could feel their collective glee before I even glanced in the mirror. My mouth fell open. I barely looked like myself. They'd put ivory powder across my cheeks and nose and heavy liner and shadow around my eyes in the ghoulish manner popular among the women here. My lips glistened with a raisin-colored gloss. My hair was in an elaborate style that made it look like a crown of sorts. I shook my head. "No, no," I whispered, reaching up to lick my fingers and begin scrubbing the awful powder from my cheeks.

The women all grabbed at my hands and shrieked in horror. "You must not!" cried the older one, chastising me like she was my nursemaid.

"I look dead!" I cried back.

"You do not. You are the loveliest thing I've ever seen," said the woman, crossing her arms across her chest. The two others stood on either side of her, wringing their hands.

I knew I'd offended them. They'd made me up like the rest of the Pacifican women. I swallowed hard. Perhaps it was best if I blended in. Maybe I'd be less of a spectacle. "The hair," I began, seeking something to soften my verbal blows. "Never, in my whole life, have I seen anything so pretty."

Smiles broke out on their faces and there seemed to be a collective sigh of relief. They nodded eagerly, so intent was their desire to please me.

"I just … I just don't feel right with all of this on my face," I said. "Please, won't you permit me to soften it a bit?"

The matron bit her lip and then nodded once. "Just a little. We want the emperor to be pleased."

I took hold of a cloth and wiped some of the powder from my cheeks, nose and chin, allowing some of my olive skin to come through again. Then I licked the tip of the cloth and wiped away the awful shadow beneath my eyes, taking a breath of satisfaction when I saw the result. The older woman shook her head, as if disappointed, but said nothing. What was it with this place that made her women want to look dead, of all things? Weren't they hungering for life? The porcelain pallor, the deep shadows ringing the eyes. It was horrifying, really, and the first thing I'd noticed about the women when I spotted them along the streets in Castle Vega.

There was a sharp knock on the door, and instinctively I rose and turned, my feet widening in fighting stance, my fists clenching. But it was only Keallach, dressed in his own ivory finery. He wore a high-necked collared tunic, with buttons down the front and crisp shoulders and long sleeves. His breeches were a rich camel color, a soft leather that disappeared into boots that almost reached his knees. His hair was pulled back, clean and shiny, and I had to admit he looked handsome.

But his eyes were only on me. Never did they waver from my face. He strode over to me, all languid grace and power, and took my hand, bowed, and kissed it softly. He straightened, still holding my hand. "My, my, Andriana, you look stunning."

I felt the hint of a blush at my cheeks. I'd not often heard the word, especially in the context of how one might look. "Thank you," I said, feeling my blush climb as I cast about for an appropriate response. "So do you."

He smiled and leaned to whisper in my ear, "I love it when you blush. It reminds me that in many ways you are innocent. I've never met an innocent in all of Pacifica. It's so ... refreshing."

I knew I had not the first idea on how to respond to that, so when he turned and offered his arm, I quickly took it. I was eager to escape these quarters, to gain information about more of the palace. It would be an opportunity to learn more—knowledge that would likely prove of great value when it came time for me to escape.

Thoughts of escaping this place and rejoining my knight made me long for Ronan but also chafed at my heart. What would he think of me, dressed up like a bridal doll? He'd clearly be torn—drawn, as I was, by the sheer luxury of it all, as well as repulsed.

We entered the long, marble-floored hallway, and I felt the soft fabric of my slippers with pleasure. They were light and gave way as I walked, not rubbing at all. If there was dancing, and Keallach succeeded in getting me out on the floor, at least they would not be a detriment.

"This way," Keallach said, veering to the right. I was counting doors, trying to keep my bearings as we turned left again, into a hallway so narrow that Keallach had to lead. But he kept hold of my hand behind him, and I felt the sense of protection that surged through him. Was he afraid for me and what was ahead?

"Do you always do that?" he said over his shoulder.

"What?"

"Try and read everyone in a room with you?"

"For the most part, yes. Do you not feel compelled to use your gift?"

"I dabble," he admitted, opening a door. We entered a large sitting parlor with gold-framed oil paintings from waist-high to the very ceiling. The tops of the walls had a heavy molding, and the walls themselves were covered in a rich fabric that appeared glued to them. On a table at the center, between a long couch and two high-backed chairs, was a vast platter full of fruit, many of which I'd never seen before. Two crystal glasses stood on one end with a green bottle between them.

Keallach moved immediately to it, unwrapping a wire and then using his thumb to edge out a stubborn cork. "We'll remain here, until it's time for our entrance," he said. "You may relax. We have a bit of time."

I turned to the paintings, moving from one to the next. Many looked like they'd been rescued from buildings before the War, from centuries before, even. "Who are all these people?" I asked, liking how a young boy in a red coat had his hand on the head of big, white dog beside him, and how the painter had made the child's dark eyes sparkle.

"They tell me they're all my ancestors," he said, coming close and handing me a goblet. I accepted it, and he clinked the edge of his lightly against mine. "To us," he said. I hesitated, and he immediately added, "Long-lost kin."

I gave him a small smile and took a sip. The liquid had an odd taste that seemed to wrinkle my tongue with its combination of tangy and sweet flavors, the hundreds of bubbles that tickled the roof of my mouth. I remembered well the Pacifican evening wine, as well as the liquor of the Aravanders, and decided to take precautions, lowering my goblet. There was no way that I'd be sidetracked or persuaded into something I didn't approve of tonight just because I was somehow impaired. There was enough against me already.

"You don't care for it?" Keallach asked, looking at the goblet in my idle hand. "Should I ring for something else?"

"No, no, it's fine," I said, moving on to the next painting. This was a vast canvas, as tall as I was, with a handsome couple in ivory clothing, which looked very much like what Keallach and I wore, and flanked by two identical boys just shy of their first decade. I studied their eyes and then looked to him. "It's you and Kapriel. With your parents."

He nodded, but his demeanor turned sober and sad. Once again, I felt the grief in him, the longing. I turned back to the painting and saw a light, black fabric that had been draped across the very top of the frame and hung down about an arm's length — an obvoius gesture toward mourning. Keallach was moving on, lifting his hand to the next, probably trying to distract me, but I stayed with his family's portrait. His mother had a soft, warm look — clearly the boys had inherited her coloring, with their dark hair and green-blue eyes. His father looked stern and vaguely unhappy. Had he known, even then, what might become of his children? The division, the horror of one turning on the other?

"Come away from that, Andriana," he said, and there was an edge of warning to his tone. "I do not wish to speak of them. Not this night."

"But some night," I said, following him. "You must speak of it, Keallach. Dig it out of the dirt. Expose it to the light. It's like a wound, festering inside — "

"I said I did not wish to speak of it!" he shouted, then winced and rubbed his forehead as if it ached.

I held my breath and forced myself not to take a step away. The rage was so sudden, so white-hot, so *surprising* that I reeled inwardly. Was it this that Sethos had capitalized on, nurtured, until it could be utilized for his own purposes?

"Do not press me, Andriana," he bit out. "I get enough of that from everyone else."

"Forgive me, Highness," I whispered flatly.

He clamped his lips shut and stared at me, knowing I didn't mean it — that I'd press him again at the first opportunity. For too long, this brother had been given sway, rather than toppled at his weak points and rebuilt like every other Ailith I knew. That had been our trainers' sole goal — destroying what was weak within us; strengthening all that was good. Keallach had been coddled and cultured by Sethos, intent on turning a Remnant into his own servant. But Keallach wasn't beyond retrieval. I knew it. There was hope in him, a longing so pure that I only needed to find the means to break him free from the gates of bondage so that he could fully embrace his calling. Kapriel would forgive him the horrors. I knew enough of him to know that. And if Kapriel could forgive him, who were the rest of us to hold past sins as the stubborn strands in the sticky web imprisoning him? I needed to free Keallach so that he could take his rightful place beside us. And if I could do that, I knew no one could stand against us. The collective power —

"This is my great-uncle," he said, pointing up to a portrait of a gray-haired man of perhaps seven decades. "He was a Community elder," he said, "and he loved me and Kapriel. We spent many afternoons playing at his house. He had a way of teaching us that didn't feel like teaching. Do you know what I mean?"

I thought of my father. That was as close as I could come. "I think I do."

He nodded, and I felt the contentment in him covering the rage from a moment ago like water on smoldering embers. "It is good to be understood, Andriana. Known." He took my hand and lifted it to his lips, kissing my knuckles softly. As gently as I could, I pulled away, but he didn't seem to mind.

We ambled over and ate from the mountain of food on the table. It could've fed twenty but it appeared to be just for us. I ate until the ribs in my corset protested, stuffing myself with cheese and soft rolls and most of all the fruits and vegetables. Keallach took great delight in naming those I'd never seen before. After a while I merely raised one or another and he'd respond, "Kiwi," or "Jicama," or "Artichoke." On and on it went.

"Is there nothing that doesn't grow in Pacifica?" I asked, sitting back, hands unladylike on my belly.

"Very little. Or that we cannot import."

"Why don't you trade out these things to the Union?" I asked.

"We find that the Trading Union doesn't have the taste for them. Your people seem to want oranges, maybe the occasional apple, but not much more. And then there's the difficulty of transporting and preserving them. Fresh produce doesn't last very long. Particularly in crossing the heat of the Expanse."

"Hmm," I said. "Seems to me that a people who have the technology you do could find some way. If you wanted to."

"Perhaps," he said lightly. "If we were one land, a united people, there'd be no reason not to try." He sat back and sipped from his goblet.

"What is this called," I said, lifting mine, still half full.

"Champagne," he said. "And you've not had much of yours."

"It's … strange." I stared at the drink dubiously, watching as streams of tiny bubbles lifted from the bottom as if bent on escaping. I'd only read about it once. "But I'm well aware of the aftereffects of your evening wine. If champagne produces similar results, I want none of it."

"It doesn't. It simply serves to loosen any tensions you feel." He reached forward and poured more in his goblet. "I find it helpful for softening the blow of events such as this evening."

"The ball?" I frowned. "You don't care for your own parties?"

"Frankly, the only thing I'm eagerly anticipating tonight is having you in my arms."

I ignored his flirtation. "So you'd rather be at Wadi Qelt."

"Indeed. But alas, the life of an emperor does not allow such hermit tendencies for long."

A knock sounded at the door and a servant appeared. "Highness, they're ready to announce you."

"Right," he said. "Thank you." He rose, straightened his tunic, and reached out a hand to help me rise.

I tensed, wondering what those on the other side of the wall would feel. I sensed their curiosity and their excitement, as well as a bit of dismay. Perhaps not all were eager to invite a Union girl into the inner empire. I tightened my grip on Keallach's arm subconsciously, and he smiled down at me as though pleased. I opened my mouth to speak to him, but then the hallway opened up into a vast ballroom, the most stunning room I'd ever been in. All the women were in gowns of white and cream and ivory, but I noted with chagrin that most were plainer than my own. The men were in versions of what Keallach wore.

"Ladies and gentlemen!" shouted the servant beside us to the silent crowd. "I present Emperor Keallach and his guest, Andriana of the Valley."

Keallach pulled away and lifted his hand to me, and I slipped my fingers onto his palm. Then we paraded forward, and the crowd parted and bowed or curtsied, leaving two chairs on the far end of the room, and three on either side, a step lower, to view. I gaped at the scene in horror. We were approaching a raised dais, and it was clear that we were to sit in them, side by side.

And as I walked past one group of young women and then another, it wasn't their whispering behind me that told me of their spite, it was their hearts. They undoubtedly saw me as competition, an interloper grabbing the most eligible bachelor in, well, anywhere. Even in most cities and villages of the Union, I knew that mothers would be pushing their daughters into Keallach's view. He represented riches beyond measure, power, protection, all wrapped up in a handsome package. Which made him dangerous on every level.

We finally reached the end of the long journey across the vast ballroom and I sank gratefully to the edge of the chair beside Keallach.

"You perch there as if ready to flee," he said under his breath, leaning slightly toward me. "They're not as bad as all that."

"Aren't they? There are women in this room who would like to eat me alive, I believe."

"Truly?" he said, cocking a brow. "How fascinating. I didn't think any of them had the gumption to have such feelings."

I thought about that as the Six were announced and strode down toward us, each with a woman on his arm who was later dispersed into a group near the dais. None of the Six were apparently allowed to keep their consort with them, which made me feel all the more awkward. But it was their combined distrust as their eyes slipped over me that made me more uncomfortable. The Six did not entirely agree with Keallach's decision to bring me into this inner circle; that much was clear. Even if they might support our union in theory, they looked upon me as an enemy at worst, a conquest at best. And I supposed I was. At least the enemy part. I would never ever succumb to Keallach's charms.

I suddenly found it difficult to breathe. I shouldn't have eaten so much. The bodice was too tight and the room too warm.

The musicians came to the end of their song and I studied them too. Never had I seen so many instruments in one place. At home there was the occasional fiddle or a guitar, but nothing as grand and varied as what the Pacificans had. I counted eighteen different instruments.

"Do you like the music?" Keallach asked, rising and bowing slightly to me, then offering his hand again.

"What are you doing?" I whispered, my eyes shifting left and right.

"We are to lead off the dancing," he said stiffly, "and you are behaving dishonorably, not taking my hand at once."

"But I do not know your dances, Keallach!" I returned. "I told you!"

"Ahh, but you shall know them," he said, a devilish smile quirking his lips upward. "Never have you had a dance partner who could move objects with his mind."

I laughed helplessly and put my hand in his, not knowing if I could believe him or not. But what did it really matter if I made a fool of myself here? They all knew I was from the Union, that I hadn't grown up with these dances. They might even expect me to trip or fall. Maybe if I did it would ease some of the frustration and fear I felt among them.

The people had moved to the edges of the room, leaving a wide expanse free that I assumed would be full of dancers in time. But for now, it was only me and Keallach, as he turned to me and firmly took hold of my waist. "Your other hand on my shoulder, please," he whispered, as the music began. "Keep your eyes on me, Andriana. Only on me. Trust me. The women say that to dance with the emperor is to float on air. See if they're right."

"You've used your gifting as a trick? A spell?" I asked.

He smiled, ignoring my agitation. "I've found it's softened many a woman's heart," he said roguishly. "See if you aren't the next."

I shook my head but we were moving, then, my feet somehow shifting in time with his, moving backward or forward as if I'd been practicing these steps since I was barely able to walk. But I sensed his power moving in me, through me, something I both wished to sever and hold on to at the same time. It was intense, his ability. Already. Even before the ceremony, the cuff.

"You've been holding back on me," I managed to say.

"I didn't want to alarm you," he returned.

I considered that. It *was* alarming, the power he wielded, even without the ceremonial armband. What might he be able to do afterward?

He smiled. "Don't battle against me, Ailith sister," he cooed, pulling me closer. "Work with me. Abide with me for a time, just a bit of time." I could feel his warm palm on the bare skin of my lower back and felt the heat rising in my cheeks again. But it was true; as I gave him sway, I was floating, sliding, and gliding across the floor with him. It was like we were one of the instruments, knowing the notes in advance, moving to them. Gradually, as the dance went on, I was aware of others joining in, swirling around us like clouds in the sky, building into a storm. But I kept my eyes only on Keallach. I smiled at him and he smiled back. Pleasure, glory surged through him. Was it my own emotion or his? It was impossible to tell. It was like we were one. One mind, one heart, one body.

Alarm screamed through me, then, and I pulled away.

Keallach faltered and reached for me, but I stepped away again.

Anger surged through him. Embarrassment. I knew I had to help him salvage how this appeared. And I didn't want what I'd felt between us — our bond — to disappear. "I'm feeling …

faint," I said, lifting a hand to my forehead. "Might we rest a minute?"

He put his hands behind his back and lifted his chin, listening to me, and his face softened. "Of course, of course," he said. Then he offered me his arm and we casually moved back to the dais as if people weren't staring at us as we went. "What's the matter?" he whispered, when we were at last clear of the bulk of them.

"Your gift," I said. "It's a bit … overwhelming."

"That is is," he said, waggling a devilish brow in my direction.

CHAPTER 24

ANDRIANA

We sat down together and Keallach waved forward a servant who poured us tall, crystalline glasses of cold water. I drank greedily, aware that I hadn't had any water all afternoon or evening. Only that bit of champagne.

"Well, at least you know the basic steps of our core dance now," he said, drinking his own glass down and then accepting a glass of champagne. He offered another to me, but I shook my head.

"I wouldn't say that," I said, staring out at the others.

"You're being modest," he chided, taking my hand and lifting it to his lips with a smile. I fought the urge to pull away again.

His eyes chilled, and he pretended to follow through as if all was merry, well aware that something was wrong. "What is it, Andriana?" he said, setting down my hand and caressing the back of it. "Surely you cannot be so unnerved by your fellow Remnant's gifting?"

I studied him. That he might be so powerful, even before he obtained an armband ... It did frighten me. "It was like I didn't have a thought of my own in my head," I muttered, trying to sort it out as much as explain. "Only your thoughts. It wasn't a leading or encouragement I felt. It was more like you were compelling me. That is not of the Maker. That is the sorceror's way." I let out a sound of exasperation. "At least some of it. Some of it feels familiar, right." I took a breath and turned more fully toward him. "Keallach, listen to me. It's all mixed up, within you."

I glanced around and found Sethos partway down the hall, talking to two matronly, fawning women. As if he sensed me, his head lifted and he glanced back at us. The women followed his gaze and then the three of them smiled and resumed their conversation. Perhaps it had only been a coincidence.

"How is my gifting not of the Maker?" Keallach asked, sipping from his crystal glass. "When you cast emotion, is that not of the Maker?"

I frowned, troubled by his logic. But then I shook my head. "I awaken emotion in another. Not drive out any other emotion at all."

"But if you could, wouldn't it be convenient? Wouldn't your power be even more potent?" He leaned closer. "Think of it, Andriana. Between my power to control a body's *motion* and your power to control their *emotions*, who could stand against us?"

I stared at him in mute horror. "You've been misguided, brother. You speak of power. Our gifts are *gifts*, and the Maker could take them away as easily as he bestowed them. They are of him and for him. To use them for our own gain—"

"But he has not revoked them, has he?" Keallach said, cocking his head. "Might we not assume that he is still showing me favor?"

"No," I said. "We should not assume that."

Keallach sighed and didn't even bother to cover his frown.

"Highness, please pardon my interruption."

We turned to look upon Lord Maximillian Jala, looking as perfectly dressed and groomed as usual. "Will you join me for a dance, Andriana?"

I hesitated. That was the last thing I wanted. I was exhausted, as if Keallach had drained every ounce of my energy in our partial dance.

Keallach leaned toward me. "It is required, Andriana. Any consort of the emperor must dance with the Six."

"Every one of them?" I said dully.

"There are only six," he said, his tone telling me he would tolerate no further debate about it. And we were getting to the crux of the matter between us. If I lost him now … *Just get through*, I told myself. *Just get through.*

I nodded numbly and accepted Maximillian's hand. Maybe after a few minutes away from Keallach, the Maker would give me the words to reach my brother, to counter the logic. Just after I sorted it out for myself.

"I must warn you, m'lord," I said, "I have no experience with your dances."

"That's all right," he said. "I am a good leader. And Keallach taught you the basics."

He placed his hand on my hip and I placed my other hand

on his shoulder as the music began. "Don't look so glum, Andriana, or you'll destroy my reputation."

"I doubt that." I concentrated on the steps, fighting the urge to watch our feet. *Forward right, forward left, left, backward left, backward right* ...

"Already the hall murmurs with echoes of your impact. They all want to be you, you know, be Keallach's favored one."

"Yes, well, lucky me."

He withdrew a few inches, studying my face as the hint of a smile danced around his eyes. "If it helps, I am not sure that I concur with the emperor that it is the best idea to have you here."

"Oh? Did my attempt to kill you make you jaded?" I said wearily.

"Perhaps," he said lightly. "But be aware — the faster you acquiesce to what the emperor wants, the easier this all shall be."

I stared into his eyes then. "I was not born to acquiesce."

"No, you were born for something far grander. To join us, rather than fight us. Together we can do much good."

"I don't think that's *quite* what the Maker had in mind."

His eyes grew cold even as his face held a light smile. I didn't know if I'd ever seen anything so frightening. His grip on my hand and waist tightened. "Do not try us, Andriana. You are here now. There is no way out."

"Keallach doesn't want me as his prisoner. At some point, there will be a way out for me."

Maximillian turned me in a tight circle, so quickly that I almost lost my footing. He leaned his head back and laughed, as if we were enjoying a private joke, then pulled me close as we came to a stop, so he could whisper in my ear. "The only way you leave Pacifica is dead. The battle is over, Andriana. Accept your new fate."

I shoved him away and several women gasped. I ignored them. "I am not blown to and fro by the *fates*," I hissed. "I am — "

"Firmly in my arms," he said, sliding back into position and turning me again. I had no choice but to grab hold or I'd fall over. "Come now, Andriana," he said, his tone grim even as he smiled at me. "Is this not far better than being my maid-servant at Castle Vega?"

A man stepped in behind him and tapped him on the shoulder, and then I was dancing with another of the Six, Lord Kendric. This one seemed nothing but utterly charmed by me. I remembered he had laughed hardest when I flipped the wiry Lord Fenris on his back. *Lord Fenris*, I thought with a sigh. I'd undoubtedly have to dance even with him this night too.

I couldn't spar with each of them; I needed to save my energy to engage Keallach later. I woodenly accepted each dance and made it through a round of steps until most — Broderick, Daivat, and even the stiff-backed, simmering Fenris — had had their required dance. I refused to speak to any of the others, but didn't miss the opportunity to search each one. I wanted to know what Keallach faced, every day, in his Council. In several there was not more than ambition, derision, and lust. In Fenris, predictably, there was hatred. But in Lord Cyrus, I found a measure of closeted hope, the tini-est slice of protection. I looked up into his dark brown eyes, and noticed for the first time that he hadn't tried to cajole or provoke me as the others had. He moved through the dance as I did, like it was something we both had to do. But since he had cut in on Fenris at a blessedly early juncture, we had the length of the song together.

"Is it true?" he said quietly, as the dance went on.

"Is what true?" I asked softly.

"That you, Keallach, and Kapriel," the last was so quietly uttered that I wondered if I'd heard it correctly, "and the others with the crescent moon mark ... are all the prophesied Remnants?"

"It is," I said. We separated for a round of the dance, weaving through three other couples, and then came together again.

"You must know that every other Remnant that has been captured has died," he said, his lips barely moving. I edged closer so that I could hear him better.

Other Remnants? Were these the ones that Sethos had mentioned? Those he held prisoner?

"What happened to them?" I asked urgently.

"They were tortured and killed."

"Killed. Did Keallach know of it?"

"Some. The Six — we — protect him from such matters."

"Such matters," I sputtered. "It is the central Call upon his life, whether he responds to it or not!"

I tripped over Cyrus's foot, but he held me aloft, face grim. I had to gather myself, if I wanted this conversation to go on. And I needed it to go on. "Why are you telling me this?" I asked.

"So that you might fully understand the peril you're in," he said.

I debated pushing him, but we hadn't time. The dance would soon end. "Who were they? These other Remnants?" I asked, leaning in still further as we turned. I desperately hoped he was mistaken.

"The first was a woman captured in the Great Expanse, trying to find you. She was killed three days later."

Killed. Dread flooded through me. "What was her name?" I asked again. If it was Tressa, or Bellona —

"Dulla," he said, barely moving his lips, smiling down at me as if I'd said something witty. "Keep dancing. Smile. I'm the one they expect to befriend you."

I tried to do what he said, smiling, pretending. But his words sent my head spinning. "Where was she from?"

"I only know she had come a great distance."

"We do not have Ailith kin by the name Dulla."

"She was not only Ailith," he said urgently, "she was a Remnant. I saw the crescent mark on her hip myself. And she claimed to be gifted."

I stared into his eyes. It couldn't be … No, not when she'd been so close to joining us … "And the other?" I managed to ask.

"A man from the South, traveling with three others to the south of Georgii Post, one of them, his knight. He went by the name of Galvarino."

I cocked my head and pretended to be engaged with what he was saying, like he shard a tender story. But inside, my stomach roiled over with his words, even though Galvarino's name wasn't familiar to me either. Yet with sickening recognition, I realized I hadn't known any of the other Remnants' names before I met them.

"And their knights?"

"They were tortured and killed too."

"You're certain — certain they each had the mark?" I asked him, feeling a bit faint. Four more of our kin, dead? There'd been a part of me that thought we were invincible, from here on out. That the Maker would somehow shield us when it came to matters of life and death. But if what Cyrus was saying was true …

"All four had the mark," Cyrus confirmed, leaning closer in a slight bow as the song ended, as if saying farewell. I shuddered, and he gave my arms an encouraging squeeze. "Know you are not alone," he whispered, turning to my side and applauding the musicians as others did around us. "Take care, Andriana," he said, taking my elbow, as his stunning words sank in. "Keallach will give you more time," Cyrus added, "because he hopes to win you. But if you do not fall into line, I fear it will not go well for you."

He smiled as we approached Keallach, and I mirrored his emotions of pretended pleasure. Keallach's face lit up as he saw my expression, apparently fooled for once. "I send you off in a muddle of contempt and you return on Cyrus's arm a woman at peace." He clapped Lord Cyrus on the shoulder. "He's a good man, this one," he said.

"Indeed. Perhaps my favorite of your Six," I said, smiling up at Cyrus.

"Hold, there," Keallach said, pretending a frown and jostling his friend as if he meant to capture him in a headlock. "Must I compete for your affections?"

"It's been made abundantly clear who I am meant to be with here," I said with a genteel nod toward him.

Keallach raised his brows in surprise, huffed a laugh, and eyed Cyrus. "Will you do me a favor and spend an hour with her every morning?" he asked. "Perhaps the rest of our days will be far less combative."

"Spend an hour with this beautiful woman?" Cyrus said, sounding far different than he'd been with me — more like he'd been like at Castle Vega. Was it an act? Which one? "Whatever sacrifice I must make, Highness," he said, holding his heart and making a pained face.

"Such an obedient man. Thank you, Cyrus. You may go now."

Cyrus bowed to each of us, and Keallach grinned after him. He felt a genuine camaraderie with the man, which fueled my hope again, even after hearing Cyrus's dire warning. Memories of it made me feel sick to my stomach. They'd killed the Remnants. What had been their gifts? If it were true, then there'd just be the five of us, not nearly as strong without those missing. Were we enough alone to turn back this tide? With this knowledge, wasn't it more imperative than ever that we bring Keallach into the fold?

"What is it, Andriana?" Keallach asked, turning to me in concern. "You suddenly appear terribly pale."

"It's been a lot to take in, this part of your life," I said. "Do you think I've been here long enough? Might I leave now?"

He studied me. "After one more dance. With me."

"On one condition," I said wearily, wondering if I even had it in me to get through one more turn on the floor. "No using your gift on me with the dance."

"No need," he said, lifting his hands in glee. "You are well versed in the steps now!" We went back to the dance floor as the music began again. Keallach held me closer than before, and it wasn't long before I felt his warm fingertips skirting the edge of my gown at the lower back. "Do you see how you have admirers already?" he asked.

I frowned at him. "I don't know what you mean."

"The women," he said, eyes on me. "They've all slipped out and scrubbed away a good deal of their powder and eye shadow. They all want to look more like you. Because I have chosen you."

My pulse quickened, and I dared to look over his shoulder

at the other women in the room. It was true. They all looked more ... human. More like me. But instead of comforting me, the sight made me feel nauseated again. What was it about Pacificans? What had made them so mindless? Is that why Keallach and the others held such sway over them? Is that why he needed me, because he knew the Trading Union was full of people far more independent than these?

A few other couples joined us on the dance floor, but the majority seemed content to break and sip from their glasses and share words under their breath, undoubtedly about me. They were both repulsed and drawn to me, it seemed.

A thought struck me then. If they were so easily swayed, could I win them over for the cause? For the Way? Might I strike at Sethos's power over them? Hope surged in me. Perhaps the Maker allowed me to be here, in this place, the heart of the enemy, so I could strike a crippling blow. And Cyrus had seemed to hint that he might be an ally. I smiled at the thought, and a surge of joy in Keallach made me look at him.

"Ah, Andriana," he said. "How lovely you are when you smile. You're understanding it now, aren't you? What we might attain, together."

Together. Something about the way he said it agitated me.

Keallach pulled me closer and we swayed back and forth. He took hold of my hand on his shoulder and brought it to his chest, gently forcing it flat until I could feel the steady rhythm beneath. "With every day that passes, you hold more of my heart," he said intently. "It's like I always knew you were coming. That I had to wait for you." Then he leaned forward, slowly, as if to kiss me. I could feel the collective intake of breath in the room. I resisted, pulling back, but Keallach's grip was sure, firm, unyielding. "Give in, my love," he said. "This is destiny."

My love? "I can't, Keallach," I said, looking into his eyes.

"Forgive me," he whispered. "But this is for your protection."

And then impossibly, I was doing as he asked. Lifting my chin. Parting my lips. Accepting his. Feeling him draw me even closer, his hands fully on my bare back. Dimly, I heard the applause around us, laughing and cheers. Felt the approval of some, the condemnation of others. And knew that once again he had compelled me, moved me, used his gift against me. I tried to move my hands, to push him away, but could not. He smiled and drew away first, leaving me as if I were stunned by his very kiss. Laughing, looking proudly at the others nearby.

I half turned, trying everything to break our bond, our connection. *Maker . . .*

I then latched on to the wish that Ronan was here. Striking Keallach down, breaking his grip on my arm. *Ronan, my knight. Ronan, my love. Ronan, Ronan, Ronan . . .*

Keallach drew away from me, frowning, then quickly forced a smile. Pretending. He'd felt it then, the internal severing of his hold on me. But still, he held on to my arm. "Come along, Andriana. I will see you to your room."

CHAPTER 25

RONAN

We had just finished our watery soup after a long day of travel to a new Drifter camp when I noticed Chaza'el get that distant look in his eyes. Others said their good-nights and padded off to their own spots to bed down by fires for the night, but I remained. Chaza'el often wished to share his vision soon afterward. I was eager to hear what he'd seen.

But when his eyes focused on me, he frowned and looked away, as if guilty.

"Chaz?" I asked gently, picking up the nickname Vidar had given him. "What is it?"

His eyes dragged back to meet mine. "It's Andriana," he said miserably.

"Andriana," I repeated.

He nodded, his lips in a thin line. Asher came and sat

down on the stump of a log beside us. So did Niero. They'd noticed Chaza'el's look too.

"What was it, Chaza'el?" I asked, my tone more angry and scared than I'd meant for it to be. *Out with it!* I wanted to shout. *Tell me!*

"Easy, brother," Asher said, reaching out to touch my arm. I shook his hand off.

"She was with Keallach," he said, closing his eyes and rubbing them.

That wasn't a surprise. "We know she's with him. What of it?"

He opened his eyes and stared dolefully at me. "She was in a white dress. A gown." He shook his head and ran his fingers through his dark hair, then clasped them together.

"A white dress," I repeated. "As in a betrothal gown?"

"Maybe," he said, lifting his hands in a helpless gesture. "No," he said, as if correcting himself. "There were many others in white too, around her."

"All right," Niero said, getting agitated himself. "Tell us all of it. Everything you saw. Don't pause."

I steeled myself.

"She was kissing Keallach. First on a dance floor, with many Pacificans looking on, applauding. Then again, in a passageway. They were in each other's arms. It was ... intimate."

I hadn't steeled myself enough for this. It was as if a hundred tiny knives had punched holes in my lungs, keeping me from taking another breath.

She was kissing him. Another man. Our nemesis. The one who had tried to kill Kapriel. The one I'd feared had imprisoned her.

I let out a humorless laugh. "Well at least she hasn't been

spending her days in a dungeon as I feared." Or *nights*. My breathing quickened at the thought of what sort of quarters Keallach might have given her, likely with easy access.

"Stop," Asher said.

His single word shushed my swirling thoughts like a dam to a river.

"You ... you love her?" he whispered. He shook his head. "I mean as more than a sister."

Niero scowled but remained silent.

"I do," I said, unable to lie when I was struggling to breathe. "Or perhaps I should say, I did." But even as I uttered the words, I knew they were decidedly false. If I didn't love her, I wouldn't feel this scalding pain.

"There is a reason the elders forbade the Ailith," Niero began, "to take up with one —"

"I know, Niero, I know!" I staggered to my feet and began to pace. The last thing I needed was a lecture on something that had been decided long ago.

"And she ... loves you?" Asher asked, seemingly unperturbed by our transgressions.

"I think so. Maybe. Oh," I groaned, wiping my face, pulling at it as if I might be able to pull free clear thoughts. "I don't know!" I said, fingers splayed, shaking my head. "She did at the last moon."

Asher nodded thoughtfully. "Tell me again of your vision," he said to Chaza'el. "Everything you can remember. Leave nothing out."

I took a breath, not certain I could get through another retelling. But Chaza'el's voice faded as I concentrated on what Dri must've looked like in that gown of white. I'd imagined her in white, of course, but with me, under a Hoarfrost moon, our hands entwined in an elder's wrapped band as we exchanged vows. But instead she was there, with *him*. Tears filled my eyes and I didn't bother wiping them away. I was only seeing them again, together … again and again *together*. Him leaning in to kiss her, her resisting, as if teasing him, then leaning in, lifting her chin, parting her lips to welcome him … the Pacificans around them applauding and smiling as if they'd just exchanged their own vows.

"Chaza'el," Niero said, drawing back my attention. "Was there any more after the passageway kiss?"

"Must there be more?" My voice cracked then, and I choked on humiliating tears of anger and betrayal. I looked to the star-filled sky, remembering Keallach pointing out constellations for her, barely keeping my legs, my breathing ragged. I backed up toward a large rock, and when I bumped up against it, I scraped downward, ignoring how my tunic rode high on my torso, how the stone scraped against the bare skin of my back. In an odd sort of way, in my grief, the pain felt like a relief, a release.

Asher turned to me and said, "For as much as Chaza'el *saw*, he saw precious little. We do not know all that led to those kisses, or what followed."

"He saw more than I wish he ever had," I said angrily, wiping my eyes with the palms of my hands, pressing in for a moment, then looking up, trying to catch my breath.

"Ahh, but you allow the enemy to make the most of that moment rather than seek what the Maker wants us to know," Asher said. "You embrace devastation and division rather than cling to the cords of your entwined hearts."

I stared at him, letting his words cycle back around and through my mind again, trying them on, like a new coat over a shirt left in shreds.

"Are you so weak, Knight, that you so easily believe the

worst of your Remnant? Or is this the time she needs you to fight for her the most?"

I sat there, stunned. Was it … possible?

"But then, why … How? Andriana is strong, Asher. Ask Niero. Very strong. And she wields emotion. Could she not ward off Keallach? Or bend him to her own heart?"

"Think, Ronan," Niero said, nodding now, as if in agreement with Asher. "What is Keallach's gift as a Remnant?"

"He can move objects."

"And people, according to Kapriel."

"He can move people," Asher repeated in wonder.

I frowned. "But he does not yet have his armband. If you are right … Could he already be so powerful as to be able to move Andriana in such a way?" But then my heart skipped a beat. Had not every Remnant had a certain measure of their gift before the ceremony? The blessing simply seemed to ignite it, expand upon it.

"Now you see." Asher gestured toward me and then out, with both hands. "The twins have always had quite impressive powers. Even before he had his arm cuff, Kapriel was able to summon the clouds and rain and wind, yes?"

"Yes," I said, remembering the Isle of Catal and both of the twins utilizing their gifting. Thoughts of what I'd seen him do since he received the cuff strengthened me. We could storm into Keallach's castle, if necessary. Free Dri …

"We must make sure that Keallach never obtains his armband," Niero said. "If we can make sure that doesn't happen, we just might have a chance to beat him." It was as if he'd read my mind.

I lifted my hands to my face and rubbed it. "I know Dri. She'll likely feel that she betrayed me and be angry at herself.

It might give Sethos, or Keallach, the exact edge they need to open that door to the dark she's wrestled with before."

"Then we must pray against it," Asher said simply. "And hope that the Maker makes Dri strong enough to endure the fiercest battle yet. Because if they claim her, it will be a terrible loss for you, friend. But it will be worse for the Remnants."

CHAPTER
26

ANDRIANA

Fury, dark and cold, flooded through me. He'd kissed me! Had made me kiss him! It was madness. How could I have fooled myself? I couldn't sway Keallach emotionally when he held physical sway over me. I tried to pull away, but he held on stubbornly. "Just a moment, Andriana," he grit out, fairly pushing me through a doorway held open by a footman and pulling me through the narrow, secret passageway. The door closed behind us. "We can have words when we are fully in private."

"This is private enough!" I skidded to a stop, put a slippered foot against his backside, and sent him sprawling. I stood there, panting, a bit stunned at my own actions.

Keallach turned and looked back at me, that wry grin again on his lips. "I suppose I deserved that." He was immediately up on his feet and moving toward me brushing off his hands.

I let out a sound of exasperation, turned and ran, but the door behind me was locked. I could feel his approach, even as I rammed on the door, yelling for someone to open it. But no one did.

Keallach's hand appeared above my shoulder, against the door. "Turn around, Dri. You have nothing to fear from me."

"Don't call me that," I said, stupidly trying the knob again, as if it would suddenly, magically open.

"Will you not face me?" he asked, pleading. "I need you, Andriana. Just as you need me. Can't you feel the pull within you?" He stepped closer, close enough for me to feel the fabric of his jacket brushing against my bare back ... and more, so much more. "Give in to it, Dri."

His use of Ronan's nickname for me made me angry, and I lifted my arm, intent on elbowing him in the belly, hoping it would jolt him out of whatever he was trying to accomplish here. But my arm froze, and slowly, I was turning, lifting my arm above my head. I tried to bring it down, to slap or strike him, but I couldn't. He lifted a hand and interlocked his fingers with mine, then used his other to stroke my cheek and across my bottom lip, forcing me to part them.

"You will yield to me," he whispered, moving his face closer to mine. "You will offer yourself to me in time, freely, without me compelling you," he said, his breath sweet and warm across my skin. "Because you know you want me as much as I want you with me."

"No, no," I said, trying to shake my head and make my lips form the words, but failing.

"Yes," he whispered back, his lips just barely grazing mine. "Let me show you. Remind you what is true."

Then I was lifting my chin, pressing my lips against his.

It began as our first kiss had, with Keallach compelling me. But as the door opened between us, as I felt the raw *need* within him, I stayed, caught up in the surprise and joy of a sudden soul-connection that I had so wanted to establish with him. He was finally as open to me as I was to him! My heart wrapped around what I felt within him — the admiration, the easing of loneliness, the excitement of recognition, all somehow funneled into this intense physical draw — and echoed it. Keallach was smart and charismatic, a born leader who only needed to get on course again. I longed to fill the gaping hole within him, to show him what it meant to be filled to all the fullness of joy and love and peace and security. And in kissing him back, in opening my mouth, welcoming his wandering touch, it was almost as if I —

I let out a cry and pushed away from him, eyes wide. I put a hand to my head. "What's happening to me?" I asked in terror. "What am I doing?"

"Come now, love," he said, smiling at me, catlike, moving in to pull me close again. "You've acknowledged it at last. This is good! Right. You understand now that the Maker has brought us together to — "

"No, no!" I said, pushing him away, turning my head to the side as he moved in to kiss me again. "Stop! I thought you said you didn't want to marry me!"

He stilled and his eyes focused on me. He shook his head and pinched his temples as if trying to sort out his own feelings. "I didn't," he said, his eyes clear, desperate. "I mean ... I wasn't ... Listen, Andriana, I'm so sorry."

I gaped at him, equally desperate to sort out what was truth and what was lie.

"Highness, may I be of service?" Sethos asked, appearing

at one end of the hallway. Had he been with us all along? How much of what I thought was Keallach's power to compel me had been part of Sethos's sorcery? And now my enemy was stepping in again before I gained the upper hand with Keallach.

My breath caught when I saw Keallach's eyes were dilating, his pupils so large that his eyes became almost black. And he was moving me again. Compelling me to wrap my arms around his neck and pull him close. "What are you doing, Keallach? Stop! This is not what I want! It's not what you want! You are my spiritual brother! Not my ... my ..."

"What, Andriana? Your ... lover?" His tone dropped, low and sultry again. It was as if Keallach — my Keallach — had disappeared, and Sethos's Keallach had replaced him. "It's so adorable that you cannot bring yourself to say it. But it's just a matter of semantics, right? You were willing to entertain a relationship with Ronan, were you not? Another of your 'brothers'? We are not biological kin. We only *feel* the pull of one another. Which just makes this feel better than I'd ever imagined it might be." He moved in again, fast, and I could feel the full force of his compelling, his attempt to open the gate between us again and flood me with feeling.

Maker, bind his gifting. Keep me safe. Help me to think!

Instantly, I felt my will harden again, as I steeled myself to resist him. I was such a fool! Relying on my gifting alone, my own strength, when what I needed was the light in this house so full of the dark.

"Keallach, listen to me," I said urgently, reaching out to him with my own gift, even as his hands roamed my back in far too familiar a fashion.

"Oh, I'm listening, love," he whispered, leaning down to

kiss my neck, holding me still so that I could not physically fight him.

"I know this thing between us is confusing," I said, closing my eyes, talking fast now, trying to will away the pleasure of his touch, his kiss. "I think Sethos has some sort of control over you. A spell maybe."

"She speaks madness, Highness," Sethos said dismissively, watching as Keallach planted kisses down the side of my neck. But his eyes were smug slits of satisfaction.

"Maybe it's because you've never met another female Remnant," I said. "Maybe he's found a way to use this pull between us for his own foul purposes!"

"This does not feel foul," Keallach murmured, his breath on my skin sending shivers down my arms.

"But you were born for so much more than this, Keallach. Here, you will only know a measure of the power the Maker created you for. And he," I spat out, looking angrily toward Sethos, "will only seek to control it."

Keallach's head came up and he faced me at last. I could see him struggling to think and watched his eyes, his pupils dilating and then diminishing. I was able to move again, breaking through —

"Leave this place, Keallach. Leave it behind you. Join the rest of the Ailith — they can help you as they have me. Help you sort things out. Then, there, you will gain what you long for most. What I feel within you here," I reached out then and touched his chest, "instead of what you attempt to do with me here," I said, reaching up to gently touch his forehead.

"Highness, really. I must interject," Sethos said as I touched Keallach, but I ignored him, even when it felt like sparks were flying from his eyes toward me. I only concentrated on the Maker, calling to him with everything in me.

"Please, Keallach," I said, resting my hand on his chest again. "I know you feel the Call. You're confusing your draw to me with the draw you'd feel toward all the Ailith. Come with me! You'll see! You've let Sethos convince you to use your gift in a way that the Maker would not sanction. Come join us — "

Keallach suddenly pulled my hand from his chest, holding my wrist away from him as if I'd burned him. His nostrils flared as he stared at me, anger building within him. Then he took a deep breath, lifted his eyes to look at the ceiling, and rubbed his temples with the other hand.

"One of your headaches again, Highness?" Sethos asked, now right behind him, his fingers curved like talons.

"Forgive me, Andriana," Keallach said, lowering his gaze to meet mine again, and I could feel the throb behind his pain-filled eyes. Had Sethos given him that headache? "We will continue this conversation tomorrow," he said, then essentially handed me off to Sethos.

"No. No, Keallach! We need to finish this. Tonight!"

He ignored me, speaking only to Sethos. "See her to her room, will you? I need to lie down."

"Of course, Highness," Sethos said soothingly, as I gaped after Keallach in horror. He was leaving me with the sorceror? Did he not remember what that man had done to me the last time? Sethos turned and dragged me toward the far end of the passageway. "No! Keallach! Don't send me with — "

But I saw then, with a glimpse over my shoulder, that he was gone, already out the other end.

Sethos let out a breathy laugh and pulled me through one doorway after another, clearly taking me out a different way than Keallach had brought me in. I tried to focus, to pay attention to glimpses of rooms, windows, but I was so tired now myself that I could barely walk. Each step felt like it was weighted by stones, and my own head began to throb. Was it Sethos? Could he cast a spell that caused headaches?

"Maker, be with me …" I said, then tried to kick Sethos's legs out from under him.

Sethos growled and slammed me against the wall, his long fingers digging into my throat, lifting me to my tiptoes. "Do … not … utter … that name … here."

I was choking, clawing at his hand, pretending like I was losing control, panicking, but in fact, uttering the Maker's name had sent power coiling through my veins and cast out the headache.

As Sethos smiled and leaned in, examining me as one might a bug pinned by the tip of a knife, I reached out and dug my thumbs into his eyes. He bellowed and released me immediately, and I fell heavily to the marble floor. "Maker!" I spat out. "*Maker! Is that* the name you fear, Sethos? Is that the name you don't want me to utter? The Maker's? The One who was, and is, and is to come?"

Hands on his knees, Sethos panted and stared at me with hatred. Then he whirled, and his fist connected with the side of my cheek and ear and sent me sprawling. When my head cleared enough for me to remember to look, I turned and saw him coming for me. I used my arms, trying to drag myself away, get my knees under me, but my head still spun. His boot was on my back, pinning me down then, and I dimly heard other footsteps running down the hall, felt the chill in my cuff grow frigid. Sheolite guards.

"Take her to her room," Sethos said.

The guards bodily lifted me, avoiding my attempts to snag a knee. My dress left me half-bound with all its fabric. I succumbed, knowing it was best to leave further battle until later, when I was stronger. *Maker, make me stronger,* I pleaded silently. We went up the stairs and down my third floor hall, and the guards essentially tossed me inside my room. But this time, I managed to keep my feet and turn to face Sethos, fists clenched. I saw that Lord Jala had joined us. He was leaning against the far wall, arms folded, waiting.

"Leave us," Sethos said to the guards. "But remain right outside the door."

"No! You leave *me*, Sethos. And you too, Lord Jala. Have you not done enough this night?"

The guards disappeared out the door, quietly closing it behind them. Sethos moved toward the window, looking out. Maximillian Jala stayed where he was.

"Why not give in to Keallach's charms, Andriana?" Lord Jala asked, his tone soothing, reasonable. "If you would but give in a little, and the emperor give in a little, you two could rule together in fine fashion."

"I remember well what happened to the last one who was to share the throne with Keallach," I bit out. "I'll end up in a cell on Catal!"

"It is different for brothers to try and rule together than for a husband and wife."

I let out a scoffing laugh. "I am not going to marry Keallach!"

"No?" Maximillian asked, lifting a dark brow. "Why not?"

"Because … because …" I winced and closed my eyes. I wanted to say I didn't love him. But I did, as I loved all the Ailith. "He is not the one who holds my heart."

"No, that is the one they call Ronan," Sethos said quietly.

I cast him a fierce look over my shoulder, but Lord Jala continued to speak. "There have been many monarchs over the centuries who find that a genuine fondness for each other is as successful an ingredient for co-regency as any passion-fueled love."

"Not that that ingredient is truly missing either," Sethos put in. "At least from what I just witnessed in the passageway."

My cheeks flamed. I bore his accusation silently, feeling it like new slices across my own bludgeoned heart. I'd betrayed Ronan. Given into Keallach ... or Sethos ... Self-loathing filled me.

"You are lost to Ronan," Sethos said, sidling closer. "Our spies tell us that he has moved on to protect the other Remnants without knights." He lifted a device before my face, flipped it open, and an image was before me. But this was more than a picture — the people shown were *moving*.

I drew back, frightened at first, but then leaned in, hungry to see every bit of my beloved kin that I could. I searched each face and tears rose in my eyes. They were all there. Even Asher and Azarel! Laughing, hugging, slapping one another on the back, clearly celebrating. Even Ronan. I froze. He moved as if he didn't have a memory of me. There was no telltale slump of his shoulders, no long look to the horizon, as if he was wondering about or worried for me.

Lord Jala shrugged as Sethos clipped the device shut. "Either they've given you up, or they believe you belong here too. Does it not make sense that your path always led here? Where you could do the most good? Where you could shape an empire? Is that not the ultimate Call on an Ailith's heart?"

"No," I said, shaking my head, my mind spinning. And yet

inside, my heart was muttering *maybe. Maybe it's true.* From a distance a realization came to me, that my enemies were working on me when I was at my weakest and most exhausted. I sank into a chair and put my head in my hands. "Go away, both of you. You seek to bind me with your lies."

"It is truth, Andriana," Lord Jala said gently, leaning toward me. "Try it, test it. You'll find it is truth."

"No," I protested. "You only want it to seem like truth to me. I do not belong here," I said woodenly. Did I belong anywhere? Even with the Ailith? When I was so easily tamed by Keallach's gift? So readily captured by Sethos? What sort of fighter was I? I was weak. So weak ...

Sethos was at my other side then, and I had the oddest sensation that he seemed to grow stronger with each breath that passed between us ... as if he was sucking in my air, leaving me more and more faint. "You think yourself invincible. You rely too heavily on the emperor's draw to you. But keep in mind, we have already killed two of your unmet Remnants. It's only a matter of time until we close in on the rest and see them to their natural end too. But there is no need for you to die with them, Andriana. No need for your bright flame to turn to cold, black ashes."

I couldn't manage to summon a response. *What is wrong with me? I'm so impotent, pathetic —*

"It will be easier for all if you simply give in, Andriana," Lord Jala said. "It can be as Keallach said. Together, you will bring peace to the empire. You've experienced the worst of the Trading Union. Help us to introduce the best Pacifica has to offer and change all that."

They were relentless. They'd only keep coming, keep

coming, keep coming, until we all bowed down to them or died fighting them.

"I am not interested in power."

"Aren't you?" Lord Jala asked lightly. He knelt in front of me, reminding me of Keallach. "You can do great things with power, Andriana. Good things. For you and everyone you love."

I looked away.

After a long moment, he sighed and rose. "This will be done easily, or it will be done with great difficulty. But Keallach has chosen you, and I now see the wisdom in his choice. So one way or another, it shall be done."

I dragged my eyes to meet Lord Jala's. Then Sethos's. They meant it. They intended to see me betrothed to Keallach. On shaking legs, I rose, fists clenched. "I shall refuse him. In Pacifica, by the emperor's own edict, no man forces a woman to wed him. Keallach's as much as told me that himself." I prayed he hadn't misled me.

The threat rose up within Sethos, so dark and overwhelming that it felt as if it reached out and choked me.

I swallowed hard, and with the last of my strength refused to shrink from him.

Sethos laughed, under his breath, slid his eyes toward Jala and back to me. "Ah, yes," he said, reaching out to stroke the line of my jaw. I moved away, disgusted, but he ignored my slight. "There is an empress within this one." He dropped his hand and leaned close, his breath cool on my neck. "She simply needs to be awakened."

They left me then, and in their wake the three maidservants entered, chattering about what an impression I'd made at the ball, congratulating themselves on a job well done. As if

I were a mere doll that they could dress and wind up and then watch dance the night away. And perhaps that's what I was.

Nothing more than a shell of what I once was.

The betrayer of all I held dear.

A fighter, vanquished.

Misery blanketed me, enfolded me in his arms.

And in his firm embrace, I slept.

CHAPTER 27

RONAN

"They won't allow this to go on," Asher said, looking behind him as we trudged up a hill days later, with more than a thousand following behind. Some were in vehicles. Many more were on foot. "Even if it's not in their official territory."

Niero looked over his shoulder and adjusted his pack straps before taking the next step. "No. They won't."

"When they come, I want to be captured," I said.

"You *what?*" Bellona asked, catching up.

"When they come, I want to be captured," I said, still not looking at anyone but Niero. He would understand me. Know what I was after. To get to Dri. The fastest way possible. Regardless of the cost.

He stood there, staring at me with his dark eyes. "You are certain," he said.

I nodded. "I belong there. With her. In any way I can."

"Wait, what?" Vidar asked. "You're saying you want the

bad guys to nab you and haul you to their dark, foul dungeon, and what? That's some part of the Maker's plan? Listen, man, we're aware you're a studly knight and all, but we're talking *dungeons*. Sheolites outnumbering you twenty to one."

"And my charge, somewhere near," I said, still not looking from Niero.

"No, Ronan," Vidar said, grabbing hold of my forearm. "No. It's suicide." But I noticed Bellona said nothing. She understood.

I only waited on Niero.

He paused, took a breath, looked down and then, once our gazes met again, he gave me a single nod.

My heart both stopped and soared in that single instant. I couldn't believe it, and yet it was as if I'd known it all along. This was my path back to Andriana.

I looked out to the plain before us as the others trudged on — Vidar still glancing back at me in consternation — and in the distance, I could see the outline of Castle Vega. Here, in the shadow of a walled city well known as enemy territory, the first step back to Dri would be taken. Finally. The hours since our parting yawned, the chasm between us widening as a horrific, dark pit. I had to get to her. We were destined to make it through — but we needed each other. Me, my Remnant; she, her knight. I swallowed. It went deeper now. I needed her as a woman. She needed me as a man. And somehow, some way, in time, the Maker would make that right.

An hour later, we set up camp.

"We're certain this is the place we're supposed to be?" Vidar asked, lifting a wary brow toward the horizon. "Isn't it a bit too much like thumbing our nose at them?"

"Probably," Tressa said, passing him and setting down a basket. "But this is where we are to be."

"Can we camp farther away?" Killian asked her, setting down another basket beside hers and nodding in the opposite direction.

"The Maker is asking us to take bigger and bigger risks," Niero said. "Do not give in to fear. Trust him, in where he leads, no matter how it appears."

Vidar stared at the silhouette of Castle Vega in the distance, then back to him. "That's screaming risk to me. Am I the only one?"

"No," I said, passing by him. "Deeper in we go. Trusting him all the while. Right?"

"Right, brother," he said, touching my fist with his. But I didn't miss that he was a little more hesitant than normal.

The people surged around us, and Killian had to bodily push men and women away from Tressa's hastily erected tent. Several other men had volunteered to help protect her from the masses, who had become more and more demanding every day. I'd thought that the more Tressa healed, the more respect she'd obtain. But in fact, the stories only seemed to fuel the frenzy. In their weakness, the people flocked to her, and in their desperation, they became like pecking hens. The men had to establish a perimeter around our camp so that she could move with some freedom among us.

They gasped over what Kapriel could summon from the skies.

They marveled at how Chaza'el could foretell the future.

But it was Tressa's gift they hungered for. The paralytics. The men with wasting diseases. Women who couldn't bear children. Children growing with deformities. And everywhere we went, the Cancer. The ever-present Cancer. Eating at people's guts. Stealing their breath. And during every waking hour, for as long as she could move, Tressa blessed and prayed and healed everyone the Maker sent to her.

Their stunning numbers only brought new pilgrims to find us.

We used the opportunity to gather them, morning and night. To tell them of the Way. To remind them what was inborn within them all, that deep, abiding hunger for something eternal. Something more than themselves and this relentless struggle to make it through another day. To hear. To serve. To experience joy, abundant joy.

Asher was preaching this night, calling out until his voice became hoarse, so eager was he that all could hear. They hovered near, eyes wide, and hope was so vivid among them that it brought tears to my eyes. I longed for Dri to be here so she could see what was happening. How people were answering the Call, just as we had.

"You come to us," Asher said, "hungry for hope. It has been a long while since hope wafted up, like the fragrance of Harvest after a long, cold Hoarfrost. But here they are." He gestured toward us. "The foretold Remnants and Knights. They gather now to serve the Maker, as you and I are called to serve the Maker."

He paused as people gasped and shouted and talked about his use of the Name, as he knew they would.

"For generations, the Maker's name has been forbidden by those who wield power. Why? Why? Because it threatens others who hold power. They seek to be gods themselves! But in fact, no one holds true power other than the Maker. And it is he who has sent the Remnants to us at last, to lead us forward. To lead us out of darkness and into the light!"

Asher and Kapriel kept preaching, dividing up so more

could hear them. People were either weeping or praising the Maker as the sun set, committing to join in Community and follow the Way from then on. Tressa healed one person after another — those in need thronged about us — and yet still more journeyed toward our camp. We could see their dancing torches in the distance, serpentine lines along the dark of the desert floor. Several self-appointed scouts rolled in, and I tensed, waiting to hear.

The first man jumped from a mudhorse and straightened his tunic.

"What'd you see?" Bellona barked, turning from helping Killian protect Tressa for a moment. "Anybody heading our way from Castle Vega?"

"Not yet. From what we can determine, people continue to pour out of desert villages, but no one from behind the city's walls."

We all seemed to take a breath of relief with this news. I turned to Vidar. "What about you? Sense anything?"

"No," he said, blinking fast, grinning in awe. "Just the presence of the Maker. Chaz is right. He wants us here now for a reason."

"Yeah, well, Tressa's not going to hold up much longer," Bellona said. "We need to call for a break until morning. Give her time to rest."

Niero nodded and circled some men and women around. He then sent them out to encourage the people to make camp, cook some dinner, and prepare to bed down, but also to keep weapons ready in case we encountered enemies during the night. Then he shouted to the crowd, several hundred deep around us, "Our healer needs to rest! She will reach as many of you as she can come morning! But for now, we ask you to send just the youngest forward! Any child who hasn't reached their first decade in need of healing, send them forward! Make way!"

His eyes met Tressa's for a moment, and she knew what he was after, nodding in understanding. The crowd grew quiet, only the weeping of mothers and frightened children audible. A circle of guards held the crowd out about ten steps from a bonfire where Tressa stood. Small children crawled between legs and ducked under the guards' entwined arms to enter in. Others were passed overhead, from person to person, until one of the Ailith took them in their arms. In all, there were seven children. Two infants, one pale and gasping for breath, frightfully thin, the other with a monstrous tumor growing on his head. Both barely opened their eyes from weakness, clearly on the edge of death. There were three toddlers, two of them unable to walk, one with the Cancer. That one cried, hot tears and snot running down his face, and clutched his belly, calling for his mother, but when Vidar picked him up, he quieted to doleful hiccups. And there were two older children, one with a leg that had clearly not been set right when broken, and another with the Cancer.

Tressa gathered the children together and took the two infants in her arms, then turned to the crowd, walking slowly past them. "The Maker is the One who has given us *all* life. It is his enemy that brings us death. But if we believe in the One who saves, if we trust him with our very lives and turn to him, commit our lives to him, he can heal us, even if there is no Remnant present at all. We have been called to awaken the Maker's people, to fight against those who hate him. There is a better way, a better life for all of us. And for these children, it begins now, with healing. Pray with me now! Pray for the Maker to come and make these children whole!"

Tressa bent over one baby, whispering words of prayer, closing her eyes and kissing him softly on the forehead, then handing him back to the crowd to send him back to his mother. Then she placed the other on the ground, covering his horrific tumor with her hands, and I prayed with her, even as I kept an eye on the masses around us. But the people were staying obediently still, or raising their hands in prayer, clearly aware, as we were, that they were experiencing something far beyond anything they'd experienced before.

The first baby reached his mother and the woman cried out, thanking the Maker, crying out her praise. "He breathes! Look at how he breathes! Look at his skin! He smiles!" She wept, then, completely breaking down. But still Tressa kept praying for the next child before her.

Tressa looked up to the sky, and I saw her smile, tears running down her cheeks too. She lifted away her hands, and we could see that the baby's skull was now normal, the tumor disappeared. She tenderly lifted the babe in her hands, smiling into his eyes and whispered, "Welcome back, little brother. Always serve the Maker who made and saved you." With a kiss she turned him, so the crowd could see, and everyone gasped and cheered.

"Keep praying with Tressa!" Kapriel called. "The Maker revels in our collective praise!"

Vidar was nodding, tears running down his cheeks, and I could tell from his expression that we were not alone. The angels were with us. Watching? Serving as witnesses? Or shielding us from the dark ones? It mattered not to me. I welcomed their presence.

Tressa turned to the others, and looked at them solemnly. "By your faith, you will be healed. Believe in the Maker, the

One who has brought you here today, with your families and friends. Believe that he will make you whole." Then, she moved from one child to the next, bending to pray over each — the one with the deformed leg, the others with the Cancer, the paralyzed. She spent no more than a few seconds with each child, laying her hands on their head, or legs, or belly and then moving on. But as she passed, each was healed.

We could all see it. Those closest to us fell to their knees, their hands reaching for the sky, praising the Maker. Others farther out, now able to see too, did the same. I grinned and took to my knees as well, caught up in the glory and miracle of the Maker, on the move among us in such a tangible way. "Thank you, Maker," I said through my tears, "thank you for the honor of serving you. You are mighty! You are holy! We are yours!"

■ ■ ■

We were sound asleep when Vidar, who'd been on watch with Bellona, shook me awake. "Company coming," he said, moving on to Killian, who was already stirring.

I was on my feet in seconds, pulling on my jacket and grabbing hold of my sword. I didn't bother to strap it on — I needed to get outside fast.

The vehicle that pulled up to our camp was in finer condition than any others we'd ever seen outside of Pacifica, the paint reflecting the waning bonfire beside me, the windows free of cracks. Killian and I shared a long look as other Drifters came up behind us, weapons at the ready. Two Aravanders drew back arrows across their bows.

"Nobody fire unless I command it," Niero said. "Understood?"

The driver's door of the enclosed Jeep opened, and we saw hands first. "Don't shoot! We mean you no harm!"

"Come out, slowly. Alone."

The man rose, and we could see he was in a Pacifican lord's tunic and boots. I stiffened.

But Kapriel sputtered a name under his breath. "Cyrus?" he said again, louder and clearer this time. "Is that you?"

Lord Cyrus's tense face broke into a smile of wonder. "Kapriel?"

Kapriel broke away from our line and went over to him. The two embraced, the sort of hug that spoke of long-separated but dear friends. When they broke apart, I saw tears in Lord Cyrus's eyes. I sidled closer to Vidar. "Anything?" I whispered, wondering if he was sensing danger that I could not.

"No. The guy's clean."

I laughed under my breath. A Pacifican lord? Why would he be here, in our camp?

"You recognize him, right?" Vidar asked me.

"No," I said, shaking my head and searching his features again. We'd met. Somewhere.

"That's Lord Cyrus, one of the Six. One of Keallach's Council."

I frowned. "You *sure* he's clean?"

"Yeah. Check out your arm cuff. Neutral, right? Maybe even a little warm?"

"Right," I said. But it didn't make any sense.

Cyrus and Kapriel spoke for several long moments, then Kapriel turned to us. "He has a woman with him. They need to see Tressa."

Understanding dawned. One thing had forced Lord Cyrus to risk everything in order to see us. To bridge the gap between him and a long-lost friend, a step that might brand him a traitor.

He needed a healer.

Kapriel came closer to us.

"He could be a spy, Kapriel," Killian said.

"He could be," Kapriel allowed, nodding. "But I choose to believe he might be the most critical friend we could make. Let us see this through and find out where the Maker is leading us, yes?"

"I don't trust it," Killian said.

"Face it, man. You hardly trust anything but the Maker," Vidar said. "I think your Rem needs to heal your *attitude*."

Killian scowled at him, but then left to wake Tressa. A woman handed him a gas lamp and soon her tent glowed with warm light. I turned to see Lord Cyrus return to his car. He'd taken a huge risk coming here — not only the fear of being branded a traitor, but also the risk of us kidnapping him or stealing his vehicle because he'd come without a single armed guard.

Cyrus lifted a woman in Pacifican dress from the other side of the vehicle, every aspect of his movement tender and caring. The sight of the dress sent a pang of longing through me, for Dri. She'd been so pretty in a gown like that, and likely wore one now.

Kapriel led Lord Cyrus into Tressa's tent, gesturing for Vidar and me to join them. The knights took up watch around the tent, and Niero leaned toward an Aravander who'd joined us. "Assemble and send four teams of Aravanders and Drifters to scout farther out than the others already in rotation. I want to know if anyone else is coming our way."

"On it," he said, padding off.

Reassured that we had reasonable protection, I entered the tent. They'd laid the woman on Tressa's bedroll, and gathered around her. She was lovely, about our age, with long, sable-brown hair that waved about her horribly pale face. My breath caught, wondering if she was already dead.

"She's been poisoned," Cyrus said to Tressa, lifting the woman's hand in his. "Please, you must save her. I love her." He shook his head. "I couldn't stay in the castle and watch her die. I knew you could save her."

"Who poisoned her?" Killian barked.

A flash of guilt appeared on Cyrus's face. "I know not. Her name is Justina. She's a consort at court. They are there to … entertain us."

I saw that he had the decency to blush a bit over this, and liked him a little more. Andriana had told me enough of the ways of the Six while at Castle Vega. It didn't take much imagination to understand what he meant.

"My family … my position … I am meant to wed another soon, in Pacifica. But this woman …" He turned desperate eyes toward Tressa. "I love her. Please, save her. She's one of you. A devotee of the Maker. It was she who whispered to me of your presence. She wanted me to come with her, to run away from Pacifica." He shook his head and brought up a hand to his face. "It's impossible, what she was asking. But she doesn't deserve to die."

"She was poisoned because someone knew her to be a follower of the Way?" Niero asked, eyes hardening.

"No," Kapriel replied grimly, for Cyrus, figuring it out. "She was poisoned because she held Lord Cyrus's heart. And he is betrothed to another."

Justina's breathing became more rapid, her color fading

to gray as we watched. Tressa knelt across from Cyrus and took up Justina's other hand. "You must know, Lord Cyrus," she said softly, "that we were sent here to bring the people back to the Maker. Are you a follower of the Maker?"

"I ..." His eyes shifted to Kapriel and then back to her. "I think ... yes, I think I am."

She gave him a knowing smile. "In a moment, I believe the Maker will affirm that belief. Pray with me. All of you, reach out and touch her and pray with me. She is moments away from breathing her last."

We all did as she asked, and I laid a hand on the woman's shoulder, her skin terrifyingly cold. And as Tressa sank deeply into prayer, pleading with the Maker who had created Justina in her mother's womb to now wash the poisons from her body, to flush the toxins away, to bring her back to us, whole again, I could feel the Spirit draw closer, surrounding us with a rush that was better than the company of angels. The hair on the back of my neck and arms stood on end and I smiled, reveling in the presence. On and on, Tressa prayed, committing Justina's life and future to the Maker, not begging him to heal her, but rather more like simply waiting on him to do what we believed he wanted to do.

Justina's flesh began to warm. I sensed that her breathing slowed. She seemed calmer, as if her entire body was allowing the tension to slide away. Her skin began to pinken again. And then her eyes opened, her long lashes fluttering in confusion, trying to focus.

Lord Cyrus wept, laughing. "Justina? Oh, my love? Justina?"

"C-Cyrus?" she said, turning her face to him. "What happened? Where ..." But then her eyes widened as she looked around at all of us. "Is it possible?" she asked, sitting up and gazing around at us in wonder, covering her mouth as if we ourselves were angels. She accepted Cyrus's embrace and kisses, but her eyes remained on us. "Am I dreaming?"

"No, sister," Kapriel said with a grin, taking her hand. "You are here, in Community. At long last."

If it was possible, her eyes widened even further, when she saw him, this time in sudden terror, then confusion. "You are not …" She glanced toward Cyrus. "This is not the emperor."

"No, this is Prince Kapriel, Justina."

Understanding dawned. "My prince," she said immediately, reverently bowing her head.

Kapriel put a finger under her chin and lifted it. "You bow to no one, Justina. You are a free woman here. Servant only of the Maker and our Community."

She nodded, smiling, but then her eyes grew curious again, clearly wondering how she got here.

But Cyrus was looking about at all of us, and rising. "I am forever in your debt. I will serve you and your cause in any way I can. I'll leave the Council immediately and —"

"No," Kapriel said, walking over to him. "I'm afraid I must ask you to do something far more dangerous than that. I need you to return to Pacifica."

My heart leaped. He was sending him back to Keallach?

"Back?" Cyrus said.

"Yes. We need a friend inside Keallach's Council. A spy. As well as a friend for Andriana."

"Someone to help us take them down from within," Killian said.

"Tell us, is Andriana well? Can you help us get to her?" I asked.

Cyrus looked at me. "She is well. But she is constantly

guarded by the Sheolites. And the emperor ..." He shook his head and ran a hand through his hair.

"I don't know how long I'd be of use to you. If they find out I was *here,* with you ..." Cyrus said, fear making his expression grim.

"They'll kill you," Kapriel finished for him. "It is frightening. I ask much of you. But will you do it?"

Cyrus looked around at all of us, and his eyes steeled with decision. "I will. I will serve you, the Maker, and your people — *our* people — in any way I can. Perhaps if you can reign, you can bring Pacifica back to the Way too."

Kapriel nodded in understanding. The two stepped away to confer in low tones for several minutes. When they returned, Justina slipped into Cyrus's embrace and he kissed her temple. "You must stay here. Whoever tried to kill you might try again."

She nodded, through her tears. "Come back to me, Cyrus."

"I'll do everything I can to do so," he pledged. "But first I must do this."

She nodded again.

Cyrus rubbed the back of his neck. "The castle wall guards know I left with her. They'll want to know why I am not returning with her."

"What reason did you tell them you were leaving, without out guard?" I asked.

His face colored. "I said I wanted ... time alone with her," he said. "It was all I could think of," he hurried on. "They thought her drunk on evening wine."

My mind raced. "Take me," I said. "Say that you two were attacked. Justina killed. And that I was your attacker, a wretched Knight of the Last Order and sworn enemy of Pacifica." I looked to Niero. "You all break camp now and disappear. We'll return to the castle just before daybreak, me as Cyrus's prisoner, to give you time to gain some distance."

"They'll take you directly to Keallach!" Lord Cyrus said, mouth partially agape. "To the Six! We're heading back to Pacifica tomorrow. You'll be beaten, man! Placed in the palace dungeon."

"I hope so," I said, waiting on him to understand my goal.

Killian was smiling now. "About as close as he could possibly get to his Remnant," he said.

"You sly dog, you!" Vidar said, punching me in the arm. "That's crazy-stupid, but also crazy-brave."

"I like it," Bellona said, taking my arm as a fellow Knight. "Let us come with you."

"No," I said, shaking my head. "I do this alone. I can't risk any more of you. And no one would buy it — that Cyrus could fight and capture more than one of us. If the Maker sees to it, we'll find some way back out of that palace." I nodded toward Cyrus. "With his help."

The young lord visibly paled again, and he looked up to the top of the tent, hands on his face for a moment, then back to Justina and Kapriel. Finally to me. He nodded once. "I'm with you. To the end."

"To the end, I am with you too, brother," I said, taking his arm in mine and cementing our pledge. Hope entered my heart for the first time since I'd watched the ship holding Andriana steam away around the river's bend.

I'm coming, Dri. Hold on. Just hold on.

CHAPTER
28

ANDRIANA

I awakened to sunlight streaming through the window and the maids arriving. I heard the sound of water running and knew that they would dip me in and see to my hair and dress me in short order. *A doll in her new clothing,* I thought grimly. *Another day, another fight to lose.*

But as I stared at the sunlight, which seemed so wrong in a place that I felt was so covered by darkness, I reached out to the Maker. *I'm so weary. I've disappointed you. Failed you. You chose me wrongly. There must have been another who would have done better.*

But the light became stronger, a stream alive with dust motes dancing, the long curtain beside the window fluttering slightly in the breeze. It was the window that Sethos had stood by last night. And yet now ... the light. I took a long, deep breath. *You cannot give in to what you feel, Andriana. You have to remember what you know to be true.*

Truth.

A maid asked me a question but I ignored her. My hand slipped to my hip and traced the place where I knew my birthmark to be. The crescent moon. A sign of something bigger to come. Of hope. Of light. Of fight.

I threw back my covers and sat up quickly. I would bathe and dress. And while they saw to me, I would concentrate on what I knew to be true. That I was born for a purpose. That I hadn't betrayed those I loved. I'd fought my adversary at every corner. Sure, I'd lost battles here and there. But this was a war. A war!

I moved toward the bath and undressed, brushing away the hands of the maids, wanting to do this myself. Naked, I stepped down into the hot, steaming waters, relishing the wince of pain as if it might sear away everything wrong and against the Maker that had crept into my mind and heart. I didn't stop, even as my body begged me to, as I entered the center of the pool where it was deepest and I could dip down and below, letting the water cover my head. I stayed under, massaging my scalp, my face, my ears, my neck, my shoulders, as if I could scrub it away. Sethos. The Six. Even Keallach, if necessary. He was distant. A pawn to Sethos, as I very nearly was myself. Was he within reach of redemption? Possibly. But he'd have to make his way himself. There was only so much I could do. And right now, all I knew was that I had to be free of this place. I had to escape. Before I became one of them.

I rose from the water, gasping for breath, and the maids wheeled back, laughing at my splashing as if I played.

"Well, someone's eager to get through her bath and see the emperor," said the matronly one. "She's smitten, I'd say!"

I bit my tongue and forced myself not to grimace. "I'd like to wear leggings today," I said.

"Leggings!" she responded. "Impossible! There's not a lady in the land that —"

"I'd like to wear leggings and a tunic," I insisted. I pretended a sly grin. "The emperor said last night that I was setting trends already. Perhaps leggings on ladies will be the next thing." I leaned my head back agreeably as the younger one reached forward to lather my hair. She worked the lavender-scented suds through the strands, and then gestured for me to dip. When I rose, I looked at the matronly one again. "So? Is it possible?"

She looked every bit as chagrined and pained as she felt, as if I'd forced her into a terrible corner. But I didn't relent.

"Well, you're tall, but you're thin. Perhaps I can find a pair that would fit."

"That'd be grand. What's your name?"

"Halla, m'lady."

"That's wonderful, Halla. I'll be certain to tell the emperor what a fine aide you are to me."

She smiled at that, and her spirits buoyed. The others sparked with agitation and jealousy, and the younger girl tried to do an extra good job as she spread an oil through my hair next, one that would keep it from tangling. After I took the sponge and bar of soap and saw to the rest of my bath myself, I rose, wrapped a long towel around me, and gave in to the two maids who would see to my hair while Halla set off to find my leggings and tunic.

"Oh, and please remember to bring me a tunic and boots too," I called lightly as she left, adding the boots to my list as if I'd already asked for them.

She froze. "M'lady, that's impossible."

"Is it?" I asked, careful to look confused. "Weren't you just thinking you knew of a way to obtain the leggings?"

She looked caught, horrified, and I smiled. "Don't worry, Halla. Remember, I have the emperor's favor, and you have mine!" I said brightly. "I only hope to entice the emperor into a bit of archery today." I waggled my eyebrows. "Or better yet, a bit of sparring. I can hardly make it interesting for him in the confines of a Pacifican gown."

"No, no, m'lady," she said, sounding anything but convinced. But she left then, presumably to do as I asked.

The girls beside me remained silent. I knew they found me shameful, unworthy with my outlandish requests. But that was all right by me. When one reached to powder my face, I blocked her hand. "No. Nothing on my face at all."

"Are you certain?" she asked, aghast.

"Beyond certain," I said, staring at my reflection. And for the first time in a long while, it seemed, I smiled an earnest smile.

■ ■ ■

Once I pulled my tunic over the leggings and cinched tight the belt, I turned toward the mirror and smiled again. I felt free. More myself than I had in days. My fingers itched to hold a sword. I actually hoped that Keallach might favor a bit of sparring. It would feel good to loosen up those muscles, to remember the ways that I seemed to have buried. I even thought that I was strong enough to do actual battle, if it came to it.

"Please, will you send word to the emperor?" I said to Halla. "Tell him I'm inviting him to the south lawn for a bit of sport?"

She wrung her hands. "There's difficulty in that, m'lady. When I stepped out for your tray a moment ago, I heard that the emperor, well, he's away on Pacifican business. He's not due back for a few days."

Her words stopped my flood of hope like a hard slap to my cheek. "What? He-he left?"

She patted my shoulder awkwardly. "Don't fret, m'lady. He'll be back in a few days. Men are like that, you know. Even men as refined as our emperor. Given to do as they please without ever informing the women."

I nodded, accepting her misinterpreted response, but chafing inside. But then it came to me. Maybe this was my perfect opportunity to escape. There'd be time for Keallach to follow if he was truly led away from the dark. If he was meant to be with us and had the strength to face his own sins. I hoped he would. But now, clearly now, I had to leave this place. Regain my strength. Rejoin the Ailith and my fellow Remnants. And tell them what I knew. The awful, awful news about our sister and brother who would never join us. Niero would know what to do, where to go, how to proceed. Niero always knew.

Thoughts of each of them sent joy through my heart. I thought quickly. "It's a shame Keallach is gone," I said. "Perhaps the Six are still here? Or did they go with him?"

"Only Lord Sethos went with him," she said uncertainly.

"Excellent," I said, thinking about the Six, and their casual, assuming ways. Would it not be something if Lord Cyrus stood with me and we turned arrow and sword on the other five? Would it not remove a critical barrier between Keallach and the Remnants? It was they who held him captive here, as surely as Sethos did. I couldn't take down Sethos without my fellow Ailith about me. But five of the Six? I smiled. They had thought they would capture me, control me. But they would find out what it meant to face a Remnant of the Maker, sent to destroy those like them and free the oppressed.

"Summon them to the south lawn. And bring refreshments." The words were odd on my tongue, a mere mimicking of what I'd heard from the men around me. But I delivered them with such force and assumption that the women scurried off to do as I bid.

I shoved away my concerns of past battles, of how emotions crippled me. I was stronger now. I'd learned a lot, and the Maker had reminded me of what I needed to concentrate on. I closed my eyes and thought of my trainer, and of Asher, and of Niero holding my hands and willing me to remember what they said.

But I couldn't take them all down. Even if Cyrus decided to stand with me. It was foolhardy. They wouldn't expect such a move from me, but would it be wiser to steal my way through the palace, killing them, one by one?

When I thought of it that way, the first pang of regret swung through me, like the pendulum on a clock. I faltered. Did I have enough warrior in me to fight this fight? If it meant I got a step closer to freeing Keallach and rejoining the Ailith?

It was complicated. But I knew if I continued to go back and forth, I might very well lose the momentum I needed to fuel my courage.

Halla returned, far too quickly to have done what I asked. She was wringing her hands. Behind her, I saw two Pacifican guards in their gray uniforms and two Sheolites in red waiting in the hall.

"M'lady, the Six are already assembled in chambers," Halla said, glancing back to the men. "They've requested you join them." I saw, then, what alarmed her, as she looked me over from head to toe, knowing the Six might hold her responsible for my unorthodox dress.

My pulse quickened. "It's all right. It will be all right." Perhaps this was just the opportunity I needed to challenge them for some sport and take them by surprise.

Halla reached out and grabbed my arm. "You must change."

"Nonsense," I said, pulling away. I felt more myself in these clothes than I ever did in the Pacifican gown.

Halla gaped at me in horror, probably fearing for her position, but I ignored her. It was high time that these people learned that a woman couldn't be tamed by simply putting her in a dress.

I strode toward the door and gestured out while looking at the Sheolites. "Well? Let's get on with it."

"We cannot take you into chambers, m'lady, without the proper clothing," sneered one red-robed guard.

"Your emperor will allow me to wear anything I wish. Shall I summon him?" I said, pretending ignorance.

"He's *away*."

"There's a reason I'm dressed this way, and it has to do with the Six. Take me to them, and I'll explain it to them myself."

The leader shrugged and gestured for us to go. Two Pacifican guards led the way, with the two Sheolites behind me.

"What did the Six say they wanted of me?"

"They didn't, m'lady," said one Pacifican congenially over his shoulder. He dared to give me an encouraging look. "I'm sure it's a small matter."

He believed his own words, I was certain of it. He was apparently as taken in by the emperor's "consort" as everyone else in the ballroom had been three nights ago; I could feel it. If I was good enough to win Keallach's heart, then I was good enough for these people. It gave me chills, their blind devotion, their mindless support. Was it Sethos's work, behind the curtains, that allowed this show to go on? As Pacifica grew, if they were able to usurp the Trading Union, that band of power would be more challenging to maintain. Undoubtedly, that is what lead them to summon me.

The men led me downstairs to the first floor, then down a northern hallway of the palace that I'd never been in. These appeared to be Keallach's public rooms and offices. At the very end of the hall we entered a large, wood paneled room, with an elaborate oil painting on the ceiling. It depicted the sky with a noble female figure dressed in white and carrying a scale in one hand and a sword in the other. *Lady Justice*, I thought she was called.

But my eyes went immediately to the Six sitting in the wooden chairs — elaborate thrones, really — that were part of the paneling on the long wall. The men, all large, looked somewhat dwarfed in them. I was led across the marble flooring to a single chair sitting dead-center in the room, a good distance from the Six. "Sit," said Jala, and I obediently did as I was told.

The two Sheolites remained on either side of me. The Pacificans went and stood to either side of the Six, their hands on the hilts of their swords. It didn't take empathic skills to find out I was in some sort of trouble.

"Three nights ago at the ball, m'lady," said Maximillian, hands on the arms of his carved chair, head straight, "you came precariously close to humiliating the emperor. We must demand your complete obedience from here on out, whether in public or private."

"On the contrary, Lord Jala," I returned. "I was manipulated and forced to do something I did not wish to do. I cannot allow Keallach to use his gift to compel me into a compromising position. *That* is not acceptable."

Maximillian scoffed at this and looked at Fenris, to his right. "Do you know how many young women would give their right eyetooth to kiss the emperor?"

"Well, I am not one of them," I said.

"That is not what I observed."

"I was compelled, and *confused*. Rest assured. I am no longer confused," I said, pausing to let each word roll off my tongue.

"It is unfortunate you see it that way," he said, rising, and stepping down to the marble floor. He came closer. "The time for wooing is over, Andriana. You must accept your fate and fully join our cause."

"I cannot do that."

"I believe you can."

It was my turn to laugh without humor. "I was born to fight against you and yours," I said. "You are somehow working with Sethos to use Keallach. That's become clear to me now. And together, you are the scourge upon our land. You choke the Union's people, use them, seek to control them. When they are destined for freedom, destined to come together to worship the Maker — "

I saw his hand coming and reached out to block it, but I was too late to stop the other. The force of his slap was so strong, I leaned hard against the left arm of my chair. Slowly, I straightened, turning back to him, hatred seething within me. I tried to lunge for him, but the Sheolites on either side of me shoved me back in the chair, hard enough to send pain from my hips upward.

"You," Maximillian said, "shall learn to keep your tongue.

To never speak that name in this palace or anywhere in the empire again. You shall turn your back on your primitive ways and learn what it takes to be a Union queen, worthy of our emperor. Only then shall you become empress."

"I don't wish to become your empress." I hissed.

Maximillian paused and dropped his hands. "Do not try us, Andriana. We brought you here today to make it clear that you will serve as the symbol of a vanquished and submissive Union. You continue to believe you have far more power than you actually do. Here, cut off from your precious Ailith, you belong to us." He leaned forward to emphasize his last words.

I said the next in a slow, low, defiant manner. "I belong to the Maker alone."

This time, when he moved to slap me, I caught his hand with my own and turned it cruelly, hearing bones crunch and watching his mouth drop open. And I recognized something—I didn't feel his emotions as I did others. It was as if he was a Sheolite. Or perhaps Sethos had blocked me from reading emotions here too, and his plan had backfired. Hope surged in me anew. If I weren't crippled by their emotions, maybe it would truly be possible to take them down one by one and be free of this place.

Maximillian backed away from me, hatred plain across his face, all trace of gentility gone. "You will learn what it means to be *owned*, Andriana of the Valley, beginning this day. It is only because you are so highly useful that you are still alive at this moment."

"You will never own me. I'll die before you do."

Maximillian pushed away a servant who'd moved forward to assist him and resumed his seat at the center of the Six. But I drew pleasure from the way he held his injured hand against his chest. "You may be surprised by the choices to come," He turned to the doorway and said, "Bring them."

I froze. Who? Were the other two Remnants alive, despite what Cyrus has said? I looked to him, but he shifted in his seat, uncomfortable, and wouldn't meet my gaze. I didn't need my empathic powers to know he was feeling guilty. I could tolerate their worst against me, but to watch a fellow Remnant abused...

But the Pacificans brought in my father.

Bedraggled, filthy, terribly skinny, but my beloved father.

Alive. Alive! Alive! He's alive! They'd only made me think they'd killed them.

They let me rise and stagger toward him. He embraced me, kissing my cheeks. He smelled foul, sickly, but I didn't care. It was Dad, *my* Dad. My precious Dad. "Where's Mom?"

When his eyes met mine, I sucked in my breath, understanding now. They had them both. They would try and use them both against me. Strong hands gripped my arms and dragged me backward, even as two others dragged him to another position in the cavernous room. But his eyes, his loving eyes, remained on me. Tears streamed down his face, cutting glistening, clearer tracks through the filth that coated his skin. "Remember, Andriana," he said, his voice strange and thin. Hoarse. "Remember who you are," he said, swallowing hard. "Remember whose you are."

Lord Jala lifted a hand.

A third soldier turned and struck my father savagely in the belly. Dad's knees buckled and he gasped for breath, turning gray and then flushing red, eyes bulging.

"There shall be no more words from you unless we ask you a direct question," Lord Jala said.

I heard his words as blows themselves. I wanted Dad to

keep talking — his voice awakening all kinds of memories that comforted and strengthened me.

Maximillian came down from his throne and patiently waited for Dad to regain himself, and then turned to me, his genteel façade back in place. "Now, there is no need to continue this, Andriana. Just one word will stop further harm from coming to your father. And that word is a simple *yes*. Yes, yes," he said, a grin spreading over his face, lifting his hands in the air and then patting his chest, playing up the drama for his chortling companions. "It feels good to say it."

"Yes, to what?" I sputtered.

Maximillian paced then, chin in hand. "*Yes*, you will wed the emperor. *Yes*, you will serve the empire. *Yes*, you will serve our cause for unification. *Yes*, you will speak to your fellow Ailith. *Yes*, you will do everything that is asked of you to end this brewing battle and help see us to peace. To peace, Andriana," he said, his voice rising. "How can you say no to that?"

"Kapriel will see us to peace. When he comes to power, he will reign over all. And you and yours will be dust."

"Those are treasonous words," he said, lowering his gaze.

"Are they?" I cried. "Or am I simply stating how we make all that went wrong, *right*?" For the first time, I wondered why Keallach wasn't here. Why he'd left without telling me. Because he'd been sent away by these men he called friends? Or because he wanted to claim innocence? "Where is Keallach? What would he say about this?"

"The emperor is away and agrees with how his Council presides over Pacifica's business in his absence," Maximillian said, perching on the edge of his chair. "He'll understand what we had to do, here."

"Beating my father? Threatening me? That does not square with what I know Keallach would *understand*."

"You confuse the emperor's fondness for you with his resolve. We cannot abide by a growing threat in the Trading Union. Neither can our emperor."

His words *growing threat* made me want to smile. These actions were born out of fear. I straightened my shoulders and lifted my chin. "I'll die before I betray the Remnants and the Maker's cause."

As I uttered the forbidden name, Maximillian rose, as did the rest of the Six.

"We are well aware of how tightly the Remnants hold to their cause, Andriana," Maximillian said stiffly. "Be advised that we had two previous encounters with your ilk and had ample time to test ... parameters. This assisted us greatly in preparing for this moment with you."

I tried to swallow, but my mouth was dry. I seethed with fury, itching for a sword, for the chance to take down this monster who gloated over torturing my brother and sister, sacred souls meant for so much more.

"What we don't know is this," Lord Jala said. "You Remnants will die for your cause. But are you willing to watch your father die if you refuse us?"

He gestured to the knights holding Dad. One forced him to his knees and brought a knife up under his throat.

I tried to rise, straining with everything in me, but the Sheolites on either side of me shoved me back and held me down. My arm cuff was growing colder by the second. There was no need for Sethos to be in attendance. His minions had full sway. I panted, desperate for breath, but suddenly felt like there was precious little oxygen in the room. *They wouldn't ... They won't ...*

Maximillian walked over to Dad and then slowly turned his head in my direction. "Tell me, Andriana. How do you think it would affect an empath to watch her loved ones die?"

I thought I might vomit.

"Do not waver, Dri," Dad said. "Do not let them hold my life — or my death — over your head like a noose. I die willingly for the Maker!"

Lord Jala grimaced and lifted a hand toward the guard holding the knife.

"No! Wait!" I screamed.

But even as I did so, Dad writhed, bodily turning the guard around after him. The guard pulled back his knife and Dad made a terrible, choking, gurgling sound and fell forward.

"Dad!" I screamed, weeping.

Blood pooled around his neck and spread. The guard backed away shaking, as if horrified at what he'd done, and dropped the knife. He moved toward the door where the other guard tried to stop him, but he shook him off.

"He's weak," Maximillian spat in disgust. "See that he's dishonorably discharged and never enters the palace gates again." He gestured for the other guard to follow him, leaving Dad's lifeless body alone — its solitary placement somehow making it all the more horrifying.

"No!" I cried. "No!" I tried to rise again, free myself from the guards, but they held me fast. It was no use. I was weeping, aching over the sight of Dad, lost to me once and now lost again ... one with the Maker at all times, in all places, and now in the Maker's presence.

But far, so far, from me. Tears ran down my face as I shuddered with the searing pain of it. *Dad. Dad ...*

The Six took their seats and remained silent as the only

sound in the room for a long while was me crying, and the only movement was a broadening pool of blood.

"Acquiesce, Andriana," Maximillian said soothingly, like a rescuer to a small child. "You clearly cannot bear to watch another of your loved ones executed like this." He gestured toward Dad's limp body and rose, slowly walking down the stairs to me again. He circled me casually, chin in hand. I noticed he left his injured wrist at his side. "Feeling grief, when you feel every emotion tenfold, it's the perfect torture for you, isn't it?"

"I will not give in to you. I will not betray my friends just so you can execute them as well! I will not be unfaithful to the Maker — the One my father just died for!"

"Don't betray them, Andriana! Help them live! This course they're on ... your precious *Way*. It will only mean death for them, in time. One by one, we shall track them down, and they will all die." Lord Jala leaned closer. "And I will see to it that you watch each one pass." He straightened and lifted his good hand. "Or you can do as we have envisioned and be the bridge between the Six and the Ailith."

We stared at each other, and I hated him then. Never had I felt rage race through every inch of me as it did at that moment.

"Bring her," he said, never releasing my gaze.

I was the first to break our stare, seeing the figure in the doorway to the left.

"No," I moaned, tears welling in my eyes. "Maker, no, no ..."
I couldn't do it. It was impossible.

But they dragged Mom into the room.

CHAPTER
29

RONAN

I heard Dri's agonized weeping and sank to my knees, wanting my guards to think I was frightened, beaten, mourning. It wasn't hard to summon the tears in my eyes, hearing my beloved keen in pain. How I hated it that she thought—

Voices rose in the next room again. Andriana, mostly. Then the low, sly voice of Lord Jala. Cajoling. Deriding. Persuading. Threatening.

Breathing quickly, I considered my options. I had to get loose. With the other guards gone with Dri's mom, it was only me and the two Sheolites alone in the room. There'd been at least four other Pacifican soldiers in the hallway at the ready, but no other Sheolites. Likely there were others with the Six.

I eased my stance, aware that my guards were listening as intently as I was, probably wishing they had a view of the horror. These creatures fed on darkness, despair, terror. And I was eager to introduce them to an eternity of it.

This was my chance, the one I'd prayed for. The one Dri's parents and I had prepared for deep in the recesses of the dungeon. Keallach and Sethos were away. If we were going to break out of the palace, there'd never be a better opportunity than this. Mentally, I moved through one motion and then the other, practicing it all in my mind, visualizing possible reactions, changes of circumstance.

Andriana shouted and Lord Jala laughed and I was on the move, ramming the man to my left, sending him sprawling, then whirling and turning and lifting the chain that bound my hands around the throat of the next. I gripped the gathered loop in one hand and as he writhed and struggled, pulled him around me just in time to take the brunt force of his comrade's sword, which came through him and nearly into me.

I tossed the injured man aside, and the second man's sword went with him. But as he fell, I pulled the first's sword from its sheath. I swung wildly at the second Sheolite, but he easily ducked it and ran into me with a growl, clearly hoping to tackle me to the ground. But I simply gave into it and lifted him up and over me, the momentum sending him sprawling. As the Maker would have it, we were close to the wall, and he came to an abrupt stop, his head and neck at an awful angle. He was still.

Panting, I eyed the doorway, amazed that the commotion hadn't drawn other guards, which likely meant that the drama that was going on in the Council room was far more engaging. Convinced I had a few precious seconds alone, I moved to the first man, still alive, but barely, and roughly turned him over. He'd tucked the key to my chains in his belt, or some pocket on his tunic. *Hurry, hurry …*

There. I found the metal bulge beneath the fabric and drew it out with shaking hands, desperate to be free and making my way to Andriana. I heard her cry out again as the lock finally gave way and the chains slipped toward the ground; I caught them just before they hit the marble and then stared toward the empty door. They'd still made a racket. But again, no one came. I pulled two daggers from the first man's belt and slammed them into my own, then a sword from the limp body. If I took those in the next room by surprise, perhaps Andriana or her parents could take up arms beside me. Even if they did, we were still terribly out-numbered. And we had only two swords and two daggers. Unless …

"Please, Maker," I whispered between gritted teeth, eas-ing up to the hallway door and peering around its edge. There were four guards in the hall, and they were all carefully watching around the doorjamb of the Council chambers. But I smiled as one looked over his shoulder and lifted a brow toward me. It was the man who had "killed" Dri's father. And his partner was the man who had been sent by Lord Jala to make certain the guard never returned.

Allies. Two most loyal to Lord Cyrus.

Seeing me emerge, the one — covered in the pig's blood he'd carried in a sack — elbowed his partner, and together they silently took down the two guards in front of them, dragging their lifeless bodies past me and into the other room where I'd been.

I moved across the floor, trying to be as silent as our trainer had taught us to be, glancing down the hallway behind us, which remained blessedly empty. I knew other guards would be on the run as soon as the Six cried for help, but apparently the lords felt adequately protected. Usually, they would be against prisoners weakened by days without food or water, in chains.

The two other men emerged again and hovered behind me. Hope surged. It was happening. Just as Lord Cyrus and I had planned. But Dri's terror made my heart race.

Andriana cried out, "I cannot! It is against everything in me to swear allegiance to anyone but the Maker!"

"Cut her mother," said Lord Jala. "but not deep enough to kill her yet."

"Now," I grunted to my companions. We charged forward, shouting. I could see Dri's dad rise, the guard's long knife in his hand, and leap upon the closest, shocked guard, freeing his wife.

I felt the Sheolites' eyes all turn toward me, but it was Andriana I watched, even as I turned, slammed the door shut, and rammed down the crossbar, then charged in to join the fight. Shock and confusion gave way to hope, and she moved as we had trained to do, season upon season, finally rising and taking down the guard to her right. My heart swelled with hope that together we just might make our way out of this hellish place.

I parried the sword of the Sheolite nearest her father and slammed a dagger into the belly of another who came up behind me, whirling to decapitate him. The Six were on their feet, drawing their own swords, shouting for aid. I had to get Dri and her parents out now. I'd decide where we were heading as soon as we made it outside. All I knew was that we had to break free of these before the other soldiers responded to the Six's alarmed cries.

I tossed a dead man's sword to Dri's mom, and she caught

it and turned to strike Lord Fenris across the arm. He'd been moving to try to apprehend her. He gaped at the woman, as if he couldn't quite comprehend that someone might dare to wound him — particularly a bedraggled, weakened woman.

"Look out!" I narrowly blocked Lord Broderick's strike from ending Dri's dad's life, and the older man turned and buried his own sword in the second lord's belly. Ten paces away, our allies killed a Sheolite together, one impaling him with his sword, the other severing his head. Dri's dad turned toward me. "We must be away," he panted.

Behind him, I saw Lord Cyrus thrust his sword through the back of a Sheolite, straight through the heart, and watched Lord Jala turn toward him, mouth agape. "Cyrus!" he cried in rage. "You've betrayed us!"

"Stick with me," I said to Dri's dad, pulling him to the side as a Sheolite charged. I grabbed hold of the last enemy's arm as he brought down his sword to strike me and whipped him to the side, breaking his arm across my leg as he fell. Dri's father pierced him through the heart. When I looked up, Andriana was facing the remaining three of the Six, who were spreading in an arc to surround her. "Stop," she said, holding the tip of her dagger toward one after the other. "Do you know what I can do with this?"

Lord Jala's nostrils flared. "This is pointless, Andriana. You have done nothing but assigned yourself a long, tortuous death, daring to attack us. And we all know that your gifting makes you weak in battle."

"Not here, now. Not where Sethos has spun a spell blocking me from reading you," Andriana grit out in rage, and she let her dagger fly. It rammed into Maximillian's chest. His face slackened in shock and he dropped his sword, lifting his hands to grab hold of the dagger. "That is your own death penalty, m'lord," she cried. "For trying to kill my father twice. This day you shall know who it is you truly serve, and suffer an eternity of consequences."

Outside, soldiers now rammed their shoulders against the door. It visibly shuddered.

My eyes moved to the windows that lined two of the walls, and I spotted men in gray uniforms running across a hill toward the palace. Toward us.

"C'mon," I said, grabbing hold of Andriana's hand, exhilarated to be by her side again, even if it was in the midst of such dire circumstances. We ran toward the far wall and I sent a chair crashing through a window, then used my sword to ram away the most threatening pieces. Andriana did not hesitate. She jumped over the sill, taking several other large, sharp pieces with her. She landed outside and drew her sword again, protecting her mother as she came out. Her father was next. Then Lord Cyrus, blessed, blessed Cyrus. As the soldiers finally burst through the cracked Council room door, my eyes shifted to what remained of the Six, hovering around Lord Jala as he collapsed, and I hurtled myself through the window.

CHAPTER 30

ANDRIANA

They were shooting at us. "Zigzag!" Dad yelled, even as we'd already begun to do so, knowing it'd be harder to hit us. We were tearing toward the hills on the far end of the expansive palace lawn, behind the sprawling building from the ocean. Making it to the trees seemed our only possible escape. The bullets passed so close I heard one whistle past my left ear, and another splintered the trunk of a tree to my right.

I dared not look back to see how far behind us they were, but I breathed better the farther into the trees we got. And yet there were still shots coming at us.

Shadowy figures emerged out of the brush as we passed them, defending us. I was moving so fast that I passed them before I could really see who they were. But as my brain caught up with the vision, I glanced back, mouth agape, along with Ronan.

Bellona and Vidar.

Here. With us.

Bellona shooting arrows, Vidar with two revolvers, driving the Pacificans away.

"We decided we couldn't let you two have all the fun," Vidar quipped when he caught up with us, standing beside a tunnel entrance in the wood, and caught my stare.

"Right!" I said with a grin.

Suddenly with them there, with us, I felt invincible. That our mad escape might just end in freedom, rather than death.

"How did you —"

"Vidar!" Bellona complained, notching another arrow. "Focus!"

Obediently he turned and took aim again.

"Take this tunnel," Cyrus said, lifting a chin in the direction we were to go. "Get down there. Take the first right. Hundred paces, take a left. We'll meet you in two minutes, or go on without us. All the way to the end." He stared hard at Ronan. "Go all the way in that same direction, and you'll emerge in a safe place. Got it?"

"Got it," Ronan said. He turned and pulled me toward the tunnel opening, the trap door artfully disguised in the brush. But I pulled away from him, insisting my parents go down first. I resisted the urge to pull them into my arms, to hold them close, even for a second. Part of me knew it was a foolish waste of time. And part of me thought that if I gave in to the dream, I just might wake.

I forced myself to focus, to not give in to relief yet. We were far from safety. But I dared to believe the Maker's dream wouldn't all end here, in Pacifica, the Maker's dream for me. We had to live. We had to see through the Call.

At last I climbed down the stairs carved into the rock and Ronan came behind. The door shut abruptly, and I fought the desire to return above and join the others to fight off the soldiers. They had counted the cost. They were giving us an edge. If we did not take it, we all might be lost and their sacrifice would've been in vain.

"C'mon, Dri," Ronan said, lighting a flare with a strike of a match. My parents' faces lit up in an eerie red, but at last I took a moment to hug them both, just for a second.

"H-how? When?" I asked.

"Later," Dad said, setting me back, firm hands on each shoulder. Gloriously firm, known hands. Hands I'd known my entire life. "Right now, let's concentrate on surviving, yes?"

"Yes," I said, tears running down my cheeks, feeling ten years old again.

"Yes," Mom said.

"This way," Ronan said. And we followed.

CHAPTER 31

ANDRIANA

We paused at the end of the tunnel, panting for breath, waiting for our friends for several long minutes, despite what Cyrus had said. "Come, Dri, we have to keep going," Ronan said, pulling at my arm, but I resisted.

"Wait. Three more counts," I said.

But after *three*, the tunnel remained pitch black and silent. We were turning when we heard a creak and soft thuds of people landing and turned back, praying it wasn't soldiers. After a bit, an eerie red light filled the other end as they turned the corner. I narrowly resisted a cry of joy and waited for Vidar and Bellona to reach us on the run, Lord Cyrus helping one of the injured, Pacifican guards who had aided us coming right behind.

Vidar looped a short, stocky arm around me, grinning, all white teeth, while I hugged Bellona in turn. Vidar then took

Ronan's arm and pulled the bigger man into a hug, lifting him off the ground, and then me. Quick introductions were made.

I sensed my parents' gratitude and curiosity, as their eyes moved from Ronan to me again. Ronan was never out of reach, constantly touching my hand, my shoulder, my back. And I longed to slip into his arms for hours.

But a creak in the ceiling directly above us sent us all scurrying forward again, with Vidar and Bellona leading the way and Ronan and Cyrus and the injured guard bringing up the rear. Every sound carried through the tunnels. At one point, we could hear the muffled shouts of soldiers, perhaps ten feet above us. Here and there, clods of dirt gave way and fell to the ground, as if complaining about the weight above. The tunnel had periodic rough-hewn posts that gave it some structure and support. But not much. Mostly it was simply a rounded tunnel dug from the soil, barely wide enough for Ronan to fit through.

We paused off and on to clear away a collapsed portion, and I grew more and more fearful that we'd find a totally caved-in block and be trapped. But fear was not of the Maker, I reminded myself, even as we stopped to wait for Bellona and Vidar to clear the next pile of debris. When it took a while, Ronan squeezed by me and the others to see if he could help them.

Mom took the moment to embrace me again, kissing my forehead. "Ah, Andriana. How we have prayed for your safety."

Dad reached around her to lay a hand on my shoulder.

"How did you survive?" I asked at last. "I went to the house, later, and there was so much blood."

"We were wounded, both of us," Mom said, and I felt the fear and pain and rage in her memories of that battle. "But they only wanted us to believe that we were vanquished, that it was hopeless to fight, and for you to think we were dead. Precisely so they could use us at the right moment against you."

"We need to keep moving," Vidar said, after sharing his canteen of water with us. The water tasted odd, metallic, but I didn't care.

"He's right. We're still a good distance from the end," Cyrus said.

I stared at him and then looked to the short tunnel, disappearing into the darkness behind him. My back already ached from running hunched over the short way we'd gone, and the taller men must really be suffering. What shape would we be in by tonight? But if it led us to freedom ...

"Vidar, how did you —" I began.

"Chaza'el," he said, playfully turning my shoulders in the direction of the others disappearing down the tunnel again. "He knew they were about to demand your sworn loyalty, or they'd kill you."

"Chaza'el," I repeated, finally understanding how the Ailith could arrive at such a critical moment. "And this tunnel? Who built this tunnel?"

"I did," Lord Cyrus said simply. "I though it wise for Keallach to have an escape route, in case of an uprising. Even most of the Six and the Sheolites did not know it was present. And the Maker knew we'd need it for an entirely different reason."

"Nice work, for a Pacifican," Bellona grunted ahead of us, and I smiled.

I reveled in the feeling of being surrounded again by people I loved who loved me in return, and by new allies too, all of us running in the same direction. It brought a strength coursing through my veins I hadn't felt since leaving the Ailith on the river. But after another hour, that strength waned; we were dirty, thirsty, and weary. Had we made much progress? I had the constant, terrible thought that those who searched for us would finally find the tunnel and come after us, easily shooting us in the back, one after the next. I prayed that the tunnel was collapsing behind us, blocking them as often as we had to stop and dig our way out.

"I'm beginning to regret my compliment, Cyrus," Bellona called back to him, when we stopped again.

"We're almost to the old tunnels, where it will open up." But there wasn't any real defense in his tone. He knew we were grateful. It was harder for the taller men, stooping constantly. Even I constantly knocked my head on the ceiling of the tunnel, caught between the overwhelming desire to straighten and yet not knock myself unconscious. The injured guard was moaning softly, even as he struggled to breathe.

The dull, thudding sound of men running above us made us all quiet again, and a big clod of dirt fell on my shoulder, then another on my back.

I held my breath as long as I could, scared to death that there were soldiers about to collapse down into the tunnel with us. I couldn't hold my breath in any longer. I inhaled. And then I choked on the billowing dust and coughed. It was awful, needing to clear my lungs, needing to breathe, but frightened that I'd give us all away. Wasn't there less earth between us and our adversaries than before?

"It's all right," Vidar whispered back to us. "They're Pacifican soldiers, not Sheolite. They don't know we're here. Let's go. But Cyrus? We need you up here now. I'll carry our brother."

The men switched places, and Vidar hoisted the now

unconscious guard over his shoulders. We went on until I thought my back or knees might give out, hunched over as we were. I could feel the grime coating my sweating face and neck. The air was stale, and just as I fought the sensation that those ahead of me were using up all the oxygen, that I was choking, we caught the scent of fresh air. The line ahead of us slowed and then stopped, presumably for Vidar and Bellona to survey the surroundings and see if Cyrus could remember our way out.

Then we heard the sound of metal upon metal and more fresh air poured into the tunnel. It was no brighter, so we clearly hadn't reached the surface yet, but in a little bit we were all standing straight and stretching in a cement cavern.

"Ah, here is familiar territory," Vidar said, as he emerged behind me and wearily, carefully set down his burden and put his hands on his hips. "Why is it that we must spend so much time in the most frightening places possible?"

"No one told you it'd be all glory," Bellona growled, tossing him a canteen. "Get over it."

We moved around, studying the graffiti on the wall as Vidar lit a new flare and Ronan lit a torch off his flame. There were grim, telling phrases everywhere. "This tunnel dates from the Great War," Cyrus said, sitting down to rest a moment. I sat down beside him, staring up at the graffiti.

The Maker has forgotten us.

Hell is here.

Forgive us. We knew not what we did.

There were curse words, names and dates, many depicting births and even more deaths, one messenger listing perhaps a hundred or more. Had there been a Community down here? Survivors? Or rebels to the Pacificans, for a time?

"Why'd you help us escape?" I asked Cyrus. "I mean, specifically. Why throw all you had away in favor of us?"

"I am indebted to the Remnants. Tressa healed someone I love very much. Someone who brought me back to the Way." He sipped from his canteen and leaned his head back against the cement wall. "I spent much time with Kapriel as a boy. His trainer had told him about this tunnel, where to find it, where it opened and ended, shortly before he died. The man knew that Sethos's power over Keallach was growing and their time was short. He feared for Kapriel's life. And then the worst happened, and I ..."

"You agreed to follow Keallach."

"I did," he said, giving me a long, sorrowful look. "I was afraid. It was the worst decision of my life. Every day has been a sort of sick torture since then. Pretending to be one with them, wishing I could be away, and yet fearing for my own life." He shook his head and pushed his hair back from his face. "I was a coward for far too long."

"But at critical moments you were brave. And wise," Ronan said, moving to stand before him. "I, for one, will be forever grateful," he said, reaching down a hand to shake Cyrus's.

"As will I," I said.

"And I," echoed the others.

"Never too late in the Maker's time," Vidar added.

His phrase reminded me of Keallach. "Despite what happened back there," I dared, "I sensed good in Keallach. Hope. He's not all bad. Is he, Cyrus?"

Cyrus paused and sighed. "I don't know, Andriana. Truly. Some days I see glimpses of the boy he used to be. But more and more I see Sethos's tentacles penetrating every part of his life, every choice. Don't you?"

I remained silent as we rose, preparing to move out again.

"You think Keallach didn't know exactly what the Six were planning to do in his absence?" Ronan asked me with a scoff, suspicion and anger radiating from him. "To you? Your parents?"

It was as if Ronan suspected me of caring for Keallach as more than a brother, even now. But he couldn't know all that happened. *Surely not* … "I don't know," I said, throwing out my hands. "Did he, Cyrus?"

Cyrus shifted, looking from me to Ronan and back again. "I don't know either. I was only a part of one conversation about what was about to happen to you and yours, and that was this morning, with Lord Jala."

"Don't you think it's convenient that he and Sethos disappeared, right before something horrific was about to happen to you?" Ronan said with a jeering tone, crossing his arms. "It was an easy way to keep his hands clean, right? Make him look innocent. He knew you wouldn't consider a *union* if you associated it with the murder of your parents."

I frowned, trying to ignore the hurt within Ronan, and turned to follow him down the wide mouth of the cement tunnel. "I believe Sethos knew what they planned. But not Keallach. I mean, yes, he … I just don't … I can't believe that he …" I let out a sound of exasperation. "Cyrus, I just can't see that it was Keallach's plan to torture me into submission. He was willing to use his gift to try and sway me, yes. But would he really have been willing to see me go through such pain? That doesn't square with what I know of him."

Ronan's shoulders stiffened before me.

"Never mind," I muttered. I dropped it. There'd be time enough to talk through what I thought about Keallach. Right now I had to focus on getting out of Pacifica with the rest of them, or we'd be killed before I ever had the chance to consider it again.

Not that I sensed any of them would give Keallach a real chance. To them, he was the one who had captured me and imprisoned my folks, as well as Kapriel, and harmed us all in one way or another. They held him responsible, even if he wasn't the one who was at the root of it all. And I supposed that was right, given that Keallach ruled. But in some ways, he was just as new to all this as we were. New to the power, experimenting, curious, trying and failing and succeeding. And if I had been with Sethos day in and day out, would I not be influenced by him?

Once Cyrus got his bearings, we moved into a jog down the dry edge of the sewer tunnel, careful to avoid the fetid stream at the center, and turned left and then right and then left again. I saw that Cyrus was following a series of casually marked lines that might have been missed by anyone coming after us, but clearly were marked by the Ailith as they passed.

"Where does it lead?" I called up to Cyrus. "Where do we come out?"

Cyrus came to a sudden stop and motioned frantically for me to be quiet. I turned to look at Vidar, and felt his rising fear before I saw it on his sweating face. A moment later the sting of my armband told me what we already knew. Someone was coming. Someone almost as powerful as Sethos. A tracker. It had to be. I hadn't felt Vidar's panic like this since that day outside the Hoodites, or in Wadi Qelt.

"Run," Cyrus growled, pushing Mom and Dad past him. "Follow the white lines until you see white stars, then follow those. Once outside, go to the white house at the top of the hill and take shelter beneath the deck." Bellona edged her bow off her shoulder, even as Vidar pulled out his revolvers and Ronan his sword. Cyrus held out his hand to me. "Come with me," he said. "I'll show you the way."

"But we can't leave them," I protested.

"Yes," Ronan said, "you can." He nodded backward, to where my folks waited at the next corner. "Keep them safe. We'll join you as soon as we can."

I heard the unearthly screech of a tracker — just like when Sethos caught up to us in Zanzibar — and chills ran down my neck and shoulders.

"Go, Dri," Ronan demanded. "You may be weaker after your time in the palace."

So that was it. They didn't trust me. They doubted me. But I couldn't help them if they were right. I could actually harm their cause if I faltered again. And the last time we'd battled trackers, in hand-to-hand combat, it hadn't gone so well.

I turned and ran with Cyrus. When we reached my parents, I took my dad's hand and Cyrus took my mom's. And as the roar of an attack echoed down the walls of the tunnel, sounding a hundred times worse than anything I'd heard before, we ran faster still.

CHAPTER
32

RONAN

There was no way I was going to lose Andriana now. Not when I'd just found her again. We threw the flare down to the right and propped the torch against the left wall, then took up our weapons and waited for our adversaries to turn the corner. With each breath, I was thankful — it meant Cyrus, Dri, and her parents could get farther away — and yet I felt I would crack open with the anticipation. Every inch of my skin was alive as my arm cuff grew colder and my muscles tensed.

"Let the Maker flow through you," Vidar said. "Force yourself to ease up, wait for him to lead, *then follow*," he said. "We do not fight alone. Remember that."

I felt a tinge of warmth on the other side of my cuff, which moved to overtake the cold. Round and round the two sensations went: frigid, then hot. I thought of the battle in the Hoodite field, when Vidar saw angels and demons and Andriana sensed the same. The hairs on my arms stood up with the sensation of others joining us unseen, and Vidar's words ran through my head, over and over. *We do not fight alone.*

Which was good. Because what rounded the corner — with even some of them splashing through the sewer muck at the center — was the most fearsome group of adversaries I'd faced yet. We were but three. They were five across and at least three lines deep.

"Not alone," I muttered to myself, as Bellona let her first arrows fly. Two Sheolite scouts went down, one male, the other female. Before the group reached us, two more were hit, one somersaulting in the stream and causing another to trip. Bellona drew her sword and took on a tracker with Vidar, as I ducked the angry strike of a scout's sword and thrust my dagger into his belly, then brought my sword around with both hands to neatly sever the head off the next.

An arrow came singing by my ear and into the throat of a gray-clad Pacifican soldier. We all wanted to take down as many as we could. But we all knew our main goal was to keep any of them from entering the tunnel after Cyrus, Andriana, and her parents. Especially the trackers, and there were four in this group. There'd been four on the Hoodite field, and we'd come against them with the entire Ailith force. *Not alone,* I repeated silently, as I blocked a tall female soldier's strike and swung her into the cement wall with every bit of strength in me. My sword severed the next man's arm, and an arrow from Bellona finished him off. I sidestepped the pointed end of a spear, caught it with my hand, and wrenched it out of the surprised man's grasp, pulling him into the end of my sword. On and on it went, one after another. I heard Vidar cry out, wounded, and saw his bleeding arm. Now he and Bellona were each battling a tracker while the other two trackers stood back, waiting. For what? For us to be so weary they could finish the task?

The next soldier I encountered was not only big, he was good. Faster than I fathomed he'd be, parrying and dodging every thrust I made. And when I turned, another Sheolite stabbed me in the side, his face an angry sneer as he twisted the short blade.

Niero leaped upon him, then, swiftly killing him as I staggered backward, the knife still embedded in my side. I stared back at our captain, wondering how he always managed to be right where we needed him ... but then gasped, my body in agony. I tried to ignore the pain, use it as fuel for retribution, but I knew my actions were now slower, weaker. And that was when the last two trackers left their positions and moved toward us.

"Niero," I began, panting. There were still two Sheolite scouts standing beside the trackers.

"I see them," he said, blocking a scout's blade, inches from his head. He punched the man in the nose, so hard that the man wheeled back and fell on his rear, blood spurting from his face. Niero whirled and took off his head, all the while keeping his eyes on the oncoming trackers. I'd never seen anything like it—so many elite Sheolite in one place.

I glanced wildly around for Vidar and Bellona. They were both down, and I hoped to the Maker that they were only unconscious, not dead. For the first time, I wondered if Niero and I would die here too. Maybe I was dead already. How else did it make sense that Niero was here with us? He was supposed to be in the Desert or elsewhere by now. *But I cannot* die, I told myself. Dri and her parents were counting on me. The least I could do was give them a few more precious seconds.

"'I do not fear those who kill the body but cannot kill the soul,'" Niero bit out, straightening to face the trackers.

The trackers froze and actually took a step back. Niero advanced. "I 'fear the One who can destroy both body and soul and send his enemies to the pit.'"

One of the trackers took another step backward and let out an animalistic cry, every inch of his face betraying fear and twined with fury. What was this? Words as weapons? But even as I thought it, weakly parrying another soldier's strike, I knew the truth of it. Niero was invoking holy words, the Sacred Words. Long forgotten words.

Every one of them resonated, as much a strengthening agent for me as they were an apparent wound to our adversaries. There was power in those words. I forced myself to stand straighter and shouted, "We fight for the One who was, and is, and is to come!"

The nearest tracker winced, and the other one now fighting Niero grimaced. But the scouts didn't seem to be as affected. They both strode toward me, studying me, my bloody hand over my wound, clearly taking into account where I might be weakest. It was as they both struck at once that I saw the first tracker whirl just out of Niero's reach and run headlong for the tunnel entrance.

He knew. That we weren't all that were left. That Dri and the others were ahead. And he was surely bent on finding them before they reached the end.

As I swung at one of the Sheolites, the other managed to drive his fist against the hilt of the knife still buried in my side, cutting it free. I bent over in agony, fighting for breath, fighting to remain conscious, falling beside the Pacifican guard who had helped free us in the palace, now dead. My vision tunneled even as I willed myself to rise again, hearing my name distantly on Niero's lips.

But my own were moving in a whisper. "Run, Dri. I'm so sorry. Run, love. *Run.*"

CHAPTER
33

ANDRIANA

We paused only when we had to stop and listened, trying to hear the battle behind us, to discern what might be happening. But we could hear nothing more than our own panting and blood pulsing in our own ears. The silence made us at first jubilant, thinking our friends had claimed victory. But when there was no whistle, no shout …

"You don't think …?" I said to Cyrus, unable to say the rest.

"No," he said firmly, but I detected the lie in his eyes before I sensed it in his heart. He hoped he could protect me, buoy my spirits to keep me from collapsing.

We heard the footsteps at a distance, and then I knew who was coming too. It wasn't Ronan, or Vidar or Bellona. It was a tracker.

I looked at Cyrus in fear, then back down the tunnel. Did I see dark wisps? Wraiths?

"What is it?" Dad asked, voice rising.

"A tracker. Like Sethos. And wraiths," I spat out. "Their favorite companions."

"Don't panic," he said, consciously lowering his voice, taking my hands and squeezing them. "Do not give in to the dark. If it comes to it, you and I will take him down together. The wraiths will follow."

"And we will help you," Cyrus said, wrapping his fingers around the shaft of an axe he'd found.

"Yes," Mom said, her own hand on a length of cloth. She'd always been a dead shot with the sling.

Hope swelled within me. I would not give in to thoughts of the worst. A tracker had slipped by our shield; that didn't mean they were all dead. I shook away the vision of Ronan alone, bleeding in that awful muck. *No.* Instead I directed my mind to my last view of him, standing tall, sword drawn, ready for whatever came his way. With Vidar and Bellona beside him. No, this lousy tracker had simply managed to slip by them as the battle raged on.

Maker, make me courageous. Give me faith!

"Let's go, get as far as we can before we take him on," I said, looking to Cyrus, but his eyes were wide and scanning the walls, even as the heavy footfalls grew louder.

"I don't see the white star," he muttered, running to the far end. "Do any of you see the star? There was once a star here, on one of these walls!" He turned one way, and then the other.

"Just choose, man!" Dad barked, voicing my own thoughts. "Dig down! Which way does your gut tell you is right?"

As if sensing our rising panic, our adversary let out a screech, sending shivers down my back. "C'mon," I said, grabbing Mom's hand. "C'mon!" I cried again, already running, choosing for Cyrus if he could not. We had to get out.

We were running, splashing down the center of the tunnel, trying to keep our feet, when we saw Vidar and Bellona enter ahead of us from the side, via another path.

"Vidar!" I cried. The two turned and slowly awaited us, leaning down, hands on knees, gasping for breath.

"Where's Ronan?" I said, my heart in my throat. I moved toward the tunnel they'd just left, but Bellona snagged my arm and forced me back.

"He'll be along shortly," she said, lying to me. "He's with Niero."

"*Niero?*"

"Niero," she repeated, drawing an arrow and shooting it into the dark mass of wraiths swirling toward us. "I don't know why I tried that," she said with an empty laugh. "But it sure made me feel a little better."

"You listen to me, Andriana," Vidar said fiercely, holding my face with both of his hands. I saw then the blood spattered across his skin and shirt, further evidence of their battle. "If you can't block the tracker, the wraiths, you concentrate on me, okay? Focus on me, and take on my feelings. Not what they try and hook you with. Got it?"

When I hesitated, he shook me a little. "Got it?"

"Yes," I whispered, agitated when he didn't believe me. "*Yes.*"

He let go of my face, took up my hand, and we ran again. Mom and Dad were right behind us, and after a while, at perhaps our fourth or fifth turn, we stopped to catch our breath.

Judging from the silence, we dared to hope that even though we were undoubtedly lost, the tracker might be as well. We were on a path that made no sense. Perhaps he had seen the marks Cyrus sought and figured it out, gone the way we were supposed to. That's what a good tracker would do, right?

But just as our hearts began to thud at a more normal pace, Mom reached out and grabbed my free hand, not out of comfort, I knew immediately, but out of terror. "Andriana, look." she whispered, nodding toward a grate ten steps away.

I turned toward it. Tendrils of dark smoke were sliding through the holes and then along the ground, curving upward at the walls. And as they met the ceiling, they arced into forms, then spun and danced toward each of us. As the first rose to my level, I let out a sound of awe. She was lovely, this spirit, perfect in form, with high cheekbones and a bow for lips and round, welcoming eyes. I didn't remember faces in those we'd seen before, only the dark, swirling smoke-like shape. But as soon as I laughed, caught up in wonder, in spite of myself, she morphed, her lips melting into teeth and then a gaping hole within the skeletal remains of a face. As she melted into her true form, she seemed to be pulling at my heart, slowing its beat, sucking out my very life.

My mother entered my line of vision, oddly coming through the wraith, until all I could see was her. "Andriana, look at me," she said. "Look at me. Remember who you are. Remember what you were born for. Remember your Call. You are stronger than these leeches! In the Maker, you are invincible!"

I watched her face, trying to digest her words as if I heard them from a distance. But as I did so, I dug into her words as anchors. *Who I was. What I was born for. My Call. My strength. In the Maker.*

Wraiths on either side of me and my mother recoiled, as if sensing my thoughts like a foul stench. But then the tracker arrived, stopping suddenly when he found us at last, his long, red cape swaying behind him like a clock pendulum coming to a stop.

Vidar was shouting, convulsing, battling both tracker and wraith. "Go to him," I said to my mother, straightening and striding toward the tracker. My father was by my side. It was he who had spent as many hours with me a day as my trainer; in the woods, along the river, climbing, digging, foraging. He and I had spent many hours sparring. I was confident that he could hold his own. At least for a time.

"Away, old man," breathed the tracker, not even looking at him. "I've come for the empath and the knower alone."

"You will fail in your mission," I said, taking a ready stance, raising my sword. I did as Vidar had asked me earlier, concentrating on him — my friend, my brother, the *knower* — rather than give this tracker any room to infiltrate my heart and mind.

"I agree," Dad said.

"I will kill you," the tracker seethed toward my father.

"You'll have to, if you want to get to them."

"As you wish," said the tracker, turning with his sword so swiftly, I didn't have time to react.

But Dad met his strike, staring up into his eyes. "Be gone, demon. You have no place here."

"On the contrary," the tracker said, striking again and again, driving my father backward, eyes only on him. "We own this land and all in it."

"Not *all*," I said, ramming my sword into his side, tip first. Then upward, through what I hoped was his heart.

He screamed and wrenched with the pain, and I faltered. He backhanded me and I whirled away, sprawling to the ground with such force I skidded several paces. When I caught my breath and turned to look at him again, he was upon me, leaning down to grip my neck and lift me up, so high that my toes left the ground. "They said I could not kill you," he whispered, coming close, the nearness of his skin like ice on a Hoarfrosted river, "but they didn't say I couldn't bring you to death's door."

He grinned, and over his shoulder three wraiths danced and smiled and then gaped with their horrible yawning mouths that seemed to suck in the very air around us. Even Vidar's torch flame curved toward them.

Vidar. Could he help me? My eyes shifted hard to the right, where I'd seen him fall. Mom was with him, rising, and he was pushing himself up to his elbows, blinking slowly, as if just figuring out where he was. Mom was swinging her sling in a circle to her right and over her head, her eyes never leaving the tracker. Meanwhile, I knew I was about to lose consciousness. I clawed at the tracker's long fingers that were digging into my throat, cutting off my air, my blood flow. I kicked against his long legs, but he didn't appear to feel it. I wasn't even entirely certain I was making contact.

I felt the rock fall against my forearm, and only vaguely understood it had bounced off the tracker's head. A big, bright spot of red dripped from his temple and his eyes shifted slowly left, slowly right, then backward, leaving only an eerie white in the sockets before me. The wraiths hissed and recoiled. The tracker's hands dropped from my neck and I fell heavily to the floor, gasping for breath as he teetered on his feet and then fell straight backward. My father staggered forward and raised his sword, praying in a whisper with fast moving lips, then brought his blade down across his neck.

I watched his blood spread, thinking it'd make much more sense if these horrific beings bled peacock blue or vermillion orange instead of the same dark red we all bled. He'd been a man once, this tracker. Just as Sethos had once been a man. And even full of the dark, they died as men.

Vidar staggered over to me and offered me a hand. I clasped it and rose, and he hooked a hand across my far shoulder, pulling me close, looking over at my parents. "So, uh, Dri, I know the elders never wanted us to be with our parents again after the Call," he said, panting. "For their safety and all. But if they want, I vote that yours can stay."

CHAPTER 34

RONAN

When I came to, Dri was binding my wound with a long, clean cloth. "Wh-what are you doing back here?" I managed. She roughly rolled me over, stealing my breath, then the other way, before I finally gathered enough air to cry out.

"I'm so sorry. I'm almost done," she said, looking miserable about causing me pain. She caught my expression. "Look, I'm sorry! You were bleeding out. I had to stop it. What would you have me do?"

I felt beads of sweat run down my scalp and fought to hold onto consciousness. And yet I was incomparably relieved that she was here, safe for the moment, even if I couldn't rise and protect her. "Where's Niero?" I asked.

"He went after the other tracker," she said sourly. "Alone. We ran and got lost — ended up back here, with you, which oddly seems safe for now. We think the Pacificans and Sheolites think they've already searched this area and moved on." She took the end of the bandage between her teeth and started a tear, then removed the rest using her fingers. "Mom, Dad, Vidar, and Cyrus are trying to find the way out again."

"Dri," I said, turning to try and rise.

"Uh, no," she said, easily shoving me back down. "You'll lie there and pray the Maker will stop your bleeding while we figure out our next steps."

"We're under the core of Pacifica," I said with a groan, lifting a hand to push the loose hair clinging to my sweating face. It wasn't hot down here in the tunnel. I supposed the wound or the pain itself was sending me into a fever. "I'm thinking our next step is to find our way out."

"That's helpful." Dri said, as she pretended to glower down at me. "We're down to two options. Vidar and Bellona went one direction, Mom, Dad, and Cyrus the other. So you rest, and that includes your tongue too. You'll need your strength when we decide which way to go."

I heaved a sigh and laid my head back on the concrete. "So we are here, alone," I said.

"Yes. Let's hope it stays that way."

"Dri," I said a moment later, reaching for her hand. She gave it to me, and I held it on my chest with both of my own, closing my eyes, preserving every bit of energy I could.

"Yes?"

"I'm sorry it took me so long to come to you."

"Hey," she said softly. "I wasn't exactly easy to reach. I know you would've come earlier if you could." She paused a second. "Right?"

"Niero ... Well Niero thought you had to do this step alone, for the most part. Sort some things out."

She stared at me a second and seemed to stop breathing. Then she looked down the dark tunnel for a long time, across all the dead bodies of those we'd defeated, and then back to me. "Maybe I did."

In that moment, I didn't think she'd ever sounded more defenseless. Open. Pure.

"Come here," I said, gesturing her closer.

She knelt, cautiously, beside me. Ignoring the pain, I lifted my hands slowly to her head and brought it down to my lips, kissing her on the forehead, where her dark hair parted in pell-mell fashion. Then I looked into her green-blue eyes. "I had to let you go," I said solemnly, "But I never want to again."

"I don't want you to either, Ronan. Try not to, okay?"

"Okay," I said, fading.

"Ronan," she said, shaking me a little. "Stay with me."

The others arrived then, in two groups, with Niero coming in last. "Found the way," Vidar crowed.

But Dri's mother looked from my bloody bandages to my eyes, leaning down to take my pulse. "How bad is it, Ronan?" she asked.

"Bad," I admitted.

She clamped her lips shut. It was the fear of any belly wound. If the intestines were caught, most died from infection within a day, even if they could survive the blood loss. If there'd been other internal organ damage …

"We need to get him to a doctor," she said to Dri.

"Right," Dri said, agitated, "Only one problem. We're still in the middle of Pacifica."

"I know one," Cyrus said, from across the tunnel. "Her home is close to where we'll emerge."

"She's trustworthy?" Bellona asked.

"As far as I know. And looking at Ronan, I'm thinking we don't have the option to tarry on a decision."

"Good," Niero said decisively. "We'll go to her first."

Bellona was already shouldering her pack, as were Vidar and Niero.

Cyrus broke out a compass — apparently obtained from a fallen enemy — and watched as the needle settled.

"We'll need two on either side of Ronan," Niero said.

He and Bellona approached and I winced, inwardly chafing that I was a burden to them all. Andriana's mother and father wordlessly took their packs from them and pulled the bags across their emaciated shoulders. With gentle strength, Niero and Bellona eased me to a sitting position and then to my feet. I bit down as hard as I could, trying not to cry out. Instinctively, I knew this wound was bad.

Andriana studied me, her beautiful eyes filling with the reflection of my own fear. I forced myself to concentrate on the Maker, on his promises, on the fact that he had brought us this far, and hope began to overtake the fear. As Dri sensed that in me, her expression eased. "Let's get on with it," I said, panting.

I could hope. But the physical pain was intense. With each of the steps we took I felt as if my gut was wrenching entirely open, that my intestines, if not sliced, would surely spill out of me. They were right. If I was to survive this, I needed to be stitched up, and fast.

ANDRIANA

Ronan lasted a fair distance — back to where we'd first

encountered our enemies and took a wrong turn as we fled — when his mouth opened in a silent gasp.

"Ronan!" I cried.

His face turned ashen and he sank down like a deadweight, nearly pulling Bellona and Niero with him. As gently as they could, they laid him out. Niero put a hand on his chest and bent down to listen to him breathe.

"No, he lives yet," I said miserably, anxiety again filling me, but the connection between us as strong as ever. Mom took my hand and squeezed it. "He just couldn't bear the pain any longer." We could all see how the blood soaked his entire tunic and down into his leggings. It was amazing he'd lasted as long as he had.

"He's so pale, he looks like the Pacifican women," Vidar said.

"Vidar!" Bellona cried.

"Sorry," he muttered. But he rose, padded over to the body of a decapitated Sheolite nearby, and pulled his cape off. "We should take several," he said, lifting it, then glancing around for others. "We can use them as a disguise. Or even one as a stretcher. It's sturdy and long."

Niero took it from him with some distaste. We all sensed the lingering stink of evil in it, but perhaps it'd serve to cloak our passing, in a way. Vidar had been right to take it, thinking of a potential disguise. I wished I'd thought to cut a couple from the scouts, or even the gray uniforms of the Pacificans. *Next time.*

Vidar suddenly froze and his face transformed into a glower. "More have entered the tunnels," he said, his eyes shifting rapidly left and right.

"How far are they?" Niero asked.

Only then did I feel the faintest warning in my arm cuff.

"I don't know. They might have reached that last battleground."

Niero sighed and reached down with Bellona, Vidar, and me to lift Ronan onto the cape, each of us at a corner. We lifted Ronan fairly easily, but I knew it wouldn't take long for our hands, arms, and shoulders to be screaming in protest.

"Let's not dawdle, shall we?" Vidar asked in a bright whisper, looking over his shoulder at the rest of us. But I was getting a sense of what he knew already. They were many, enough to spread out and fill every tunnel in their efforts to capture us. We would not manage to escape them again. Not down here.

"This way," Cyrus whispered, running ahead of us.

And as best we could, we hurried after him.

CHAPTER 35

ANDRIANA

Near the end of the tunnel, we heard troops running and pulled to one side, setting Ronan down, freezing in place, and dousing our torch, hoping that anyone who looked in our direction might not see us. But within a few breaths we knew they were on the other side of the wall.

My armband grew colder and colder, and we heard a muffled voice call a halt from the other side of the concrete. I closed my eyes, reaching out to sense them, to try and get an idea of their number. But it was best obtained through Vidar, beside me. I reached out and laid one hand on his shoulder and the other on the wall.

"Andriana, no," he whispered, but it was already done. I absorbed what he inherently knew. Eight on the other side, one of them a tracker, two of them scouts, the rest Pacifican soldiers. And the tracker — I could almost *see* him pausing, leaning toward the wall that separated us, lifting his nose in the air and inhaling deeply, as if he could smell us. When he put his hand on the wall as I had, a shock ran through me and I pulled away, scrambling to the far side of our tunnel, fearing he might come through the wall itself.

Vidar struck a match and lit his last flare. He motioned to Bellona that our enemies were on the other side and then tossed her his flare. Vidar's eyes met mine for a moment of recognition. It had been a while since we chose this passage-way. The turn was a good half-mile back. We had only the time it'd take for them to double-back and enter our tunnel to get away. Our only hope was to outrun them.

Collectively, we turned toward Cyrus, praying he'd make the right choices. All our lives depended on it. And then, we forced ourselved onward, as fast as we could go.

My mouth and throat were parched, but I ignored my thirst. The last of the canteens had been drained hours ago, the water that flowed by our feet undrinkable. And then around the next corner, light. I blinked, wondering at first if it was a trick of the mind, or an electrical light, like those in the palace. But it wasn't. Hope surged within us all, and we immediately moved forward, but more cautiously now, fearing exposure to any who might be outside.

It had been hours since we'd been in the sun, and I blinked repeatedly as we neared the grate.

"This is it," Cyrus said excitedly. "Come quickly. We need to get a couple of us up there and lift the rest to safety."

"Where are we?" Niero asked him.

"If I'm right, on the border of the city, near a canyon I once knew. And that doctor," he said.

We four carrying Ronan set him down, and Niero and

Vidar bent down to give Cyrus a leg up. He grabbed hold of the bars and lifted himself up, peered around, then shifted and looked some more. I could feel his satisfaction before he dropped down and panted, "It's good."

Niero and Vidar lifted Bellona up next. She swung over to the right and then lifted her legs to a small ledge in the concrete, too small to rest her body on, but enough to release some of the weight. Then she set to reaching through and unscrewing one nut and then the next, until the grate swung open and there was an empty hole showing nothing but glorious sky. Moving swiftly, she swung through and disappeared a moment, then reached over, just her face and arm visible. "It's clear. Send up Vidar first."

Niero hoisted him alone, practically tossing him up. Then, with the two of them up top, they easily lifted my parents and me. Below us, Niero and Cyrus lifted the corners of the cape around Ronan — now fashioned into a seat — up to us.

"C'mon, c'mon," Vidar hissed down at them as we set Ronan to one side. "They're coming!"

Grimacing, Cyrus placed a muddy boot in Niero's hands and he lifted him up to us with a grunt. He crawled past us, and they reached down again. "Jump, Niero," Vidar grunted. Together, they caught hold of his arms and lifted him up, and I closed my eyes in relief. We were all out. Bellona carefully closed the grate, wincing as the rusty hinges squeaked in protest. Swiftly, she set to putting the nuts back in place as we hurried to a small copse of trees and hunched down, waiting.

"They have to be *right* there," Vidar whispered, fear evident in his eyes.

I prayed for a shield of angels as Vidar slowly rolled to the side and stilled, listening, feeling, eyes wide, nostrils flared.

I dared not reach out myself, and instead attempted to sever any tie to any emotion at all, scared to death that I might open a door the Sheolites would recognize as me and betray us all.

Niero moved between me and Cyrus and grunted at us to get back, and we sank farther in and among the trees.

I stared at Niero as we settled in to wait. For good or bad, this was where we would take our stand, or slip from our enemies' grasp. The muscles in Niero's neck and jaw tensed and relaxed, the pulse in his neck visible. Other than that he was utterly still, in a crouch, as if poised to leap upward in flight. And for the first time, I wondered about the sense of comfort and protection I always felt around him. The same way I felt when ...

We could hear voices, shouts. Vidar slipped his hand in mine, waiting, ready to leap and run. But after a time, the voices faded.

Vidar's eyes widened. "Impossible," he whispered. "They're moving on. Passing us."

"Not impossible," I whispered back, even as I reached down to check Ronan's pulse, faint but steady. "*Angeli* over *demoni*."

Vidar grinned then, in the familiar dimpled-cheek-all-big-teeth way I'd come to know as his relaxed grin. I smiled too.

But after a moment my eyes shifted back to Niero. And stayed there.

CHAPTER
36

ANDRIANA

We left the tunnel behind and took a faint trail down a shallow canyon. But we were deep enough to be hidden, and that gave me a sense of peace and hope that I clung to. At the end, I saw that the sun was sinking on the horizon. The day was coming to a close and we were still in Pacifica. And deep inside, I thought that if we didn't get Ronan help soon, he wouldn't live to see another sunset.

"Take heart," Niero said, squeezing my hand. "We must be close."

"Closer than you think." Cyrus said. We'd come out on the edge of what appeared to be a vast ranch, fenced all around, with horses that were much taller than the mudhorses of home. I recognized them as like those the Sheolites rode and tensed.

A woman left her small house, and we ducked behind several boulders, watching as she moved to the barn.

"It's her," Cyrus said. "If I don't return, bring Ronan to the barn when it's dark. We can't risk more than me crossing this distance and being seen."

"And what if there's someone else in the barn and they capture you?" Vidar asked, a frown wrinkling his forehead.

"She's a doctor, Vidar, not a soldier. And I'm one of the Six."

"And if there's somebody else? Somebody hunting one man, in particular, of the Six?" he pressed, staring warily at the barn.

"Is there?"

He closed his eyes a moment and then opened them, shaking his head. "I still don't like it."

"Fortunately, you don't have to like every one of our plans," Bellona groused. "What other choice do we have? We'll be lucky to keep Ronan alive until nightfall." She tensed as the last words left her lips and looked over at me. "Sorry."

I opened my mouth to say it was okay, but then closed it. It wasn't okay. I needed them all to be praying. Believing that Ronan would get through this.

With a nod from Niero, Cyrus moved off and Niero turned to place a hand on my shoulder. "It will be all right," he said, and his familiar strength seemed to move from him to me, warming me.

I moved out from under his hand and to Ronan's side. I leaned down and put my head to his, noting that at least he wasn't sweating anymore. But then the clammy chill of him made me worry anew. "Stay with me, Ronan," I whispered in his ear. "Stay with me."

■ ■ ■

Cyrus didn't return. The woman left the barn, carrying a heavy pail, but she never looked our way. We paced, waiting for the sun to set and twilight to fade. Finally, when it was utterly dark, when I thought one more second of waiting might kill me, we were on the move again.

Cyrus opened a side door for us, one that rolled on wheels on tracks at the top and bottom. As soon as we were all in, he closed it again, and I sighed in relief as I saw what he had prepared for us. Fresh hay lined the room. A table, at the center, had obviously been cleared and cleaned. We placed Ronan atop it. A horse stuck his head over the wall of a stable and then shifted left and right, whinnying his agitation, ears back, unnerved by his sudden visitors and perhaps the scent of blood. Niero moved over to him and with low tones and a slow hand, reached up to calm the beast, much like he had me.

The ranch woman arrived then, and we all looked to her. Niero put a hand on the hilt of his battle axe, but Cyrus reached out a calming hand. "There is no need. Galen is our friend, a sister in the Way."

"You are deep in enemy territory," Vidar said with uncustomary hostility, staring hard at the woman.

"A fact for which I believe you should be thanking the Maker right now," she returned. She was perhaps four decades and five, trim and dark, and edged past him to put her armload of clean rags and a tool box on the table beside Ronan. From the box, she pulled a bottle of clear liquid, uncorked it, and took a long swig. Wiping her lips with the back of wrist, then splashing more on her fingers, as if washing, she offered the bottle up. "Who will be assisting me?"

"I can," Mom said. She took the bottle, and without dropping her gaze, swallowed a mouthful too, and followed her lead in washing her hands in the stuff. The acrid smell of alcohol wafted through the room, momentarily even overpowering the hay. Galen also set up a bag of what appeared to be blood, attached to a long tube, and set out instruments. She intended to insert it into Ronan? I'd heard of transfusions; I'd just never seen one done.

"Good," said Galen. "I'll need others around us, each holding a leg or arm, in case . . . ?" She looked at me.

"Ronan," I supplied.

"In case *Ronan* awakes." I walked around the table to take position beside the doctor and hold one arm. Bellona and Vidar each took a leg and Niero the other arm.

Moving efficiently, Galen unbelted Ronan's trousers and pulled the right side down. She paused, momentarily, at the sight of the perfect crescent moon, and then moved on to fold under the bloody shirt, well away from the wound. She placed a clean cloth, scissors, a knife with a tiny blade, and several needles and thread on Ronan's torso. Then she cut away the old bandage and slid it neatly from under his back. I wanted to weep at the amount of blood dripping from the bandage. It was a wonder Ronan remained with us now. Bellona had been correct. By all rights, he should've been dead hours ago. *Please, Maker,* I pleaded silently as Galen poured alcohol over the three-inch wound. Ronan didn't flinch. Had he been awake, I knew the pain would've made him scream. *Please please please please please please. Save him. Don't take him yet.*

Galen bent and, using a metal instrument, pulled apart the skin to peer inside. She paused, then probed the wound with her finger a moment, then bent again to look inward. Blood poured out of Ronan and onto the table, so much so that it began to drip on the floor. "I need light," she said. Dad brought the kerosene lamp as close as he could, holding it over her shoulder. "There," she said, pouring more alcohol on Ronan, inside him this time. She nodded grimly. "It's his gut. But I don't think they got his intestines."

I tried to swallow and failed.

Galen lifted a small, sharp knife and made a swift incision. I gasped and turned away until I was certain I wouldn't vomit, then turned back to see her grab hold of the first needle and bend to begin stitching slippery, bloody flesh. Even then, Ronan did not move. Were we losing him?

"Pray, Dri," Niero said quietly, looking at me steadily. "Do not give in to fear. Remain true in your hope in the Maker. He holds it all in his hands, does he not? Even your Ronan?"

I could feel my father's eyes on me as he said this.

"He does," I said to Niero.

"Did he not bring this world into being?"

"He did."

"Did he not cause the seers of old to tell of the day the Ailith would be born?"

"He did."

"Did he not keep the Community alive, waiting for the Remnants' Call?"

"He did," I said softly, my eyes moving to Ronan.

"Has he not brought us this far?"

"He has."

"Remember all of *those* things," Niero said, "as you pray." He turned and looked at the rest in the room. "All of you do so. There is a time for us to act, and a time that we leave our lives in the hands of the Maker. Truly, they're there all the time. We only delude ourselves in thinking we have more power, more control. But in the end, we come to this. The Maker breathed life into us, and when we breathe our last, he will welcome us in the hereafter. But here or there, we are never alone. We are his."

Galen reached for another needle and thread, not pausing long enough to knot off the first. I knew she was trying to stop the bleeding by sewing up one cut at a time, from the innermost out. And if she was trying to repair intestines, her work was delicate indeed. She only left the wound once to open up a vein at Ronan's arm and insert the end of a tube. Then she set a small, battery-operated pump to forcing blood into his body.

I turned to Ronan, and, while keeping one arm wrapped around his, reached out to lay a hand on his head. And as Galen continued to toil, hour after hour, and I watched the bottle of alcohol poured and poured again, I did as Niero had directed and prayed for mercy from the Maker, for healing. Then I concentrated on finding faith and trust in my heart again and passing those into Ronan. Then strength. And courage. Calm.

Much, much later, the doctor was done, stitching up the last of Ronan's wounds and wiping away the blood, and binding him anew with clean cloths plastered over his side. The blood bag had long been empty. She attached another one now.

Ronan's pulse was terribly faint, his breathing rapid and shallow. He was a ghastly shade of gray. But he was still with us.

Galen straightened and arched backward, obviously in pain. Then she covered Ronan with a thick, clean blanket, studied his face as if memorizing it, and wearily moved to a bucket of water, washing her bloody hands and forearms, and then her face.

"There's more here," she said, gesturing toward the pump and other buckets and looking around at all of us. "You all look like you've been in surgery yourselves with the amount of blood on you."

"Surgery. Right," Vidar said, giving her a faint smile.

"Anyone else need stitches this night?" she asked. But we all shook our heads. I knew that I'd mostly suffered blunt force trauma. But fortunately no cuts. Perhaps the rest were the same. Or more afraid of her needle and thread than any bleeding wound from the fight.

Galen brought the pink-stained cloth to her face again, pushing back her sweaty hair. Then she reached for a basket she'd set by the door when she first came in. "There's bread and cheese in here. Enough for all of you. You can rest here tonight. But come morning, you have to be gone."

I frowned and shook my head. "That's impossible. Ronan —"

"You'll have to leave him with me," she said. "I'll hide him in here, best I can. But there was already a patrol here earlier in the day. Told me there were subversives out and about and I was to report anything unusual I saw, anyone I didn't know. Lucky for me I only saw family."

Niero smiled at that. Vidar was leaning his whole head under the faucet, washing his hair and neck and face. He rose and shook out like a dog, sending drops of water flying in the air. But my mind was on the conversation at hand.

"We can't leave Ronan behind," I said, going to Niero and grabbing his big arm. "We can't. We might never get inside Pacifica again!"

Bellona was now washing, filling a bucket as our hostess had. "He's a knight, Andriana. He made it into Pacifica. When he's well enough, he can make it out again too."

I shook my head. "He's a knight. He's not supernatural."

"He is, in a way," Niero said, leaning back on an old bench, "as an Ailith."

"You know what I mean," I said. "We all need one another. None of us is strong enough to do what we were called to do alone."

"You might be surprised," Niero returned before moving to take his turn at the pump.

CHAPTER 37

ANDRIANA

I knew I was getting nowhere. I'd let them eat, and then I'd revisit the subject. They might be leaving him behind. But there was no way I would.

When we'd all washed, Galen handed out bread and a hunk of cheese to all of us. Bellona passed out cups of water. I ate numbly, shoving bite after bite down my throat while feeling no hunger. I only ate because I knew it would help me and my kin if I had the energy it would provide. It was the same with the water. Where I'd once been parched, desperate for a drink, now I drank as if I was trying to remember what it meant to be thirsty, even as I distantly noted my chapped lips and shriveled tongue.

"What else have you heard?" Vidar asked Galen, food in his mouth. "From the Union? Or here, about our cause?"

"There are stories," Galen began. "Not many of them on

this side of the Wall, but here and there I hear whispers of your healer, your seer. And you," she said, looking at me. "The beautiful girl who feels every emotion as her own. The people of Pacifica can hardly stop talking of Andriana and how you've caught the emperor's eye. They see it as destiny, you both being Remnants. Some even dare to call it a holy union."

She stared hard at me.

"While Keallach or the Six had that in mind," I said, "I never did. I was only trying to survive."

She lifted a brow again. "You refer to the emperor by his given name?"

I let out a short laugh. "He is no different to me than Vidar or any of the other Remnants. A wayward brother, nothing more."

"A brother," she said carefully. She was suspicious, I realized.

"What do they say about me?" Vidar said with a scowl. "The *knower*?" he prodded.

Galen shook her head a little, as if confused, and Bellona laughed under her breath.

"How about the *discerner*?" Vidar pressed.

Still, Galen shook her head, lifting her eyebrows and half smiling, as if in apology.

Vidar grew more intent. "The guy who knows good from evil?"

"Give it up, Vidar," Bellona said, leaning back in the hay and closing her eyes.

"How is that fair?" he railed. "Everyone gets a story but me?"

"Your story is still being written," Niero said gently.

"Sleep now, my friends," Galen said. "Morning will come soon enough, and you will need your strength for the journey. Know that I will guard your friend with my life until he's well enough to come after you."

I swallowed hard and turned to her. "Thank you," I said. "I'm so grateful."

She smiled a little and nodded once. But there was sorrow in her too, apology. "I did what little I could. If you could've gotten him to me sooner ..."

I closed my eyes, willing myself not to cry. "I know," I said. But the tears ran then, making my nose drip. I lifted a hand to it, even as the slight woman pulled me into her arms for a moment.

"You never know how the Maker will answer our pleas," she said. "Never in my life did I believe my path would lead to sheltering or treating Remnants. If he saw me to this place, he will see Ronan through this place too."

I couldn't say anything, knowing if I did, I was liable to cry and never stop. Mom and Dad joined me, wrapping their arms across my shoulders. Galen backed away, wiping her hands on her skirt. "I need to get back. If anyone's watching the house, they'll notice my lights are on late. Turn down that lamp, would you, especially as I leave?"

Bellona did as she asked, and we were plunged into near darkness.

Galen turned and slid open the barn door, and we heard it roll shut until wood met wood. The others settled down in the hay, each grabbing a blanket. Vidar was asleep in seconds, snoring softly with his pistol in his hand across his chest. Bellona rolled her eyes and turned over in the opposite direction, her sword at her side. Cyrus went up to the hayloft, intent on "keeping an eye on the road" when he wasn't sleeping. Apparently there was a window up there.

Mom and Dad gave me another squeeze and went over to Ronan, and I started crying anew when I sensed their fervent hope, their faith, their trust. I soaked it in as my own until

I almost believed my knight would make it until morning. When they were finished, Mom cast me one last, weary smile, and the two of them cuddled together in the far corner, one blanket across them both, their weapons on either side.

But I couldn't bear to leave Ronan, weary as I was. He was shivering now, with beads of perspiration dotting his forehead and upper lip, more making his neck and chest shine. I brought the lamp closer and gently folded the blanket back. Only the appearance of the blood on the bandage, seemingly halting in the size of a fist, gave me hope. If he wasn't losing blood any longer, could his body begin to concentrate its efforts on the wounds themselves?

Niero came closer and watched me a while. When I bent my head to pray in silence, he did too. But he went to his knees. It seemed right, such action, and I went to my knees too, my hands on Ronan's arm near my forehead, running hot with fever. The only sound in the room was Vidar's snore, the slow, steady breathing of our companions sleeping, and Ronan's chattering teeth, but I could have sworn I could almost hear Niero's unspoken prayer.

It filled me like a song, so rich, so deep … and yet as if it were in a different language. It was crystalline. Untainted by human sin or desire. Only joy. Only praise for the Maker. And as I became one with the words, they filled every corner of me, driving out my pain, my sorrow, my fear. Every inadequacy became a realized dream. Every weakness was usurped by strength. I was as I was created to be. Andriana, daughter of the Maker. With a Call upon my very life. A Call I could not ignore, no matter how torn it left me.

I opened my eyes to look up at Niero, who was standing now and staring intently at me. There was only tender care in his dark eyes. "Daughter of the Light," he said quietly, and

I didn't know if he spoke the words, or somehow whispered them into my mind. "Do not be afraid."

The words made no sense. But as he grabbed hold of his tunic and slipped it over his head, leaving his powerful chest bare, my eyes ran again over the scarred flesh I'd seen before. I remembered the cave, and how he healed so quickly, and how it made no sense that a man so young could have born so many wounds.

He shifted his shoulders, took a deep breath, clasped his hands, and bowed his head. My eyes grew wide as he continued to pray silently — prayers I could somehow feel within my own mind and heart — prayers so beautiful that tears streamed unbidden down my cheeks. And that was when I noticed that Raniero was practically glowing, lighting up the far side of the room, brighter and brighter by the moment. But then I saw something at his shoulder, spreading, widening, lifting. My mouth fell open as the creamy feathers of wings rose and unfurled in the most majestic vision I'd ever seen.

Niero lifted his head and looked me full in the face. "If the Maker asks it of you, you must go," he said.

I nodded slowly, aware now that I was in the presence of one of the Maker's messengers. That this was a Word directly from the Maker.

"But the Maker cares for you, Andriana, just as he does his servant, Ronan." He reached across Ronan's body and let his hand hover over the wound. The light grew brighter, and I had to look around at the others, wondering how none of them awoke to it. Was I dreaming? Wouldn't Vidar awaken if he sensed an angel here?

I glanced back to Niero's hand, but it was too bright to look at for long, so I looked up into his eyes. And there, I saw the barest hint of my friend Niero, the one I'd walked so many miles alongside, the one who had saved me, taken a bullet for me, protected me.

"No matter how it feels," he said softly, "you are never alone, Andriana. Never alone. Remember that."

"I will," I promised.

Then he bent over Ronan's face and I stilled. It looked like he was going to kiss him. But Niero only breathed air into his mouth and nose from inches away. I could almost smell it, that breath from his lips. It smelled of freshly turned earth. Of water off of snowmelt. Of air at the top of the mountain. Of sun warming rock. Of life. *Life*.

"Rise, son of Light," Niero said to Ronan.

My eyes moved to Ronan's beloved face and in wonder, I watched his eyelids flutter, then blink open. Ronan grimaced, shifted as if stiff, and then stretched. *Stretched*. Like there was no pain at all. Then he sat up, looked over at me and said, "Dri. What's happened?"

Raniero smiled then, from Ronan's other side. He lifted a finger to his lips, even while his wings folded back in and disappeared.

"How did you do that?" I whispered, tears of wonder streaming down my face. For Ronan, restored. For Niero, so much more than our leader. So much made sense now. "How did I not know it before?"

"Know what?" Ronan asked, hopping off the table.

"That Niero is the best possible leader for us," I mumbled.

But Ronan was studying the bandage at his belly, not really hearing me. "What's this?" he asked in confusion, pulling back the glued edge to peer beneath. He peeled it all the way off while I fought back a shout for him to leave it in place. I half-believed he would still be bleeding. But what I'd just seen told me it'd be far different.

It was. There was bruising, but the wound looked as if it had been stitched months before, barely a pink line, the stitches disintegrated. Vidar had risen behind me and ambled closer, rubbing his eyes. Perhaps Niero's ... *glory* had awakened him? Niero and I shared a long look.

But Vidar's eyes were on Ronan's wound. "Whoa. How'd *that* happen?" He leaned in to take a look, then even closer.

"Vidar," Ronan complained, shoving Vidar's head back as he tried to get a look himself. "What happened?" He looked up at me, then Niero.

"It's a long story," I said.

"It can't be that long," Ronan said. The others were rousing around us, blinking at us as if we were a dream. Which I suppose we could legitimately be. For a moment, I wondered again if I was asleep and this was all in my head.

"Ronan?" Bellona asked. "*Ronan?*"

"We have to be going," Niero said firmly to me and Vidar, pulling on his shirt. He put on his shoulder sheath and slid his swords in. "Now." He moved over to unhook Ronan, who was even more confused as he traced the tube from his arm to the drained blood bag above him.

"Now?" I asked, even as I moved to grab a pack and rouse my parents.

"Yes," Niero replied, giving me a steely look. There was a reason. A very good reason.

"All right," I said, but I couldn't resist pulling Ronan in for a quick embrace as he rose off the table, wincing, moving as if he was only sore — not rising from a surgery that should have killed him. I shook my head in amazement. Everyone else readied to go, but stared our way.

Ronan glanced down at me, and I understood his fear that

Niero would see. That we'd be chastised again, even separated. "Hey, what's that for?"

"For not ... for being here. With me. I'm so glad you're *with* me, Ronan."

I saw as he noticed the tears in my eyes. "Hey," he whispered, turning away from Niero, so that our guide would only see his back. "You all right?" he asked urgently, searching my eyes, lifting a quick hand to my cheek.

"Never better," I said brightly, taking his hand in my own. "Come on, Knight. We need to gather our things. We've been called."

"And we will answer," he muttered behind me, still clearly trying to figure out what was going on as my mother and father came over to him and embraced him like a long-lost child. I was sure Ronan had no idea why everyone was acting so strangely.

Niero grinned over his shoulder at me as he slid open the barn door. We ran out in a line, scurrying across the field, back to the safety of the canyon. And as we climbed and climbed, heading north and east under a velvet sky laden with stars, I felt nothing but hope, even in the heart of enemy country. We would make our way out and onward to wherever the Maker called.

Whenever he called us.

Because we had a mission to accomplish, we Remnants and Knights.

A people to gather.

Hearts to kindle. Stories to tell.

An enemy to vanquish, one way or another.

And they had barely begun to see the fight we would bring to their very door.

Lisa invites you to join her and other Remnants readers
on the fan page found here:

Facebook.com/RemnantsSeries

You can also learn more about Lisa Bergren and the Remnants
Series by connecting with her online:

www.LisaBergren.com
Twitter: @LisaTBergren
Facebook.com/LisaTawnBergren

Check out the final book in this series
when it releases in winter 2016.

REMNANTS
SEASON OF GLORY